MODERN HUMANITIES RESEARCH ASSOCIATION
LIBRARY OF MEDIEVAL WELSH LITERATURE

GENERAL EDITORS
ANN PARRY OWEN
ERICH POPPE
SIMON RODWAY

HYSTORIA GWERYDDON YR ALMAEN
THE MIDDLE WELSH LIFE OF
ST URSULA AND THE 11,000 VIRGINS

EDITED BY
JANE CARTWRIGHT

MODERN HUMANITIES RESEARCH ASSOCIATION
LIBRARY OF MEDIEVAL WELSH LITERATURE

ALREADY PUBLISHED

Welsh Court Poems
edited by Rhian M. Andrews (2007)
(available from University of Wales Press)

Selections from Ystorya Bown o Hamtwn
edited by Erich Poppe and Regine Reck (2009)
(available from University of Wales Press)

Early Welsh Gnomic and Nature Poetry
edited by Nicolas Jacobs (2012)
(available from www.mhra.org.uk/series/LMWL)

Historical Texts from Medieval Wales
edited by Patricia Williams (2012)
(available from www.mhra.org.uk/series/LMWL)

A Selection of Early Welsh Saga Poems
edited by Jenny Rowland (2014)
(available from www.mhra.org.uk/series/LMWL)

Arthur in Early Welsh Poetry
edited by Nerys Ann Jones (2019)
(available from www.mhra.org.uk/series/LMWL)

texts.mhra.org.uk

Hystoria Gweryddon yr Almaen

The Middle Welsh Life of
St Ursula and the 11,000 Virgins

Edited by Jane Cartwright

Modern Humanities Research Association
2020

Published by

*The Modern Humanities Research Association
Salisbury House
Station Road
Cambridge CB1 2LA
United Kingdom*

© Modern Humanities Research Association 2020

Jane Cartwright has asserted her right under the Copyright, Designs and Patents Act 1988 to be identified as the author of this work. Parts of this work may be reproduced as permitted under legal provisions for fair dealing (or fair use) for the purposes of research, private study, criticism, or review, or when a relevant collective licensing agreement is in place. All other reproduction requires the written permission of the copyright holder who may be contacted at rights@mhra.org.uk.

First published 2020

*ISBN 978-1-907322-59-4 (HB)
ISBN 978-1-907322-74-7 (PB)*

Copies may be ordered from www.mhra.org.uk/series/LMWL

CONTENTS

Preface vii
Abbreviations ix
Introduction 1
Text 51
Notes 60
Glossary 97
Index of Personal Names 118
Index of Place Names 121
Bibliography 122

I'm mab / For my son
Ifan Rhydderch Hughes

PREFACE

The purpose of this volume of the Library of Medieval Welsh Literature is to make available to students and scholars interested in Middle Welsh and medieval literature an edition of one complete saint's Life, *Hystoria Gweryddon yr Almaen*. Although a section of the text appeared in T. H. Parry-Williams, *Rhyddiaith Gymraeg Y Gyfrol Gyntaf Detholion o Lawysgrifau 1488–1609* (Caerdydd, 1954), the Welsh version of the Life of St Ursula has never been edited in its entirety with full critical apparatus. Hagiography was one of the most important literary genres in medieval Europe, and Welsh culture celebrated the cults of both native and universal saints. The cult of St Ursula and the 11,000 Virgins originated in Cologne in Germany, and various versions of her legend proliferated in Latin as well as European vernaculars following the discovery in the twelfth century of a Roman cemetery which was interpreted as the mass grave of Ursula and her martyred companions. In most versions of the legend Ursula is an Ancient Briton and sails from Britain on her final pilgrimage, never to return to her homeland. It was perhaps a natural step for a saint presumed to have Celtic roots to be appropriated by the Welsh, but her Life does not appear to have been adapted into Welsh until the early sixteenth century.

Since the text is extant in only one manuscript, Aberystwyth, National Library of Wales, MS Peniarth 182, it has not been possible to compare this to other Welsh manuscript versions, as is usually the case when discussing Middle Welsh texts in this series. The Introduction, Notes and Glossary aim to help Welsh speakers as well as non-native speakers to understand the *Hystoria* and appreciate its wider literary context. The text was adapted into late medieval Welsh by the poet, cleric and hagiologist Huw Pennant so that lovers of literature could enjoy the legend of St Ursula in their own language. My aim is to rescue the Welsh version of the text from obscurity by working with the original manuscript and making an accessible edition available for lovers of Welsh culture as well as hagiography. I also hope to highlight the work of Huw Pennant in this period since his work has attracted very little attention. The text is interesting not only because it is representative of a Welsh hagiographical text produced shortly before the Reformation, but also because it is both a translation and adaptation of a Latin text which also appears to incorporate Welsh sources.

My thanks are due to the staff of the National Library of Wales for permission to view the original manuscript Peniarth 182. Many thanks to Gerard Lowe, the staff at the Modern Humanities Research Association and the series editors for their patience. I am particularly indebted to Erich Poppe, who checked the typescript; his cheerful encouragement, helpful comments and suggestions for numerous improvements were much appreciated. I am grateful to my colleagues at the Centre for Advanced Welsh and Celtic Studies and the University of Cambridge who worked on the AHRC-funded projects on *Saints in Wales/Vitae Sanctorum Cambriae*, especially Ann Parry Owen and Jenny Day, who checked sections of the text and answered numerous queries. Thanks also to Simon F. Davies for careful copyediting. Magdalena Öhrman and Morfydd Owen kindly answered questions regarding the Latin texts. My students at the University of Wales Trinity Saint David have responded enthusiastically to lectures on St Ursula and Welsh hagiography and allowed me to 'test' sections of the edition in seminars with them. I would also like to thank Joanne Dudley, Cinzia Sertorio, Rory Geoghegan, Lynne Irvine, Einir Wyn Kirkwood, Eleri Davies, Chris Forster-Brown, Tracey Lovering, Andrea Mills, Paul Mills, Paul Jackman, Emily Wooster, Luned Davies, Tristan Gray Hulse, Dafydd Johnston, Simon Rodway, Cathryn Charnell-White, Janet Burton, Angela, Jo and Tom Ansted, Gwen Davies, Julie Christopher, Mike Cartwright, and Rhys Williams for their support. I alone am responsible for any errors which remain.

Jane Cartwright

ABBREVIATIONS

AHRC	Arts and Humanities Research Council
AS Octobris	Victor de Buck et al. (eds), *Acta sanctorum octobris tomus IX* (Antwerp, Brussels, Tongerloo, Paris: Brussels Greuse, 1858), pp. 73–303
BBCS	*Bulletin of the Board of Celtic Studies*
CE	Charles Herbermann et al. (eds), *The Catholic Encyclopedia*, 15 vols (New York: Encyclopedia Press, 1913)
EETS o.s.	Early English Texts Society, original series
GPC Online	*Geiriadur Prifysgol Cymru/A Dictionary of the Welsh Language*, Canolfan Uwchefrydiau Cymreig a Cheltaidd Prifysgol Cymru <http://www.geiriadur.ac.uk> (accessed 30 October 2019)
GMW	D. Simon Evans, *A Grammar of Middle Welsh* (Dublin: Dublin Institute for Advanced Studies, 1964)
LA	Jacobus de Voragine, *The Golden Legend*, ed. and trans. by W. Granger Ryan, 2 vols (Princeton: Princeton University Press, 1993)
NLA	*Nova Legenda Anglie* (London: Wynkyn de Worde, 1516), Early English Books Online
NLW	National Library of Wales
Pen. 182	Aberystwyth, National Library of Wales, MS Peniarth 182
RepMW	Daniel Huws, *A Repertory of Welsh Manuscripts and Scribes c. 800–c. 1800*, 3 vols (Aberystwyth: National Library of Wales, forthcoming)
TYP	Rachel Bromwich (ed.), *Trioedd Ynys Prydein*, 3rd edn (Cardiff: University of Wales Press, 2006)

INTRODUCTION

Hagiography

Hagiography, stemming from the Greek ἅγιος, 'holy', and γράφία, 'writings', is one of the richest and most significant literary genres of the medieval world. The narratives that recount the biographies or legends of the saints, their Lives (Greek βιος, Latin *vita*, Welsh *buchedd*), survive in large numbers and record in detail the various traditions and miracles associated with the holy men and women who were revered throughout the medieval period in both the East and the West. As noted by Thomas Head: 'Hagiography provides some of the most valuable records for the reconstruction and study of the practice of premodern Christianity'.[1] Given that hagiography was one of the principal forms of literary activity in the Middle Ages and studying these texts is, therefore, essential in order to gain a holistic understanding of medieval spirituality in any given community, it seems appropriate that a hagiographic legend should be added to the repertoire of texts currently available in the Library of Medieval Welsh Literature. Before considering the importance of the genre in Wales and discussing the particular text presented here, *Hystoria Gweryddon yr Almaen* (the Welsh Life of St Ursula and the 11,000 Virgins; literally 'The Story of the Virgins of Germany'), it would be useful to consider briefly both the origins and principal characteristics of hagiography as a genre.

The first Christian saints were the early martyrs who died for their faith, including, as one might expect, biblical figures such as St Peter and St Paul. One of the earliest hagiographical texts recounts the martyrdom of Polycarp, bishop of Smyrna, who was burned alive c. 150–180 for his religious beliefs, but whose flesh smelled miraculously of bread baking, according to his hagiographer.[2] Another historical martyr, St Perpetua of Carthage, was thrown into prison c. 203 when she refused to sacrifice to pagan gods, and much of the account of her terrifying experiences is thought to have been composed by her during the period in which she was incarcerated with her young child. Perpetua was eventually thrown to wild animals, along with other Christians including Felicity and Saturninus, at the military games organized in celebration of

---

[1] Thomas Head (ed.), *Medieval Hagiography: An Anthology* (New York and London: Routledge, 2001), p. xiii.
[2] Herbert Musurillo (ed. and trans.), *Acts of the Christian Martyrs* (Oxford: Clarendon Press, 1972), pp. 2–20. This volume contains editions and translations of the acts of all the 'genuine' early Christian martyrs. See also the discussion in Robert Bartlett, *Why Can the Dead Do Such Great Things? Saints and Worshippers from the Martyrs to the Reformation* (Princeton and Oxford: Princeton University Press, 2013), pp. 4–22.

Emperor Septimius Severus's birthday.[3] Persecution of Christians in the Roman Empire began with Nero in 64 CE and ended after the Christian conversion of Constantine (306–337) when Christianity was finally legitimized by the Edict of Milan in 313.

In the fourth century veneration of the saints' relics began to be formalized, since, as noted by Peter Brown, the dead bodies of saints were perceived to bridge the gap between heaven and earth.[4] One of the principal roles of the saint was to act as an intercessor, mediating between ordinary Christians and God. Although strictly speaking all Christians could be regarded as saints once they had entered the kingdom of heaven, the honorific title came to be reserved for a selection of particularly worthy holy men and women who gained direct access to heaven because of their personal sacrifice and great virtues. Pope Damasus (366–384) began publicizing the sacred remains of particular saintly bodies in the catacombs of Rome and including their names in the liturgy.[5] Ambrose of Milan (c. 340–397) discovered the remains of the twins St Gervasius and St Protasius, translated them to his own newly-built basilica in Milan (where he was later buried between them), and actively promoted their cults and the healing powers associated with their relics. Fragments of their relics were distributed throughout Italy and Gaul and many other churches were dedicated to the martyred twins: effectively Ambrose set a precedent demonstrating how saints' cults could spread, proliferate and become international.[6]

When it was no longer necessary to die for one's Christian beliefs, a new form of 'martyrdom' became prevalent among the early saints: this involved sacrificing personal wealth and property, one's sexuality, emotional ties, and familial bonds. Confessors, or early Christian ascetics, took over the role previously played by the early martyrs, and one of the principal trail-blazers was

---

[3] Musurillo (ed.), *Acts of the Christian Martyrs*, pp. 106–30. See also Petr Kitzler, *From 'Passio Perpetuae' to 'Acta Perpetuae': Recontextualizing a Martyr Story in the Literature of the Early Church* (Berlin: De Gruyter, 2015), and, on the authorship of the text, Thomas J. Heffernan, 'Philology and Authorship in the *Passio Sanctarum Perpetuae et Felicitatis*', *Traditio*, 50 (1995), 315–25.

[4] Peter Brown, *The Cult of the Saints: Its Rise and Function in Latin Christianity* (Chicago: University of Chicago Press, 1981), p. 1 and ff. in which he explores what it meant to contemporaries to join heaven and earth at the graves of dead humans.

[5] L. Duchesne (ed.), *Liber Pontificalis*, 2nd edn, 3 vols (Paris: E. de Boccard, 1955–1957), I, pp. 212–25; Victor Saxer, 'Damase et le calendrier', in *Saecularia Damasiana: atti del convegno internazionale per il XVI centenario della morte di papa Damaso*, Studi di antichità Cristiana 39 (Città del Vaticano: Pontificio istituto di archeologia cristiana, 1986), pp. 61–88; M. Sághy, '*Scinditur in partes populus*: Pope Damasus and the Martyrs of Rome', *Early Medieval Europe*, 9 (2000), 273–87; Alan Thacker, '*Loca Sanctorum*: The Significance of Place in the Study of the Saints', in *Local Saints and Local Churches in the Early Medieval West*, ed. by A. Thacker and R. Sharpe (Oxford: Oxford University Press, 2002), pp. 1–43 (pp. 3–5).

[6] Thacker, '*Loca Sanctorum*', pp. 5–12.

St Antony (d. 356), often referred to as 'the Father of Monks'.⁷ He withdrew from human habitation and spent many years in the service of Christ in the Egyptian desert. His Life, composed by Athanasius of Alexandria *c.* 360, who had known and admired St Antony, was originally written in Greek, but was translated into Syriac, Coptic, Latin and other languages.⁸ Athanasius records that Antony's example was so influential that 'the desert became a city of monks' as many other ascetics were keen to follow his example. One such individual who relinquished his military career in favour of the monastic life was St Martin: his Latin Life by Sulpicius Severus was composed *c.* 396 during Martin's lifetime (d. 397) and recounts his many miracles as well as how he became bishop of Tours.⁹ The Lives of St Antony and St Martin proved immensely popular and were widely disseminated. As noted by Bartlett, 'Between 360 and 400 Athanasius and Sulpicius Severus, along with Jerome, who composed Lives of the Egyptian hermit Paul and other ascetics, shaped Christian hagiography for good'.¹⁰

The Lives of Antony and Martin were hugely influential and set models of sanctity for others to emulate. In the fifth and sixth centuries numerous legendary martyrs were celebrated and by 800 it had become common practice to commemorate the feast of the saint on the day on which he/she died and hear a reading about the saint's life. The saints became the celebrities of their day, offering solace and support to the faithful, and it was natural for people to seek local heroes in their quest for saintly candidates. As noted by Sarah Salih, knowledge of hagiography 'spanned the social spectrum' and appealed to all ranks of society — oral and pictorial as well as written narratives recounted the Lives of local and universal saints. Hagiography was 'a multilingual and multinational phenomenon', and throughout the Middle Ages the number of saints created and the hagiographical texts composed about them in Greek, Latin and the various vernaculars multiplied exponentially.¹¹

Noteworthy examples of Merovingian, Irish and Anglo-Saxon saints' Lives

---

⁷ Bartlett, *Why Can the Dead Do Such Great Things?*, p. 20.
⁸ Athanasius of Alexandria, 'Life of St. Antony of Egypt', trans. by David Brakke, in *Medieval Hagiography* ed. by Head, pp. 1–30; Bartlett, *Why Can the Dead Do Such Great Things?*, p. 19, estimates that 165 manuscripts of the Greek version alone are extant.
⁹ Sulpicius Severus, *Sulpicious Severus' 'Vita Martini'*, ed. by Phillip Burton (Oxford: Oxford University Press, 2017). For a detailed discussion, see Clare Stancliffe, *St Martin and his Hagiographer: History and Miracle in Sulpicius Severus* (Oxford: Clarendon Press, 1983). *Vita Martini* was also translated into Middle Welsh; see Jenny Day (ed.), *Buchedd Marthin Seintiau yng Nghymru / Saints in Wales / Vitae Sanctorum Cambriae* website <http://www.seintiaucymru.ac.uk/> / <http://www.welshsaints.ac.uk/> (forthcoming).
¹⁰ Bartlett, *Why Can the Dead Do Such Great Things?*, p. 20.
¹¹ Sarah Salih, 'Introduction: Saints, Cults and *Lives* in Late Medieval England', in *A Companion to Middle English Hagiography*, ed. by Salih (Cambridge: D. S. Brewer, 2006), pp. 1–23 (p. 13).

were produced in the early medieval period, such as Stephanus's *Life of St Wilfrid*, Ursinus's *Passion of St Leudegar*, Cogitosus's *Life of St Brigit*, Muirchú's *Life of St Patrick*, Bede's *Life of St Cuthbert* and Felix's *Life of St Guthlac*, to name but a few.[12] While many of the hagiographical texts produced throughout the whole of the Middle Ages remain anonymous, perhaps the most influential collection of saints' Lives, the *Legenda aurea* (Golden Legend), is accredited to Jacobus de Voragine, a Dominican friar who became archbishop of Genoa (d. c. 1298).[13] Justifiably described by Sherry Reames as a medieval 'bestseller', more than eight hundred manuscript copies of the Latin versions alone are extant, and between 1470 and 1500 one hundred and fifty-six editions of the *Legenda aurea* were printed by the earliest printing presses.[14] The collection was translated or adapted into many European vernaculars, such as Jean de Vignay's French *Légende dorée* (c. 1333–1340), which was itself translated into Middle English and known as the *Gilte Legende* (1438).[15] Other medieval collections of saints' Lives, such as the Middle English network of texts known as the *South English Legendary* (c. 1270–1285), are thought to draw on the *Legenda aurea* as well as other sources.[16] The fact that so many slightly different versions of the same saints' legends were in circulation by the late Middle Ages means that it is often difficult to unpick direct lines of transmission, particularly when translation is also involved, and as tempting as it is for scholars to assume that the *Legenda aurea* is the main source for almost any 'standard' saint's Life,[17]

---

[12] Stephanus, *The Life of Bishop Wilfrid*, ed. and trans. by Bertram Colgrave (Cambridge: Cambridge University Press, 1927); Ursinus, *Passio Leudegarii*, ed. by B. Krusch and W. Levison (Hanover and Leipzig: Impensis Bibliopolii Hahniani, 1910); Cogitosus, 'Cogitosus: Life of Saint Brigit', trans. by J.-M. Picard, *The Journal of the Royal Society of Antiquaries of Ireland*, 117 (1987), 11–27; Muirchú, *Muirchú Moccu Macthéni's 'Vita Sancti Patriccii' Life of Saint Patrick*, ed. by David Howlett (Dublin: Four Courts Press, 2006); Bede, *The Life of St Cuthbert*, trans. by J. Stevenson (London and New York: Burns & Oates, 1887); Bertram Colgrave (ed. and trans.), *Two Lives of Saint Cuthbert: A Life by an Anonymous Monk of Lindisfarne and Bede's Prose Texts, Translations and Notes* (Cambridge: Cambridge University Press, 1940); Felix, *Felix's Life of St Guthlac*, ed. and trans. by Bertram Colgrave (Cambridge: Cambridge University Press, 1956).

[13] Jacobus de Voragine, *The Golden Legend*, ed. and trans. by W. Granger Ryan, 2 vols (Princeton: Princeton University Press, 1993), hereafter *LA*.

[14] Sherry L. Reames, *The Legenda Aurea: A Reexamination of its Paradoxical History* (Madison: The University of Wisconsin Press, 1985), pp. 3–5.

[15] Brenda Dunn-Lardeau (ed.), *La légende dorée: édition critique, dans la revision de 1476 par Jean Batailler, d'après la traduction de Jean de Vignay (1333–1348) de la Legenda aurea (c. 1261-1266)* (Paris: H. Champion, 1997); Richard Hamer (ed.), *Gilte Legende, volume 1*, EETS (Oxford: Oxford University Press, 2006); Hamer (ed.), *Gilte Legende, volume 2*, EETS (Oxford: Oxford University Press, 2007); Hamer (ed.), *Gilte Legende, volume 3*, EETS (Oxford: Oxford University Press, 2012).

[16] Manfred Görlach, *The Textual Tradition of the South English Legendary* (Leeds: University of Leeds, 1974).

[17] For example, Glanmor Williams, *The Welsh Church from Conquest to Reformation* (Cardiff: University of Wales Press, 1976), pp. 101, 103.

this is, of course, not always the case — as we shall see when discussing some of the idiosyncrasies apparent in the Middle Welsh version of the legend of St Ursula and the 11,000 Virgins.

Saints' Lives often share common themes or patterns: they frequently begin by outlining the saint's noble lineage; they provide an account of the saint's unusual conception and birth as well as his/her precocious childhood; they explain details relating to the saint's education, piety and humility; they narrate the many miracles performed by the saint both during his/her lifetime and posthumously; the saint is usually forewarned of his/her death and although the saint always welcomes death, this is regularly accompanied by a description of the great lamentation performed by the saint's community; details of the saint's martyrdom or natural physical demise are provided, sometimes accompanied by episodes involving the discovery or translation of the saint's relics, as well as descriptions of how the relics are venerated or the many miraculous events that have occurred at the saint's shrine, church, holy well or cemetery. As an exemplary Christian, the saint's deeds often mirror the life of Christ: miracles involving healing, controlling the elements or the natural world, walking on water, miraculously producing food or wine, and even resurrecting the dead are regularly performed by the saints, and common hagiographical motifs frequently reappear in different saints' Lives. Miracles, episodes and even whole sections are often borrowed from one saint's Life and applied to another. Régis Boyer has defined a 'kind of typology of medieval hagiography'[18] and Jocelyn Wogan-Browne has analysed the blueprint for a female saint's Life.[19] Folkloric elements and similarities between saints' Lives and secular heroic tales have been usefully identified in Welsh and Irish hagiographic texts by Elissa Henken and Dorothy Ann Bray.[20]

Lack of perceived originality in literature associated with saints has often led to criticisms of the genre as a whole, which, at times, has either been seen as inferior to native vernacular literature or read as a kind of misleading and unreliable form of history. In *The Sources for the Early History of Ireland* J. F. Kenney, for example, dismisses hagiography since he believes its main source is 'legend':

---

[18] Régis Boyer, 'An Attempt to Define the Typology of Medieval Hagiography', in *Hagiography and Medieval Literature: A Symposium*, ed. by Hans Bekker-Nielsen et al. (Odense: Odense University Press, 1981), pp. 27–36.

[19] Jocelyn Wogan-Browne, 'Saint's Lives and the Female Reader', *Forum for Modern Language Studies*, 4 (1991), 314–32. On feminine sanctity, see also Jane Cartwright, *Feminine Sanctity and Spirituality in Medieval Wales* (Cardiff: University of Wales Press, 2008).

[20] Elissa R. Henken, *Traditions of the Welsh Saints* (Cambridge: Brewer, 1987); Henken, *The Welsh Saints: A Study of Patterned Lives* (Woodbridge: D. S. Brewer, 1991); Dorothy A. Bray, *A List of Motifs in the Lives of the Early Irish Saints* (Helsinki: Suomalainen Tiedeakatemia, 1992).

> Legend belongs to the realm of folklore, where the transmission of facts is exceedingly erratic. The folk-mind sometimes retains the record of an event with extraordinary accuracy from generation to generation, sometimes within a few years distorts it beyond recognition. It is a medium that cannot be trusted. Yet we may say that, as a rule, folk-lore transmutes the personality which appeals to it — and the saint is such — into something different, something associated with a world of wonder and make-believe and primitive ethics, created out of the people's oldest and most elementary ideas.[21]

Particularly within the nineteenth and early twentieth centuries, there was a tendency to mine hagiographical texts for any information that might shed light on the period in which the saint was perceived to have lived (even if those texts had been composed some five hundred years after the saint was believed to have died).[22] Yet rather than see hagiography as an imperfect record of monastic tradition 'contaminated [...] by popular legend',[23] most scholars now appreciate that hagiography, when viewed within its literary and historical context, is a valuable source for the religious, social and cultural history of the period in which it was written, rather than the period it purports to describe.[24] As such, it sheds light on contemporary religious beliefs, literary tastes and influences, as well as the patronage, reception and transmission of medieval texts and the socio-political concerns and ecclesiastical preoccupations of the day.

Kenney's pejorative claim that hagiography reflects 'primitive ethics' represents the oft-made criticism that the religious element in medieval saints' Lives consisted of a mixture of 'magic' and 'superstition' designed to appeal to the lowest common denominator in medieval society. It also reflects

---

[21] J. F. Kenney, *The Sources for the Early History of Ireland* (New York: Columbia University Press, 1929), p. 301.

[22] Sabine Baring-Gould and John Fisher, *Lives of the British Saints*, 4 vols (London: Cymmrodorion, 1907–1913), provides useful accounts of the extant sources and dedications associated with saints from the Celtic regions, but tends to treat them as historical characters.

[23] Kenney, *The Sources*, p. 301. In the late nineteenth century Carl Horstmann, who edited two important collections of saints' Lives, the *Early South-English Legendary* and *Nova Legenda Anglie*, anticipated criticism of the hagiographical texts, but was also keen to defend the value of the genre: 'I know most Englishmen consider it not worth while to print all these Legends; I know they regard them as worthless stuff, without any merit [... yet] every epoch, every faith, has its *raison d'être*, and every poetry its beauty. If the present English public cannot see any merit in these Legends, it does not follow that there is no such merit', Carl Horstmann (ed.), *The Early South-English Legendary*, EETS o.s. 87 (London, 1887; reprinted Millwood New York, 1975), pp. ix.

[24] Hippolyte Delehaye was one of the first scholars to appreciate this: Delehaye, *Cinq leçons sur la méthode hagiographique* (Bruxelles: Société des Bollandistes, 1934), Delehaye, *Les légendes hagiographiques*, 4th edn (Bruxelles: Société des Bollandistes, 1955). See also J. Wyn Evans, 'The Early Church in Denbighshire', *Transactions of the Denbighshire Historical Society*, 35 (1986), 61–81 (p. 65); Salih, ' Saints, Cults and Lives', pp. 15–23.

the supposition that saints' Lives were devoid of any theological depth. Yet hagiographical texts could be both theologically and structurally complex and sophisticated. Thomas O'Loughlin has shed light on the scholarly erudition of Rhygyfarch (1057-1099) and the intricate layering of biblical references in *Vita Dauidis* (the Life of St David of Wales), and Elizabeth Krajewski has carefully analysed the earliest Lives of SS Brigit, Samson and Cuthbert to uncover the deep biblical influences within the narratives, arguing that the texts were intended to educate and be both metaphorical and illustrative rather than factual.[25] In the case of Cogitosus's *Vita Brigitae*, for example, she proposes a deliberate chiastic structure in which Brigit's Kildare is portrayed as a monastic city of refuge, the locus of the New Jerusalem where Christians from all over Ireland could come to celebrate holy days in imitation of the tribes of Israel.[26] The medieval hagiographer deliberately intended to echo passages of scripture and miracles or images associated with Christ or other biblical and saintly figures. Many of these would have had specific resonances with their medieval audiences that may not readily be apparent or easily interpreted by a modern audience: this 'recycling' of common motifs was intentional and, no doubt, not perceived as a weakness by contemporary audiences.

What made a saint a saint rather than a particularly pious Christian was his/her ability to perform miracles, and any miracle was a sign that God was acting through the agency of his chosen individual, that is the saint. Miracles, by their very definition, were meant to be incredulous, not merely good deeds capable of being performed by any devout Christian. The *virtus* of the saint gave him/her special powers: the ability to heal the sick, provide food during a famine, ease emotional and physical pain, and intercede on behalf of the faithful devotee or repentant sinner. The fact that the saint was a merciful fellow human being, who had often also suffered hardship, meant perhaps that he/she was perceived by devotees as being more amenable than Christ or God himself. Praying to a sympathetic human, who was already a resident in heaven, inevitably appealed to Christians keen for the saint to intercede on their behalf and use his/her influence to grant requests, especially when the saint was renowned for assisting with specific problems. Hagiographic texts served several purposes, but they primarily made a case for why a particular individual should be considered a saint — laying out the criteria necessary for this role and emphasizing how the holy person in question fulfilled these characteristics. Therefore the text, to a certain extent, may be seen to embody the virtues of the saint. And the individual responsible for copying, compiling, translating,

---

[25] Thomas O'Loughlin, 'Rhygyfarch's *Vita Dauidis*: An Apparatus Biblicus', *Studia Celtica*, 32 (1998), 179-88; Elizabeth M. G. Krajewski, *Archetypal Narratives: Pattern and Parable in the Lives of Three Saints* (Turnhout: Brepols, 2018).
[26] Krajewski, *Archetypal Narratives*, p. 90.

commissioning or even reading the saint's Life was implicated in this virtue — for all of these activities constituted an act of veneration, and to venerate a saint was also to worship God.

While many hagiographies and multiple versions of many hagiographical texts are extant from the medieval period, it is also possible to argue that the term 'hagiography' covers more than one genre. The Bollandist Hipployte Delehaye, in his seminal study of the Lives of the saints, classified hagiographical texts into six categories, and 'authenticity' appears to have been his main criterion for allocating a particular Life to a specific category: that is, whether the Life was a genuine eye-witness account about a real person, an imaginative account about a person that existed or a fictional account about a person that never existed, etc.[27] For Delehaye 'every writing that bears on the saints' could be classified as hagiography.[28] Thomas Head noted that it was best to refer to hagiography as 'a collection of genres' rather than a single genre, since hagiographical literature included the passions (or *passio*, 'suffering', of the martyrs), Lives of the saints, collections of miracle stories, accounts of the discovery or movement of relics, bulls of canonization, liturgical books, sermons, visions, etc.[29] Hagiography, therefore, covers a broad range of texts and some hagiographical texts (such as *Hystoria Gweryddon yr Almaen*) combined several elements from this range of genres.

Hagiography in Wales

A substantial corpus of hagiographical literature written in Latin and Welsh is extant from Wales. Numerous *vitae* and *bucheddau* record the biographical legends of various native Welsh saints, as well as the universal saints of Christendom, and medieval Welsh poetry is also an important hagiographical source.[30] The earliest Life of a Welsh saint, however, was written in Brittany

---

[27] Hippolyte Delehaye, *The Legends of the Saints*, trans. by Donald Attwater (Dublin: Four Courts Press, 1998), pp. 86–89. His six categories may be summarized as: (i) passions of the martyrs based on official reports, (ii) authentic Acts based on eye-witness accounts, (iii) Acts based on written documents, (iiii) Acts that are not historical but based on a real person, (v) imaginative romances in which the person is also an invention, (vi) forgeries.
[28] Delehaye, *The Legends of the Saints*, p. 3
[29] Head (ed.), *Medieval Hagiography*, p. xiv; Head, 'Hagiography', The ORB: On-Line Reference Book for Medieval Studies <http://www.the-orb.net/encyclop/religion/hagiography> (accessed 23 April 2018).
[30] Guy Philippart's ambitious international survey of Western hagiography refers only to a few of the Welsh saints' Latin *vitae*: Philippart (ed.), *Hagiographies: International History of the Latin and Vernacular Hagiographical Literature in the West from its Origins to 1550* (Turnhout: Brepols, 1994–2010). However, two projects funded by the AHRC will make scholarly editions and translations of more than one hundred Middle Welsh and Latin texts about Welsh saints available online (including verse and prose *bucheddau* and prose *vitae*): Seintiau yng Nghymru / Saints in Wales / Vitae Sanctorum Cambriae <http://www.seintiaucymru.ac.uk/> / <http://www.welshsaints.ac.uk/> (forthcoming).

rather than Wales in the seventh or possibly early eighth century. *Vita I S. Samsonis* recounts how St Samson was born and bred in Wales and studied, along with SS David, Gildas and Paul Aurélian, under the tutelage of St Illtud (traditionally thought to be at Llanilltud Fawr/Llantwit Major). St Samson reputedly left Llanilltud Fawr for the stricter monastic regime on a nearby island (generally assumed to be Caldey Island),[31] before travelling extensively in Cornwall and finally settling in Brittany. St Illtud's reputation as one of the first great teachers of Britain is established in the early medieval Breton sources for *Vita S. Paul Aureliani*. Written by Wrmonoc at Landévennec *c*. 884, this Life claims that St Paul studied at Llanilltud. Illtud is referred to in the section on wonders and miraculous events in *Historia Brittonum* (*c*. 829/30), and John Reuben Davies suggests that this drew on a lost Latin Life of Illtud that would have pre-dated the *Vita S. Iltuti* (*c*. 1200) which is found in London, British Library, Cotton Vespasian A. xiv.[32] At least five versions of the Life of St Malo, another Welsh saint, were composed in Brittany by different authors from the ninth to twelfth centuries, and Barry Lewis suggests that the reference to *ystoria* in an anonymous Middle Welsh poem to St Mechyll, who was identified with Malo from at least the fourteenth century, may imply that there was once a Welsh version of the Life of this saint. Although the identification of Mechyll of Llanfechyll in Anglesey with Malo is not unproblematic, the poem clearly conflates St Malo and the Anglesey saint and attributes Malo's principal miracles to Mechyll.[33]

Inevitably, many Welsh saints' Lives will have been lost over time and the texts that survive may well represent 'the tip of the iceberg' in relation to Welsh hagiographical output. It is generally assumed that the Latin Lives of Welsh saints preceded their later Middle Welsh equivalents and that poetic narratives, or snippets of hagiographical traditions preserved in poetry, may have drawn on lost Welsh Lives or oral versions of saints' Lives that were never committed to writing. There were also, no doubt, Latin *vitae* that have vanished: Fiona Winward and Patrick Sims-Williams argue convincingly that the Middle Welsh *Buchedd Beuno* (*c*. 1346) was based on a lost Latin Life of Beuno, and Jonathan

---

[31] Jennifer Bell, in 'Here, There or Nowhere: The School of St Illtud' (unpublished paper delivered at the XVIth International Congress of Celtic Studies, University of Bangor, 23 July 2019), suggests that St Illtud's school may have been located on Caldey Island rather than Llanilltud Fawr.
[32] John Reuben Davies, 'The Saints of South Wales and the Welsh Church', in *Local Saints and Local Churches in the Early Medieval West*, ed. by Thacker and Sharpe, pp. 361–95 (p. 383).
[33] Barry Lewis (ed. and trans.), *Medieval Welsh Poems to Saints and Shrines* (Dublin: School of Celtic Studies, Dublin Institute for Advanced Studies, 2015), pp. 72, 132–33. On the various Lives of St Malo and the process of rewriting hagiography in Brittany, see Bernard Merdrignac, 'The Process and Significance of Rewriting in Breton Hagiography', in *Celtic Hagiography and Saints' Cults*, ed. by Jane Cartwright (Cardiff: University of Wales Press, 2003), pp. 177–97, especially pp. 191–95.

Wooding proposes that references to St Brendan in Bili's Latin Life of Malo imply that Brendan enjoyed a cult in Wales before 900 CE.[34] Kathleen Hughes suggests that Lives of St Brendan and St Maedog appear to have been familiar to a hagiographer in west Wales *c.* 1090,[35] and Ben Guy argues that a Life of St Dyfrig may have been written in Moccas shortly after *c.* 850.[36]

While in modern Wales only the feasts of St David, and to a lesser extent St Dwynwen (patron saint of lovers), may be familiar to people, in medieval Wales the feast of a different saint was celebrated every day, and these would vary from one region to another. The feasts of native and universal saints are commemorated in Welsh calendars, and appropriate readings for the liturgical commemoration of saints' cults would have been required by monastic and ecclesiastical communities. Given that a royal injunction of 1549 declared that all medieval service books should be destroyed, it is little wonder that relatively few liturgical texts survive.[37] However, among the texts that do is an early fifteenth-century breviary that contains liturgical material and an office intended for the celebration of St David's Day, 1 March.[38] A decree in 1398 records that St David's feast day was celebrated throughout the province of Canterbury, although his main sphere of influence was largely confined to south Wales in the medieval period (as indicated by his church dedications);[39] SS Beuno, Deiniol and Gwenfrewy held greater influence in north Wales, and the cults of Illtud, Teilo and Dyfrig predominated in the south-east. Fashions

---

[34] Fiona Winward, 'Lives of St Wenefred (BHL 8847–8851)', *Analecta Bollandiana*, 117 (1999), 89–132; Patrick Sims-Williams (ed.), *Buchedd Beuno* (Dublin: School of Celtic Studies, Dublin Inst. for Advanced Studies, 2018), pp. 17–32; Jonathan M. Wooding, 'The Figure of David', in *St David of Wales: Cult, Church and Nation*, ed. by J. Wyn Evans and Jonathan M. Wooding (Woodbridge: Boydell Press, 2007), pp. 1–19 (p. 13).

[35] Kathleen Hughes, 'British Museum MS. Cotton Vespasian A. XIV ('Vitae Sanctorum Wallensium'): its Purpose and Provenance', in *Studies in the Early British Church*, ed. by Nora Chadwick et al. (Cambridge: Cambridge University Press, 1958), pp. 183–200 (p. 190); James Conway Davies, *Episcopal Acts and Cognate Documents Relating to Welsh Dioceses 1066–1272*, 2 vols (Cardiff: Historical Society of the Church in Wales, 1946), II, pp. 500–01

[36] Benjamin David Guy, 'The Life of St Dyfrig and the Lost Charters of Moccas (Mochros), Herefordshire', *Cambrian Medieval Celtic Studies*, 75 (2018), 1–34 (p. 37). Although now in Herefordshire, Moccas was the site of an early Welsh monastery claimed to have been founded by St Dyfrig.

[37] See Daniel Huws, 'St David in the Liturgy: A Review of the Sources', in *St David of Wales*, ed. by Evans and Wooding, pp. 220–32 (p. 221) and ff. for a review of extant liturgical sources.

[38] Owain Tudor Edwards, *Matins, Lauds and Vespers for St David's Day: The Medieval Office of the Welsh Patron Saint in National Library of Wales MS 20541E* (Cambridge: Brewer, 1990); Edwards, 'The Office of St David in Paris, Bibliothèque Nationale, MS Lat. 17294', in *St David of Wales*, ed by Evans and Wooding, pp. 233–52.

[39] See Heather James, 'The Geography of the Cult of St David: A Study of Dedication Patterns in the Medieval Diocese', in *St David of Wales*, ed. by Evans and Wooding, pp. 41–83.

for particular saints could come and go, and ecclesiastical politics often determined which saints' Lives were composed and promoted.

The earliest Latin prose Life of St David was written by Rhygyfarch (d. 1099), a monk from Llanbadarn Fawr, whose father Sulien was twice bishop of St Davids. At the synod of Llanddewibrefi David is appointed archbishop 'by the consent of all the bishops, kings, princes, nobles, and all the ranks of people of the whole British nation' and his monastery is declared 'the metropolitan church of the whole country, so that whoever might govern it should be accounted archbishop'.[40] Rhygyfarch left the audience of the *vita* in no doubt as to the pre-eminence of the patron saint of St Davids. Bernard, the first Norman bishop of the diocese (1115–1148), was also keen to establish the metropolitan status of Menevia and despite swearing an oath of obedience to the Archbishop of Canterbury, it would appear that he harboured a desire to secure archiepiscopal independence for the see of Menevia.[41] He was also determined to re-discover the corporeal relics of St David, which had most likely disappeared in a raid by Orkneymen *c.* 1089.[42] His failure to find the relics was, no doubt, a source of frustration, since his main rival Urban, bishop of Llandaf (1107–*c.* 1134), had succeeded in acquiring the relics of St Teilo and St Dyfrig. Dyfrig (or Dubricius), who is described as a holy bishop in the early Life of St Samson, is presented in his own *vita* as the founding father of the Welsh Church and is accredited with founding the see of Llandaf. Dyfrig is appointed archbishop of the whole of 'southern Britain' by St Germanus and St Lupus, and consecrates other bishops such as Deiniol (patron of Bangor cathedral) and David. Before he expires Dyfrig retires to Bardsey Island and his Life ends with an account of the translation of his relics to the cathedral erected by Urban in Llandaf in 1120.[43] Prior to the ninth century, a monastery that venerated Teilo at Llandeilo Fawr in Carmarthenshire appears to have owned the Book of St Chad (the Lichfield Gospels) and an ancient altar of St Teilo, but in the twelfth century Teilo became 'archbishop of Llandaf'. The

---

[40] Richard Sharpe and John Reuben Davies (eds), 'Rhygyfarch's *Life* of St David', in *St David of Wales*, ed. by Evans and Wooding, pp. 107–55 (p. 147).

[41] Menevia was the Roman name for St Davids and corresponds to the diocese of St Davids. On Bernard and his attempts to obtain metropolitan status for St Davids, see J. Wyn Evans 'Bishops of St Davids from Bernard to Bec', in *Pembrokeshire County History II*, ed. by R. F. Walker (Haverfordwest: Pembrokeshire Historical Society, 2002), pp. 270–303 (pp. 271–78), but cf. also the different view proposed by John Reuben Davies, 'Cathedrals and the Cult of Saints in Eleventh- and Twelfth-Century Wales', in *Cathedrals, Communities and Conflict in the Anglo-Norman World*, ed. by Paul Dalton et al. (Woodbridge: Boydell Press, 2011), pp. 99–116 (p. 103).

[42] Kathryn Hurlock, *Medieval Welsh Pilgrimage, c. 1100–1500* (Basingstoke: Palgrave Macmillan, 2018), pp. 18–19.

[43] G. H. Doble, *Lives of the Welsh Saints*, ed. by D. Simon Evans (Cardiff: University of Wales Press, 1971), pp. 56–87; J. G. Evans and J. Rhŷs (eds), *The Text of the Book of Llan Dâv* (Oxford: John Bellows for J. G. Evans, 1893).

twelfth-century *Liber Landavensis* (Book of Llandaf, NLW 17110E) promoted Urban's newly founded diocese and gave it an air of archaic authenticity. As well as charter material confirming land grants, it also includes the Lives of SS Teilo, Euddogwy, Clydog and Aelfgar.[44] The cult of St Euddogwy (Oudoceus), a 'long forgotten bishop of that name, who turned up in charter-memoranda' was, according to John Reuben Davies, 'raised from the dead' by Urban, who was keen to promote the cults of native Welsh saints and associate them with his diocese when this suited his own political game.[45] The hagiographical texts in the *Liber Landavensis* functioned as one of the main propaganda tools employed in this struggle for diocesan lands and supremacy.

The Latin Life of Cadog was composed by Lifris, son of Bishop Herwald, c. 1090. It was revised by Caradog of Llancarfan c. 1140 and a composite version of the two Lives appears in London, British Library, Cotton Vespasian A. xiv c. 1200. Lifris's *Vita Sancti Cadoci* was described by Phillimore as 'infinitely the most important of all the Welsh Lives of saints written in Wales'.[46] In much the same way as Sulpicius Severus's Life of Martin stood at the head of the genre of Latin hagiographical texts in the western world, so too may Lifris's Life of Cadog be considered, to a certain extent, the uber text of the *vitae* of Welsh saints. A complete and fairly lengthy Life, many of the motifs and miracles re-occur in other saints' Lives, and the re-occurrence of certain common motifs, such as the hanging of a mouse and maiming of horses, in secular native tales led Glenys Goetinck to speculate that Lifris may even have been the author of the Mabinogi.[47]

Vita Sancti Cadoci appears in the important collection of saints' Lives found in Cotton Vespasian A. xiv, compiled in Monmouth priory, that also includes the *vitae* of SS Gwynllyw, Illtud, Dyfrig, David, Teilo, Padarn, Clydog, Cybi, Carannog, Brynach and Aedan.[48] According to Kathleen Hughes, Cadog 'is clearly the most important saint in the collection'.[49] Llancarfan was granted to Gloucester between 1093 and 1100. Kathleen Hughes has suggested that at some point before the Vespasian A. xiv manuscript was compiled the Lives

---

[44] On the charters, see Patrick Sims-Williams (ed.), *The Book of Llandaf as a Historical Source* (Oxford: Boydell Press, 2019).
[45] Davies, 'The Saints of South Wales', p. 391. See also Davies, *The Book of Llandaf and the Norman Church in Wales* (Woodbridge: Boydell Press, 2003).
[46] Egerton Phillimore, 'Notes by the Editor', in J. W. Willis-Bund, 'The True Objects of Welsh Archaeology', *Y Cymmrodor*, 11 (1890–1891), 125–32 (p. 127).
[47] Glenys Goetinck (ed.), 'Pedair Cainc y Mabinogi: Yr Awdur a'i Bwrpas', *Llên Cymru*, 15 (1987–1988), 249–69.
[48] A. W. Wade-Evans (ed. and trans.), *Vitae Sanctorum Britanniae et Genealogiae* (Cardiff: University of Wales Press, 1944); see also the forthcoming editions in the Seintiau yng Nghymru / Saints in Wales / Vitae Sanctorum Cambriae projects <http://www.seintiaucymru.ac.uk/> / <http://www.welshsaints.ac.uk/> (forthcoming).
[49] Hughes, 'British Museum', p. 191.

of Welsh saints were collected at Gloucester, and that the selection of saints in the legendary reflects the interests of Gloucester as well as Monmouth.[50] However, more recently, the nature and extent of Gloucester's involvement has been queried and it has been suggested that its relationship with Llancarfan and Llandaf is most likely to have been predominantly financial.[51]

Another important collection of saints' Lives is found in London, British Library, MS Cotton Tiberius E i from the mid-fourteenth century: *Sanctilogium Angliae, Waliae, Scotiae et Hiberniae*. This vast corpus of saints' Lives, attributed to John of Tynemouth (*fl.* 1366), includes the Lives of Welsh saints such as Cain, Caradog, Cennydd, Winefride, Gildas, David, Justinian, Cadog and Teilo, among others. It was envisaged as a national collection of saints' Lives and also included a Life of Ursula, considered no doubt by Tynemouth as a 'British' saint (i.e. deriving from Britain) rather than specifically included here as a Welsh saint.[52] The *Sanctilogium* was later to be reordered by John Capgrave (1393–1464) and re-cycled as *Nova legenda Anglie*.[53] The collection was printed by Wynkyn de Worde in 1516 but included a different version of the Life of Ursula which, as we shall see, shared similarities with the Welsh text.[54]

Two Latin Lives of Winefride (or Gwenfrewy as she was known in Welsh) appear to have been produced independently of each other in the first half of the twelfth century; both relate the legend of how St Winefride was decapitated by Prince Caradog when she refused his advances, but later resurrected by St Beuno (her uncle according to the saintly genealogies known as *Bonedd y Saint*). Appended to the anonymous Life is a series of posthumous miracles that took place at her holy well, most of which involve either miraculously healing the faithful or enacting retribution on those that abuse the church or its property at Holywell (i.e. Treffynnon in Welsh, the place which took its name from her well). The other *vita* was compiled by Prior Robert of Shrewsbury sometime between 1137 and 1142. In addition to the standard Life of St Winefride, Prior Robert's *vita* also describes how he, accompanied by the prior of Chester and a Welsh priest, journeyed to Gwytherin, where Winefride was buried, and persuaded the bishop of Bangor and the local Welsh prince (either Gruffudd ap Cynan or his son Owain Gwynedd) to exhume Winefride's relics and have them translated to Shrewsbury. In the context of Welsh hagiography the *vita*

[50] Hughes, 'British Museum', p. 193.
[51] Benjamin David Guy, 'The Vespasian Life of St Teilo and the Evolution of the *Vitae Sanctorum Wallensium*' (unpublished paper delivered at the *Vitae Sanctorum Cambriae* Conference, University of Cambridge, 26 September 2019).
[52] The fragments of Ursula's *vita* can be found in London, British Library, MS Cotton Tiberius E. i, fols 88r–89r.
[53] Carl Horstmann (ed.), *Nova Legenda Anglie*, 2 vols (Oxford: Clarendon Press, 1901), I, p. xii.
[54] *Nova Legenda Anglie* (London: Wynkyn de Worde, 1516), Early English Books Online (hereafter *NLA*).

is unusual because in this instance the hagiographer is a character in the Life. Prior Robert's Life is preserved in three manuscripts; David Callendar argues that Laud Misc. 114, a twelfth-century manuscript associated with Pershore Abbey in Worcestershire, most closely resembles Robert's original Life.[55]

It is this version that most closely resembles the Middle Welsh *Buchedd Gwenfrewy*. The Welsh Life is preserved in four manuscripts: (i) Aberystwyth, NLW, MS Peniarth 27ii, compiled by an unknown scribe in the second half of the fifteenth century, which ends with Gwenfrewy's death and burial at Gwytherin and brief fragmentary references to healings at her well at Holywell; and (ii) Aberystwyth, NLW, MS Llanstephan 34, a manuscript compiled by Roger Morris of Coedytalwrn in Llanfair Dyffryn Clwyd at the end of the sixteenth century. This includes the account of the translation of her relics to Shrewsbury by Prior Robert and is a more 'complete' account, although the phraseology in Peniarth 27ii occasionally mirrors the Latin text more closely than Llanstephan 34 does.[56] The other two manuscripts, (iii) Aberystwyth, NLW, MSS Peniarth 225 and (iv) Llanstephan 104, are effectively copies of the Llanstephan 34 text.[57]

Given that so few native Welsh female saints have extant Lives, in the context of feminine sanctity, St Winefride may perhaps be considered a Welsh super saint. Many female saints were known and revered in medieval Wales, but few traces of their cults survive: often their names are preserved in place names, church dedications and genealogies, or they are mentioned briefly in poetry or the Lives of other saints. Winefride, on the other hand, has a substantial hagiographical dossier, including the Latin *vitae* and Welsh *buchedd* discussed above; she also features strongly in *Buchedd Beuno* (c. 1346) and poems were composed in her honour by Ieuan Brydydd Hir (*fl*. 1450–1485), Tudur Aled (*c*. 1465–*c*. 1525) and Siôn ap Hywel ap Llywelyn Fychan (*fl. c*. 1490–1532), as well as various *cywyddau* by anonymous poets.[58] Her well at Holywell, now considered

---

[55] David Callander (ed. and trans.), *Vita Sancte Wenefrede*, Seintiau yng Nghymru / Saints in Wales / Vitae Sanctorum Cambriae website <http://www.seintiaucymru.ac.uk/> / <http://www.welshsaints.ac.uk/> (forthcoming).

[56] Jane Cartwright, '*Buchedd Gwenfrewy*: The Life of St Winefride in NLW MSS Peniarth 27ii and Llanstephan 34' (unpublished paper delivered at XVI Celtic Congress, University of Bangor, 25 July 2019).

[57] Moses Williams (1685–1742) clearly had possession of Llanstephan 34 at some point and compiled an index to the manuscript. His amanuensis copied the Life almost word-for-word into Llanstephan 104. Peniarth 225 is an adaptation Thomas Wiliems made which is incomplete and ends with a miracle emphasising the sanctity of the burial ground at Gwytherin. See Jane Cartwright (ed. and trans.), *Buchedd Gwenfrewy*, Seintiau yng Nghymru / Saints in Wales / Vitae Sanctorum Cambriae website <http://www.seintiaucymru.ac.uk/> / <http://www.welshsaints.ac.uk/> (forthcoming).

[58] The *cywydd* (plural *cywyddau*) is one of the most important metrical forms in traditional Welsh poetry. Paul Bryant-Quinn (ed.), *Gwaith Ieuan Brydydd Hir* (Aberystwyth: Canolfan Uwchefrydiau Cymreig a Cheltaidd Prifysgol Cymru, 2000), pp. 141–45; T. Gwynn Jones

to be one of the Seven Wonders of Wales, is undoubtedly the most well-known of all Welsh holy wells, and the medieval poets, just like her hagiographers, referred to the many healing miracles that took place at Holywell, as well as the refurbishing of the well chapel in the early sixteenth century. One can clearly understand the motives that led to Prior Robert's compilation of *Vita S Wenefede*, after having acquired her relics for his own priory church, as well as why the monks of Chester and Basingwerk Abbeys, who vied for ownership of the well throughout much of the Middle Ages, may also have had reason to promote her cult. Winefride was a rare example of a Welsh female saint who acquired political clout. She was deemed suitable to be venerated by royalty: Richard II, Henry V and Edward IV all went on pilgrimage to Holywell, and Henry VII's Lady Chapel within Westminster Abbey contains a statue of St Winefride. Although, in the twelfth century, the diocese of St Asaph had its share of 'absent' bishops or those that may not have engaged with local saints given the apparently hostile relationship they appear to have shared with the local populace,[59] by the fifteenth century, when *Buchedd Gwenfrewy* was most likely composed, Winefride appears, alongside St Asaph, on the fifteenth-century seal of the Chapter of St Asaph, demonstrating her authority within the diocese in that period.[60]

Perhaps one of the reasons why so few *vitae* or *bucheddau* survive for native female saints is that these female characters lacked political clout and did not come to be considered as patrons of the dominant dioceses. This is also true of the majority of local native male saints and may explain why so few Welsh *bucheddau* are extant for them, although traditions about them are preserved by poets familiar with local and oral traditions. The only other native female saint for whom a prose *vita* survives is Melangell, patron saint of hares. Three complete copies and two incomplete copies of her Latin Life, *Historia divae Monacellae*, are extant in manuscripts dating from the late sixteenth century, and there is also a printed copy of a seventeenth-century manuscript which was destroyed in a fire in 1858.[61] Her relics were venerated in France in the early eighteenth century and described in a series of letters by the Jesuit Father Louis de Sabran, who also refers to a play that was performed in her honour at

(ed.), *Gwaith Tudur Aled*, 2 vols (Caerdydd: Gwasg Prifysgol Cymru, 1926), II, pp. 523–26; Henry Lewis et al. (eds), *Cywyddau Iolo Goch ac Eraill* (Caerdydd: Gwasg Prifysgol Cymru, 1937), pp. 104–06; A. Cynfael Lake (ed.), *Gwaith Siôn ap Hywel ap Llywelyn Fychan* (Aberystwyth: Canolfan Uwchefrydiau Cymreig a Cheltaidd, 1999), pp. 73–75.
[59] Hurlock, *Medieval Welsh Pilgrimage*, p. 128.
[60] Cartwright, *Feminine Sanctity*, Plate 13.
[61] Cardiff, Central Library, MS 3.11, p. 1 (incomplete); London, BL, Harley MS 2059, fols 111r–v (incomplete); Aberystwyth, NLW, MS 1641B I, pp. 63–8; R. Williams, 'Historiae Monacellae', *Archaeologia Cambrensis*, 3 (1848), 139–42; Huw Pryce, 'A New Edition of the Historia divae Monacellae', *Montgomeryshire Collections*, 82 (1994), 23–40.

St Omers.[62] The relics appear to have been lost, but the play is still extant.[63]

There are far fewer Middle Welsh prose *bucheddau* than Latin *vitae* that record the traditions of native Welsh saints. Thirty-two *bucheddau* are extant as well as three series of miracles or *gwyrthiau* (the Miracles of the Blessed Virgin Mary, the Miracles of St Edmund and the Miracles of the Archangel Michael). Approximately three quarters of the *bucheddau* record the Lives of universal saints (such as, for example, the Lives of Mary Magdalene, Martha, Mary of Egypt, Margaret of Antioch and Katherine of Alexandria, which are all found in the White Book of Rhydderch, Aberystwyth, NLW, MS Peniarth 5, *c.* 1350), and Welsh adaptations of the Lives of the apostles and evangelists, Martin, Nicholas, Dorothy, Andrew, Laurence, Silvester, Ursula, Simon and Jude, are preserved in manuscripts from the fifteenth and sixteenth centuries.

In addition to the Middle Welsh Lives of St David and St Beuno, which were adapted into Welsh and copied *c.* 1346 by an anonymous scribe known as 'the anchorite of Llanddewibrefi' for a Welsh layman named Gruffudd ap Phylip ap Trahaearn (Oxford, Jesus College, MS 119), and *Buchedd Gwenfrewy*, discussed above, the only Welsh Lives that venerate native saints are *Buchedd Collen, Buchedd Ieuan Gwas Padrig, Buchedd Llawddog* and *Buchedd Curig*. All of these Lives are found in Llanstephan 34 (1580 x 1600), the most important recusant collection of Welsh *bucheddau*.[64] Of the twenty-seven *bucheddau* in this manuscript, twenty-six are in the hand of Roger Morris and one (*Buchedd Margred*) was copied by Thomas Evans Hendreforfudd. The Life of Collen, which is also found in other manuscripts from the first half of the sixteenth century,[65] tells how Collen fought the pagan Byras and became Abbot of Glastonbury before deciding to live as a hermit and retiring to Glastonbury Tor, where he was obliged to overcome Gwyn ap Nudd.[66] Although Collen is associated with Llangollen and Ruabon in north-east Wales, Delpino suggests that St Colan in Cornwall is the same saint and that the Welsh Life may have derived from a Latin *vita* of Colan produced at Glasney, Penryn in Cornwall —

---

[62] Geoffrey Holt (ed.), *The Letter Book of Louis Sabran, S. J. (Rector of St Omers College) October 1713 to October 1715* (St Albans: The Catholic Record Society, 1971), pp. 8, 36–37, 53, 58, 66, 78, 80, 95–97, 99, 101, 108–10, 112, 118, 272, 277.

[63] Clitheroe, Stonyhurst College, MS 'Tragedies, Gallicanus, etc.', fols 148–66. Russell, 'The After-Life' of St Melangell/Monacella' (unpublished paper delivered at the *Vitae Sanctorum Cambriae* Conference, University of Cambridge, 26 September 2019).

[64] A recusant was a Roman Catholic who refused to attend Protestant services of the Church of England during the post-Reformation period and continued steadfast to his/her faith during the period in which Catholics were persecuted.

[65] Cardiff, Central Library, MS 2,629 (1535–1536) and Aberystwyth, NLW, MS Llanstephan 117 (1548), as well as six other later manuscripts.

[66] Alaw Mai Edwards (ed. and trans.), *Buchedd Collen*, Seintiau yng Nghymru / Saints in Wales / Vitae Sanctorum Cambriae website <http://www.seintiaucymru.ac.uk/> / <http://www.welshsaints.ac.uk/> (forthcoming).

that is, the same monastic college that produced the Cornish Lives of Meriasek and Ke.[67] The Life of Ieuan Gwas Padrig, a pupil of St Patrick, tells how he drove snakes away from Denbighshire, sailed over from Ireland miraculously on a slate slab and landed in Anglesey, before founding a church in Cerrigydrudion which he dedicated to Mary Magdalene.[68]

The earliest Welsh hagiographical poems are found in the work of the Poets of the Princes in the twelfth century. The poets Cynddelw, Llywelyn Fardd and Gwynfardd Brycheiniog composed *awdlau* to SS Tysilio, Cadfan and David, respectively, that recorded miracles and events associated with these saints.[69] In addition to the spiritual benefits associated with praising these saints, the poets were kean to emphasize the power and protection that Tysilio, Cadfan and David offered to the specific *clas* churches and communities with which they were associated, namely Meifod (Tysilio), Tywyn (Cadfan) and Llanddewibrefi (David). Individuals seeking *nawdd*, protection, could be offered sanctuary within the geographical boundaries that belonged to the church in question, and partisans are known to have fled to the church sites for protection during periods of conflict.[70] Nerys Ann Jones and Morfydd E. Owen have unravelled the complex political situations that appear to have led to the composition of these particular poems, and the ways in which the poets invoked the local native saint 'as a force to be used as a weapon in secular political manoeuvring' in twelfth-century Meirionnydd, Powys and Deheubarth.[71]

It is, however, in the work of the Poets of the Nobility in the fourteenth and fifteenth centuries that prolific references to the Welsh saints appear. As well as venerating the universal saints of Christendom — including, for example, all

---

[67] Mary I. R. Delpino, 'A Study of "Ystoria Collen" and the British Peregrini'(unpublished PhD thesis, University of Pensylvannia, 1980), p. 16.
[68] Jane Cartwright (ed. and trans.), *Buchedd Ieuan Gwas Padrig*, Seintiau yng Nghymru / Saints in Wales / Vitae Sanctorum Cambriae website <http://www.seintiaucymru.ac.uk/> / <http://www.welshsaints.ac.uk/> (forthcoming). He is also associated with Mary Magdalene and Cerrigydrudion in a *cywydd* by the Anglesey poet Gutyn Cyriog: D. J. (Gwenallt) Jones, 'Buchedd Mair Fadlen a'r *Legenda Aurea*', *BBCS*, 4 (1929), 325–29 (p. 329); Jane Cartwright (ed. and trans.), *Mary Magdalene and her Sister Martha: An Edition and Translation of the Medieval Welsh Lives* (Washington, DC: Catholic University of America Press, 2013), p. 20.
[69] An *awdl* is a long poem or ode written in *cynghanedd* (a complex system of alliteration and internal rhyme unique to Wales), plural *awdlau*. See the forthcoming editions and translations by Ann Parry Owen (ed. and trans.), 'Canu i Ddewi', 'Canu i Tysilio' and 'Canu i Cadfan', all at Seintiau yng Nghymru / Saints in Wales / Vitae Sanctorum Cambriae website <http://www.seintiaucymru.ac.uk/> / <http://www.welshsaints.ac.uk/>.
[70] For example, the chronicle *Brut y Tywysogyon* records that in 1109 the partisans of the local nobleman Cadwgan and his son Ithel fled to the sanctuary of the church of Llanddewibrefi for protection: T. Jones (ed.), *Brut y Tywysogyon (Red Book of Hergest Version)* (Cardiff: University of Wales Press, 1952), p. 60.
[71] N. A. Jones and M. E. Owen, 'Twelfth-Century Welsh Hagiography: The Gogynfeirdd Poems to Saints'in *Celtic Hagiography and Saints Cults*, ed. by Jane Cartwright (Cardiff: University of Wales Press, 2003), pp. 45–76 (p. 68).

aspects of the Life of the Virgin Mary — the poets composed numerous poems to lesser-known local Welsh saints (such as Dwynwen, Cawrda, Dyfodwg, Einion Frenin, Tydecho, Cynhafal and Mwrog). Only one poem to St Cathen of Llangathen in Carmarthenshire, for instance, appears to be extant, and this is recorded in a single manuscript in the poet's own hand: there is no prose Life.[72] In vivid detail Dafydd Epynt (*fl. c.* 1460) describes the excruciating physical pain he was suffering: it was almost as though a witch was chipping away unceasingly at his rib cage. He appears to have been suffering from a form of ague or malaria common in Britain and boggy areas of Wales in the fifteenth century and he appeals to St Cathen to heal him, noting at that time that Cathen was believed to have been buried at Llangathen:

> Cathen wyn, caeth yw 'nannedd,
> Gwared fi ar gwr dy fedd!
> Mae tân o'm iad i'r adain
> [   ]
> Ton yw 'mron yn ymrannu,
> Torred dan ddant teirton ddu.
> Gwrach oedd (gweywyr awch iddi!)
> Yn cael ymafael â mi[...]
> Gyr, ni allaf yn glafach,
> Gathen wyn, y gwythi'n iach.
>
> [Blessed Cathen, my teeth are locked rigid, | Succour me at your graveside! | I am on fire from my crown down to my arm | [   ] | My chest is broken, splitting in two, | It was broken under the bite of the black ague. | A witch (the sharpness of spears to her!) | Was having a bout of wrestling with me. [...] | O blessed Cathen, I cannot be sicker, | Make my sinews well again.][73]

Dafydd Epynt, a poet possibly from Merthyr Cynog on the edge of Mynydd Epynt, along with the fifteenth-century Breconshire poet Hywel Dafi, record interesting traditions associated with St Cynog that do not survive in any of the medieval Welsh prose *vitae* or *bucheddau*. For instance, Cynog, having fled to Wales from Ireland, one night encountered a cannibalistic giant moving from house to house in Caerwedros, eating an inhabitant from each of the houses as he passed through. Cynog rescues the son of a widow and is injured himself in the affray, but God sends him a miraculous golden torque with which he slays the giant before he too is martyred by decapitation. One of the Welsh cephalophore saints, Cynog is said to carry his own head around on a tether. Hywel Dafi appeals to him to defend Brycheiniog and ensure peace for

---

[72] Aberystwyth, NLW, MS Peniarth 54, pp. 124–27.
[73] Lewis (ed. and trans.), *Medieval Welsh Poems*, pp. 121–22, 392–94. See also Owen Thomas (ed.), *Gwaith Dafydd Epynt* (Aberystwyth: Canolfan Uwchefrydiau Cymreig a Cheltaidd Prifysgol Cymru, 2002), pp. 32, 94.

the inhabitants, while Dafydd Epynt appeals to Cynog to protect him with his torque should the poet ever encounter the devil.[74] Although Gerald of Wales (1146–1223) refers to Cynog's torque, the 'legend' recounted in the two poems was not preserved in prose form until recorded by the antiquarian herald Hugh Thomas c. 1702, who notes that he was drawing on an oral source provided by 'the poor Ignorant Country People where he suffered Martirdom'.[75] In Hugh Thomas's version the cannibal giant 'Instantly fell downe Dead and his Bowells which had Devoured much Innocent Blood like Judas's burst in sunder & fell to the Ground'.[76]

The fact that the poets also drew on local oral traditions means that some of the details in the poems are occasionally different from the *vitae/bucheddau*, although they usually record the same basic miracles and events when both verse and prose hagiographical texts are extant. Gwynfardd Brycheiniog's *awdl* to St David places greater emphasis on Llanddewibrefi than St Davids, and tantalizingly refers to some miracles that were not recounted in David's prose Lives: he is said, for example, to have visited Rome and lodged in Palestine, where it appears that he suffered a mighty blow with a fist from an unpleasant young girl with cruel teeth.[77] The wider context for this, which might have already been familiar to the poet's audience, is not explained. St David is also described in the *awdl* as guarding his tutor Peulin's corn fields and enclosing a flock of wild birds in a barn. This common hagiographical motif occurs in the Lives of Illtud, Paul Aurélian and Ieuan Gwas Padrig, but it is not mentioned in any of the prose Lives of David, although the miracle was clearly familiar to other poets such as Lewys Glyn Cothi and Iolo Goch.[78]

On other occasions it is not the light the poets shed on individual saints' miracles, but rather the collective naming of saints that is impressive: Dafydd Nanmor, for instance, invoked a whole army of saints to protect Henry VII as he gathered support in Wales for his campaign prior to the Battle of Bosworth. The power of approximately one hundred saints is unleashed and although the vast majority of the saints named are local native saints (such as Caron, Curig, Peblig, Tybïe and Non), a number of international saints also happily intermingle in his list of *saint yr ynys hon*, 'saints of this island', for example SS Gregory, George, Thomas, Stephen, Mary and Michael.[79] Since sanctity was

[74] Lewis (ed. and trans.), *Medieval Welsh Poems*, pp. 102–07, 242–60.
[75] London, British Library, MS Harleian 4181, p. 129; see pp. 129–32 for Cynog's story. On Hugh Thomas and the traditions he preserves about a number of native Welsh saints, see Jeanne Mehan, 'The Enduring Meme of the Saintly Daughters of Brychan Brycheiniog' (unpublished PhD thesis, University of Wales Trinity Saint David, forthcoming).
[76] London, British Library, MS Harleian 4181, p. 130.
[77] Parry Owen (ed. and trans.), 'Canu i Ddewi', lines 21–24.
[78] Parry Owen (ed. and trans.), 'Canu i Ddewi', lines 168–75; Wade-Evans (ed. and trans.), *Vitae Sanctorum*, pp. 212–15; Cartwright (ed. and trans.), *Buchedd Ieuan Gwas Padrig*.
[79] Thomas Roberts and Ifor Williams (eds), *The Poetical Works of Dafydd Nanmor* (Cardiff: University of Wales Press, 1923), pp. 46–50.

locally conferred in Wales, some of the universal saints' cults took on a regional flavour, and it is possible that the medieval populace did not differentiate between 'native' and 'non-native' saints in the same way that we do today, particularly in the late Middle Ages. They were embraced wholeheartedly for the important services they provided to the faithful, and approximately eighty Middle Welsh poems are extant that venerate saints in this period.[80]

Whilst poetry helped promote pilgrimage sites in Wales, it seems that canonization of the saints or formal recognition by the papacy was not deemed necessary. Canonization in the Middle Ages was a costly and cumbersome business and it is little wonder that Gerald of Wales's attempts to canonize St Caradog failed.[81] Documentation relating to St Davids provides only a glimpse of this process of seeking papal approval and relates to the granting of an indulgence at St Davids, not, as has often been assumed, the attempted canonization of St David.[82] As noted by Bartlett, it was generally accepted that requests to the papacy needed to be frequently repeated and insistent. To provide one example, it is recorded that the inquiry into the canonization of Louis IX, over a fourteen-year period, produced 'more written material than one ass could carry'.[83] During the entire period between 1200 and 1525 fewer canonizations occurred than they did during the papacy of Pope John Paul II (1978–2005).[84]

In Wales, as elsewhere in Europe, veneration of saints continued to flourish in the late fifteenth and early sixteenth centuries. As noted by Duffy, up to the very moment of the Reformation:

> Traditional religion had about it no particular marks of exhaustion or decay, and indeed in a whole host of ways, from the multiplication of vernacular religious books to adaptations within the national and regional cult of the saints, was showing itself well able to meet the new needs and new conditions.[85]

---

[80] See Lewis (ed. and trans.), *Medieval Welsh Poems*, as well as the forthcoming editions and translations of poetry by Lewis, Salisbury and Johnston in Seintiau yng Nghymru / the Saints in Wales project.

[81] See Hurlock, *Medieval Welsh Pilgrimage*, pp. 18-25, for a useful discussion of the development of pilgrimage sites in Wales and Gerald of Wales's attempt to canonize Caradog.

[82] Bishop Godwin erroneously claimed that St David was canonized and this was then repeated: Francis Godwin, *De praesulibus Angliae commentaries* (London: William Stansby and Eliot's Court Press, 1616), p. 601; Silas M. Harris, 'Was St. David Ever Canonized?', *Wales* (June 1944), 30-32.

[83] Boniface VIII, *Sermones et bulla canonisatione sancti Ludovici, Recueil des historiens des Gaules et de la France* 23 (Paris: Imprimerie Nationale, 1894), pp. 151-52, quoted in Bartlett, *Why Can the Dead Do Such Great Things?*, p. 64.

[84] As noted by Bartlett 'the "age of canonization" is not to be sought in the Middle Ages at all, but in the late twentieth century', *Why Can the Dead Do Such Great Things?*, p. 60; for a discussion of the frequency and complexity of medieval canonization, see pp. 59-64.

[85] Eamon Duffy, *The Stripping of the Altars: Traditional Religion in England 1400-1580*

It is in this period that we see adaptations such as *Hystoria Gweryddon yr Almaen* produced in the vernacular for Welsh audiences. But before turning to Ursula's Welsh Life, let us briefly consider the development of her legend and cult.

The Development of the Cult and Legend of St Ursula and the 11,000 Virgins

The origins of the cult of St Ursula may be traced to the Clematius inscription. This is a carved stone now preserved in the south wall of the choir in the church of the 11,000 Virgins in Cologne which has generally been thought to date to the fourth or fifth centuries, although recent work on the inscription has suggested that it might be later — possibly from the eighth century.[86] The inscription records that Clematius restored a basilica on the site where an unnamed and unnumbered group of holy virgins were martyred:

> Divinis flammeis visionib(us) frequenter admonit(us) et virtutis magnae maiiestatis martyrii caelestium virgin(um) imminentium ex partib(us) orientis exsibitus pro voto Clematius v(ir) c(larissimus) de proprio in loco suo hanc basilicam voto quod debebat a fundamentis restituit. Si quis autem super tantam maiiestatem huius basilicae, ubi sanctae virgines pro nominee XPI sanguinem suum fuderunt, corpus aliciius deposuerit exceptis virginib(us), sciat se sempiternis tartari ignib(us) puniendum.[87]

> [Frequently admonished by divine visions of flame and by virtue of the most majestic heavenly martyred virgins coming from the east, in fulfilment of a vow, the virtuous Clematius restored this basilica on their land from the foundations up. It should be known that if the body of anyone other than the holy virgins is deposited in this majestic basilica, built on the site where the holy virgins spilled their blood in the name of Christ, he will be punished by eternal hellfire.][88]

Ursula was not established as the leader of the group until the tenth century. A ninth-century calendar claims that there were in fact 11,000 virgins in this group and that their feast was held on 21 October.[89] This vast number is

---

(New Haven and London: Yale University Press, 1992), p. 4.

[86] The dating is problematic because the inscription appears to have been re-chiselled. For a discussion of the various dates proposed, see Klaus Militzer, 'The Church of St Ursula in Cologne: Inscriptions and Excavations', in *The Cult of St Ursula and the 11,000 Virgins*, ed. by Jane Cartwright (Cardiff: University of Wales Press, 2016), pp. 29-39 (pp. 32-33).

[87] Scott B. Montgomery, *St. Ursula and the Eleven Thousand Virgins of Cologne: Relics, Reliquaries and the Visual Culture of Group Sanctity in Late Medieval Europe* (Bern: Peter Lang, 2009), p. 10.

[88] Montgomery, *St. Ursula*, p. 10 n. 2.

[89] Milano, Bibl. Pinacoteca Ambr. MS 12 *sup.*; Kristin Hoefener, 'From St Pinnosa to St Ursula: The Development of the Cult of Cologne's Virgins in Medieval Liturgical Offices', in *The Cult of St Ursula and the 11,000 Virgins*, ed. by Cartwright, pp. 61-91 (pp. 65, 74-76).

generally thought to derive from a misreading of the Roman numeral XI and the letter M for *martyrum*, 'martyrs' — the M was possibly misinterpreted as *milium*, 'a thousand' — so eleven martyrs became eleven thousand.[90] In a ninth-century martyrology by Usuardus of Paris (*c.* 860) Martha and Saula are named as the principal martyrs, and in an early tenth-century sermon, *Sermo in natali SS. Virginum XII milium*, Pinnosa (or Winnosa), the daughter of a British king, is the leader of the troupe of virgins. These early sources betray the fact that the story of the martyrdom of the virgins was in flux and not stable at that time.[91]

The sermon was written for a community of religious women who had moved from Gerresheim to Cologne. The purpose of the sermon appears to have been to explain the Clematius inscription and resurrect the memory of a group of 'nearly twelve thousand' virgins who had been martyred on the site for their steadfast adherence to their faith. The anonymous preacher acknowledged that 'a certain amount of information about the holy virgins was handed down to us that was neither very extensive nor very detailed, but open to many interpretations'.[92] He notes that while some suggest that the virgins came from the east, others claim that they were originally from Britain and that they fled the country during the persecution of the Christians under Maximian (235–238), only to suffer martyrdom whilst on pilgrimage in Cologne. Clematius is praised for funding the rebuilding of the church to honour their bodies when the original church was burnt to the ground by barbarians. Relatively few details are provided, but the leader, Pinnosa, was joined by all the sisters ('we know very few by name') and the throng from Britain was 'known to God'. The phrase *Deo notus*, 'known to God', would later become the name of the leader's father (Deonotus or Nothus), but in the *Sermo* it implies only that the virgins were Christians. In 922 the nuns for whom the sermon was written were in possession of 'the leader' Pinnosa's relics. It was not in fact until after Pinnosa's relics had been translated from Cologne to Essen *c.* 947 that Ursula usurped the position of principal virgin.[93]

---

[90] Wilhelm Levison, 'Das Werden der Ursula-Legende', *Bonner Jahrbücher*, 132 (1927), 1–164 (pp. 27, 39–42); Montgomery, *St. Ursula*, pp. 11–12.

[91] The martyrology by Usuardus lists their feast on 20 October rather than 21 October. Usuardus, *Acta sanctorum iunii VII, Martyrologii Usuardini*, ed. by Jean-Baptiste Sollerius (Antwerp: J. P. Robin, 1717), p. 613. Another ninth-century source that refers to the virgins' tomb in the basilica is the Life of St Cunibert, bishop of Cologne 619–623, claimed to have been written some two hundred years after his death: Victor de Buck et al. (eds), *Acta sanctorum octobris tomus IX* (Antwerp, Brussels, Tongerloo, Paris: Brussels Greuse, 1858), pp. 73–303 (p. 212), hereafter *AS Octobris*.

[92] Pamela Sheingorn and Marcelle Thiébaux (trans.), *The Passion of Saint Ursula and The Sermon on the Birthday of Saint Ursula*, 2nd edn (Toronto: Pergrina Publishing, 1996), p. 47.

[93] Guy de Tervarent, *La légende de Sainte Ursule dans la littérature et l'art du moyen-âge*, 2 vols (Paris: Les Éditions G. van Oest, 1931), I p. 16; Montgomery, *St. Ursula*, p. 15.

The first passion related to the story, *Passio I: Fuit tempore pervetusto*, was written by a Flemish author, Herric, and dedicated to Archbishop Gero of Cologne, between 969 and 976. This tale replaced Pinnosa with Ursula, whose father was by now called Deonotus, a Celt and ruler in ancient Britain. While in the *Sermo* the virgins flee the Roman occupation of Britain and are murdered by Roman soldiers in Cologne, in *Passio I* the Huns are introduced as the perpetrators of the crime and Ursula is slaughtered because of her refusal to submit sexually to the leader of the Huns. Cordula, the virgin martyr who is so afraid that she hides onboard the ship, only to be martyred the next day, is also introduced for the first time in this passion. Not only are the virgin martyrs said to originate from Britain, but the legend itself is given a British provenance, since Herric claims that the Archbishop of Canterbury told the tale to Count Hoolf, who had travelled from Germany to England to secure the hand of Edith, daughter of King Edward, for Emperor Otto I. Hoolf then transmitted the legend to the religious community in Cologne and, some fifty years later, the nuns requested that the British legend about the virgins martyred in Cologne be written down by the hagiographer Herric.[94]

Ursula's pre-eminence had become well established by *c.* 1100 when a second passion, *Passio II: Regnante Domino*, confirmed that Ursula led 11,000 virgin martyrs to Cologne. Whilst the first passion, extant in six manuscripts, would appear to have had a limited circulation, the second passion is extant in over one hundred manuscripts and contains most of the 'standard' elements of the Ursuline legend that would be transmitted in various languages and multiple versions throughout the Middle Ages. As we shall see, although the hagiographical tale would continue to evolve, acquiring new characters and different emphases, it was relatively stable by the time the second passion was circulating.

According to the second passion, Ursula's father Deonotus is a Christian king in Britain who is threatened and intimidated by 'a certain foreign king' who wishes his son to marry Ursula, renowned for her great beauty. Ursula, keen to relieve her father's anxiety, agrees but informs him that 'Nonetheless, I shall die unmarried with the seal of virginity intact'.[95] She requests a three-year period of respite while the two kings gather a fleet of 11,000 virgins to accompany her to Rome. The virgins, described here as 'a novel kind of army', practise nautical manoeuvres — sometimes simulating flight and at other times combat. In this version of the legend Pinnosa is relegated to second in command and no mention is made of Cyriacus, the British pope who welcomes them to Rome in later versions of the Life (including the Welsh text). One unusual detail here is that the young maidens call at Tiel as well as Cologne en route to Rome, where

---

[94] Sheingorn and Thiébaux (trans.), *The Passion*, p. 7.
[95] Sheingorn and Thiébaux (trans.), *The Passion*, p. 20.

they buy utensils, 'for Tiel had a market fair'.[96] In Cologne Ursula learns that it is pre-destined that her holy troupe will be martyred on their return journey. They disembark in Basel and travel on foot to Rome, and when they return they discover that the city of Cologne is under siege. The barbarians slaughter the virgins 'like wolves descending upon a sheepfold'.[97] The prince of the Huns offers to marry Ursula, but when she rejects him he shoots her with an arrow, and all of the virgins are said to have been tortured and slain by the barbarian horde. However, once the mass martyrdom is complete, the 'fierce' Huns become terrified when they witness a vision in which an army of virgin soldiers rises up and ousts them from the city. Once they have fled, the inhabitants of Cologne burst through the city gates and gather up the 'lacerated limbs of the martyrs'. The virgins are given an honourable burial (some in the ground and others in sarcophagi) and, after a certain period of time has passed, Clematius is exhorted by God to build a church in honour of the holy virgins. Cordula's story is appended and she is said to have appeared in a vision to a recluse named Helmdrude, whom she instructs to pass on her testimony to the nuns who keep vigil at the virgins' burial place.[98]

In 1106 an abundance of bones was discovered in Cologne when a section of the city walls was rebuilt to the north of the city. This Roman cemetery was naturally assumed to contain the skeletal remains of Ursula and the 11,000 virgins. Abbot Gerlach of Deutz carried out a medieval archaeological excavation between 1155 and 1164 which was recorded by his sacristan Theoderich.[99] Since the bones of men and children, not only women, were found in what was assumed to be the *ager Ursulanus*, this proved problematic. Abbot Gerlach sought the help of Elizabeth of Schönau (*c.* 1129–1164), a Benedictine mystic, who had begun experiencing ecstatic visions when the relics of one of the virgins, St Verena, were translated to her convent at Schönau. Elizabeth would enter a trance-like state and communicate directly with Verena and the martyrs: she thus explained that Ursula and her troupe of virgins were accompanied by a much wider entourage of bishops, princes, prelates, and their wives and children. Numerous inscriptions on the gravestones were explained, including the name of Ursula's betrothed, Etherius, who set out from Britain to join her and Cyriacus, the pope who welcomed the virgins in Rome but relinquished his post so that he could accompany them to Cologne.[100] New characters were added to the legend and these visions were recorded by

---

[96] Sheingorn and Thiébaux (trans.), *The Passion*, p. 25
[97] Sheingorn and Thiébaux (trans.), *The Passion*, p. 27.
[98] Sheingorn and Thiébaux (trans.), *The Passion*, pp. 33–6.
[99] Levison, 'Das Werden', pp. 35, 107–39; Montgomery, *St. Ursula*, pp. 19–23; Militzer, 'The Church', pp. 34–35.
[100] Elizabeth of Schönau, *The Complete Works*, trans. by Anne L. Clark, Preface by Barbara Newman (New York: Paulist Press, 2000), pp. 213–33.

Elizabeth's brother Ekbert.[101] In the *Liber revelationum Elizabeth de sacro exercitu virginum Coloniensium* Elizabeth expresses her anxiety at the tasks that Abbot Gerlach frequently presented and anticipates that her visions would be met with scepticism and criticism. She says that she will:

> disclose what has been revealed to me through the grace of God about the virginal company of Saint Ursula, queen of Britain, who in days of old suffered martyrdom near the city of Cologne for the name of Christ. Although I was very resistant, certain men of good repute pressed me with their demand to investigate these things at length and they do not allow me to be silent. Indeed, I know that those people who oppose the grace of God in me will take this occasion to scourge me with their tongues.[102]

She indicates, however, that she was motivated by the spiritual rewards that she expected to receive as a result of honouring the virgins and publicizing their martyrdom. Elizabeth was familiar with *Passio II: Regnante Domino* and refers to this several times in her work. Her mentor, Hildegard of Bingen (1098–1179), composed at least thirteen hymns for the feast of the 11,000 virgins.[103]

Passio II: Regnante Domino is often claimed to be one of the sources used by Geoffrey of Monmouth in his alternative secular version of the murder of the 11,000 virgins found in *Historia regum Britanniae* (1136–1138).[104] Purporting to be a history of the British kings based on an 'ancient book in the British language',[105] Geoffrey's *Historia* makes Dionotus, Ursula's father, king of Cornwall. Set during the period when Maximianus had left Britain denuded of troops due to his military campaigns in Brittany, Gaul and Germany, the story recounts how Maximianus was keen to establish a 'second Britain' in Brittany and repopulate the region with British offspring. Having successfully conquered Brittany, he gave the region to Conanus Meiriadocus, who sent a message to Dionotus seeking his help in finding British wives for himself and his men. Conanus had long admired Ursula, Dionotus's beautiful daughter, and thus he requested her hand in marriage. Ursula, his betrothed, set sail for Brittany with 11,000 virgins as well as 60,000 commoner women. They

---

[101] On the dissemination of Elizabeth's visions and the nature and extent of her collaboration with Ekbert, see Anne L. Clark, *Elizabeth of Schönau: A Twelfth-Century Visionary* (Philadelphia: University of Pennsylvania Press, 1992).

[102] Elizabeth of Schönau, *The Complete Works*, p. 213.

[103] See William Flynn, 'Hildegard (1098–1179) and the Virgin Martyrs of Cologne', in *The Cult of St Ursula and the 11,000 Virgins*, ed. by Cartwright, pp. 93–118.

[104] For example, Levison, 'Das Werden', pp. 90–107; Reeve in Geoffrey of Monmouth, *The History of the Kings of Britain: An Edition and Translation of De gestis Britonum [Historia regum Britanniae]*, ed. by Michael D. Reeve, trans. by Neil Wright (Woodbridge: Boydell Press, 2007), pp. lii, lviii n. 63.

[105] This is usually assumed to have been a Welsh source, although doubts have been cast on whether the 'book' actually existed. See Karen Jankulak, *Geoffrey of Monmouth: Writers of Wales* (Cardiff: University of Wales Press, 2010).

were, however, shipwrecked en route and most of the women drowned. The remaining survivors were then brutally slaughtered or sold into slavery by Wanius, king of the Huns, and Melga, king of the Picts, because they refused to participate in sexual intercourse.[106]

Described by Bryan as 'a dynastic tragedy' rather than a martyrdom, Geoffrey of Monmouth's legend is 'set in the mundane world of political (if providential) history rather than the sacred register of hagiography'.[107] Geoffrey mentions that some of the female travellers would have preferred to remain unmarried virgins, but Ursula and her troupe are not described as saintly heroines who specifically considered themselves to be brides of Christ.[108] Ursula is far more vocal and proactive in the hagiographical tales, whereas she remains silent throughout the *Historia* and we do not learn whether she objected to her betrothal to Conanus. Indeed, in Geoffrey's tale we do not know if Ursula drowned or was murdered (for her death is not specifically dramatized) and she is not even given a name in one of the two earliest manuscript recensions of *Historia regum Britanniae*.[109] While the hagiographical tale originated from the relics of the virgins and is centred on the cult site at Cologne, Geoffrey's version does not mention Cologne, and the bodies of the victims are presumably merely washed away or cast aside. Having murdered the women, Wanius and Melga then sail to Scotland and launch an attack on Britain, since the land has been left undefended. The *Historia*'s Ursula is not only British but may be read as a character who parallels the realm of Britain, 'as it and she are caught up in the fallout of Roman imperial politics'.[110]

Translated into numerous vernaculars (including Welsh),[111] Geoffrey of Monmouth's alternative *Brut* version of the tale continued to be adapted and altered to meet the various purposes of its authors and audiences. Bryan traces the development of the tradition up to and including the fifteenth-century Middle English prose *Brut*. In one particularly unusual English version of the *Brut* by Laȝamon, Ursula is not murdered, but instead is horrifically gang-raped by Melga and his men; read by Bryan as 'colonial metaphor', Ursula's (and Britain's) oppression is avenged by an army of British women who laugh loudly as they hack Melga's body into pieces, *& þus heo areden þæsne kinedo[m]. of Wanis & of Melgan*, 'and thus they rid the kingdom of Wanis and of Melga'.[112]

---

[106] Geoffrey of Monmouth, *The History of the Kings of Britain*, pp. 104–11.

[107] Elizabeth J. Bryan, 'Ursula in the British History Tradition', in *The Cult of St Ursula and the 11,000 Virgins*, ed. by Cartwright, pp. 117–42 (p. 117).

[108] Geoffrey of Monmouth, *The History of the Kings of Britain*, pp. 108–9.

[109] Geoffrey of Monmouth, *The History of the Kings of Britain*, pp. xii, lii, lviii n. 63; Bryan, 'Ursula in the British History Tradition', p. 138 n.1.

[110] Bryan, 'Ursula in the British History Tradition', p. 122

[111] Henry Lewis (ed.), *Brut Dingestow* (Caerdydd: Gwasg Prifysgol Cymru, 1942); Brynley F. Roberts (ed.), *Brut y Brenhinedd* (Dublin: Dublin Institute for Advanced Studies, 1971).

[112] Laȝamon, *Laȝamon: Brut*, ed. by G. L. Brook and R. F. Leslie, EETS o.s. 250, 277 (London:

As noted above in the general discussion of the genre of hagiography, one of the most influential collection of saints' Lives in the medieval period was Jacobus de Voragine's *Legenda aurea*. Completed *c.* 1265 and introduced into Britain in the 1270s, the compendium inevitably included a version of the Life of St Ursula that incorporated elements from *Passio II: Regnante Domino*, as well as some of the characters from Ursula's wider entourage identified from the funerary inscriptions by Elizabeth of Schönau, including Cyriacus, the British pope, Etherius, Ursula's fiancée, and minor characters such as Babilia, Juliana, Victoria and Aurea.[113] The popularity and wide dissemination of the text spawned various adaptations, including the *South English Legendary*, which Marx argues is more dramatic and vivid than the *Legenda aurea*, since the compiler has deliberately altered the narrative in order to render it more engaging for a popular lay audience.[114] Marx traces the development of the Life of Ursula in a variety of Middle English texts, including the *Gilte Legende* (1438), Osbern of Bokenham's *Legendys of Hooly Wummen* (1392–1447) and Caxton's *Golden Legend* (1483).

The explosion in the cult of relics following the discovery of the mass graveyard in the twelfth century meant that the cult of the 11,000 virgins became one of the most relic-rich of all medieval saint cults. Just as the relics of the martyrs were transported far and wide, so too the legend of St Ursula proliferated, evolving and adapting to a variety of different and often 'local' contexts as it was transmitted. For example, despite the fact that the Huns are the perpetrators of the massacre in most versions of the legend, the assumption that Huns and Hungarians were related meant that Ursula was deemed to have a special relevance in Hungary, and she frequently appeared in Hungarian codices from the thirteenth century onwards, as well as numerous frescoes and altarpieces.[115] The image of Ursula and her seaborne companions as a military force unwaveringly accepting martyrdom in battle rather than relinquishing their faith also appears to have ensured that Ursula had a special relationship with the military orders, at a time when the Hospitallers were waging war against Islam at sea. Nicholson argues that Ursula's veneration among the Templars, Hospitallers and Teutonic Knights was linked to local devotions: for example, St Cordula became the patron saint of the Hospitallers' commandery

---

Kegan Paul, Trench, Trübner & Co, 1963), line 6427; Bryan, 'Ursula in the British History Tradition', p. 131.
[113] *LA*.
[114] William Marx, 'Saint Ursula and the Eleven Thousand Virgins: The Middle English *Legenda aurea* Tradition', in *The Cult of St Ursula and the 11,000 Virgins*, ed. by Cartwright, pp. 143–63 (p. 147).
[115] Anna Tüskés, 'The Cult of St Ursula in Hungary: Legends, Altars and Reliquaries', in *The Cult of St Ursula and the 11,000 Virgins*, ed. by Cartwright, pp. 187–204.

in Cologne after her relics were discovered in their vineyard.[116] Of the plethora of medieval art objects depicting Ursula and the 11,000 virgins, one of the most renowned artefacts is Hans Memling's shrine of St Ursula. Completed in 1489, it depicts a fictive chapel on both its short ends, which perhaps was intended to evoke the chapel of the Hospital of St John in Bruges, where the shrine containing the relics was originally kept.[117] The narrative cycle painted in oil on the panels of the shrine depicts the various stages in Ursula's pilgrimage and encourages the viewer to take part in a spiritual pilgrimage with the virgins.[118]

In Germany and elsewhere in Europe, large numbers of ornate reliquaries and reliquary busts are extant that encase the remains of what are believed to be the skulls or bones of Ursula and the 11,000 virgins.[119] Many of these are preserved in the awe-inspiring Golden Chamber in the church of St Ursula in Cologne, where thousands of bones, skulls and reliquaries decorate the walls of the church. Although this will be a familiar site to most readers, the Golden Chamber was only erected in the western end of the church in 1643 at the behest of Johann Crane, a wealthy local nobleman.[120] A simple inscribed gravestone, thought to belong to the fifth or sixth centuries, recorded the death of an innocent or unmarried girl named Ursula aged eight years, two months and four days, and this was discovered in 1893, built into the nave of the church.[121] Ursula's young age was not referred to by Elizabeth of Schönau, although she noted, when she interpreted the gravestone of Etherius, that Ursula's betrothed was aged twenty-five when he was martyred alongside Ursula.[122] Militzer suggests that a Romanesque shrine would probably once have been positioned over the relics of St Ursula, and that this was probably replaced by the Gothic shrine of SS Ursula, Etherius and Hippolytus. Before the construction of the

---

[116] H. Nicholson, 'St Ursula and the Military Religious Orders', in *The Cult of St Ursula and the 11,000 Virgins*, ed. by Cartwright, pp. 41–59 (pp. 45–53).

[117] Montgomery, *St. Ursula*, p. 134; Jeanne Nuechterlein, 'Hans Memling's St Ursula Shrine: The Subject as Object of Pilgrimage', in *Art and Architecture of Late Medieval Pilgrimage in Northern Europe and the British Isles*, ed. by Sarah Blick and Rita Tekippe, 2 vols (Leiden: Brill, 2005), I, pp. 51–75 (p. 62).

[118] Vida J. Hull, 'Spiritual Pilgrimage in the Paintings of Hans Memling', in *Art and Architecture*, ed. by Sarah Blick and Rita Tekippe, 2 vols (Leiden: Brill, 2005), I, pp. 29–50.

[119] One of the precious objects singled out to advertise the British Museum's exhibition *Treasures of Heaven: Saints, Relics and Devotion in Medieval Europe* (23 June–9 October 2011) was a magnificent painted reliquary bust of one of the 11,000 virgins; see Samantha Riches, 'Relics of Gender Identity: Interpreting a Reliquary of a Follower of St Ursula', in *Matter of Faith: An Interdisciplinary Study of Relics and Relic Veneration in the Medieval Period*, ed. by James Robinson, Lloyd de Beer and Anna Harnden (London: British Research Publication No. 195, 2014), pp. 143–50.

[120] J. J. Merlo, 'Johann Crane und seine Stiftungen in der Ursulakirche zu Köln', *Zeitschrift für christliche Kunst*, 2 (1889), 105–10.

[121] Militzer, 'The Church', p. 34.

[122] Elizabeth of Schönau, *The Complete Works*, p. 221.

Golden Chamber, pilgrims would probably physically pass under this less elaborate saints' shrine in their quest to be blessed by the holy relics.[123]

In 1535, Angela Merici (1477–1540) founded the Company of St Ursula in Brescia, Italy. Orphaned at the age of fifteen, she dedicated her life to the religious education of young women who were initially educated in their own homes, but the association went on to found numerous schools and orphanages. By the time of her death there were twenty-four communities belonging to the Company, and her Rule was approved by Pope Paul III in 1544. The members of the Company did not take religious vows or wear a habit; however, in 1572 the women consented to becoming a monastic religious order known as the Ursulines.[124] In 1969, the feast of the 11,000 virgins was suppressed and omitted from the Roman Calendar, although it survives in the Roman Martyrology. In 1807, Angela Merici was canonised by Pope Pious VII, and the Ursulines continue to operate in several countries, including Wales.

The Welsh Life of St Ursula and the 11,000 Virgins: *Hystoria Gweryddon yr Almaen*

Hystoria Gweryddon yr Almaen is extant in only one manuscript, Aberystwyth, NLW, MS Peniarth 182, in the hand of Syr Huw Pennant. The dates 1509, 1513 and 1514 all occur at various points throughout the manuscript,[125] and the *Hystoria* has often been dated confidently to 1514 on this basis.[126] However, the manuscript was clearly in Huw Pennant's possession for some time, and it would appear that Huw added texts to it over a number of years. One cannot be certain, therefore, in what year precisely *Hystoria Gweryddon yr Almaen* was composed, and it is plausible that Huw continued to add texts shortly after 1514. The Welsh Life of St Ursula is positioned towards the end of the manuscript, between a short herbal based on *Macer Floridus* (pp. 250–60) and the Latin hymn praising Ursula and the virgins, *O vernantes Christi Rosae*

---

[123] Paul Clemen (ed.), *Die Kunstdenkmäler der Stadt Köln. Im Auftrage des Provinzialverbandes der Rheinprovinz und der Stadt Köln* (Düsseldorf: L. Schwann, 1934), p. 49; Militzer, 'The Church', Figure 3.

[124] Quericiolo Mazzonis, 'The Impact of Renaissance Gender-Related Notions of the Female Experience of the Sacred: The Case of Angela Merici's Ursulines', in *Gender, Catholicism and Spirituality: Women and the Roman Catholic Church in Britain and Europe, 1200–1900*, ed. by Laurence Lux-Sterritt and Carmen Mangion (Basingstoke: Palgrave Macmillan, 2011), pp. 51–67.

[125] Aberystwyth, National Library of Wales, MS Peniarth 182 (hereafter Pen. 182), pp. 45, 178 and 246; Daniel Huws, *A Repertory of Welsh Manuscripts and Scribes c. 800–c. 1800*, 3 vols (Aberystwyth: National Library of Wales, forthcoming; hereafter *RepMW*), I, Peniarth 182.

[126] T. H. Parry-Williams, *Rhyddiaith Gymraeg Y Gyfrol Gyntaf Detholiad o Lawysgrifau 1488–1609* (Caerdydd: Gwasg Prifysgol Cymru, 1954), p. 18. J. Gwenogvryn Evans records 1514 as the date of the manuscript, *Report on Manuscripts in the Welsh Language*, 2 vols in 7 parts (London: Royal Commission on Historical Monuments, 1898–1910), I, part iii, p. 1003.

(pp. 301–12). Two different sections of the manuscript include several medical recipes treating a condition known as *tostedd*, 'bladder stone', and one wonders whether Huw Pennant may have been suffering from this affliction himself if he was keen to collect and record various cures for the same illness.[127] Other texts include poetry, such as the *Afallennau* and verse by Dafydd ap Gwilym, as well as a poem and an *englyn* by Huw Pennant himself. Huw would appear to have made considerable personal use of this manuscript, which is small in size and easy to handle and transport.

The manuscript is clearly written in a good hand but contains very little decoration: the initial letter <H> in the title *Hystoria Gweryddon yr Almaen* has been decorated and there is rubrication on the first two letters. The ascenders of some letters (usually <h> but also <ll> and <b>) in the first line of certain pages have been decorated, but these are closer to personal doodles than formal decoration. At one point near the middle of the Life the letter <h> has been extended in the word *Archdiacon* ('Archdeacon'), and Huw Pennant has sketched the face of a cleric or a monk above the word.[128] Other 'doodles' include the face of a dragon or a monster, a bird sitting on a branch (probably a hawk), and a hand pointing at a particular section of text.[129] The author refers to himself several times throughout the manuscript: for example, *hügh pennant offeiriad*, 'priest', p. 45; *Syr hugh Pennant*, p. 165; and *hugo pennant Capellan*, 'chaplain', p. 246. The title *Syr* ('Sir') is more likely to indicate that he was an ordained member of the clergy than a knighted nobleman. At one point in Peniarth 182 he records receiving funeral expenses in 1514 at his house in Llanfihangel (literally 'the Church of St Michael'), and thus it would seem that at that time he was serving as curate at one of the many places in Wales known by that name — possibly Llanfihangel-ar-arth in Carmarthenshire, since Thomas Eynon Griffyth Lloyd of the parish of Llanfihangel-ar-arth later signed the manuscript.[130] This is notable given that, along with the Life of St Ursula, Huw had also chosen to adapt the Miracles of the Archangel Michael from Latin into Welsh, and included these miracles venerating his church's namesake in the same manuscript.

---

[127] Pen. 182, pp. 57–58, 236–44; Diana Luft, 'Treating the Stone in Sixteenth-Century Wales (According to the Vicar of Gwenddwr)', The Recipes Project <https://recipes.hypotheses.org/tag/diana-luft> (accessed 1 October 2019).

[128] Pen. 182, p. 286.

[129] Pen. 182, pp. 67, 68, 163 (a dragon or monster), p. 143 (a bird), pp. 26, 27 (pointing hand). There is also another face, p. 73, and the face of a dog or dragon, p. 160.

[130] This, of course, could also be a coincidence, but it is plausible that the manuscript stayed in the same parish. One would not necessarily expect to find a reference to the incumbent at Llanfihangel-ar-arth in 1514. However, episcopal registers of the diocese of St Davids do record that Sir Gruffin ap David took over the vicarage of Llanfihangel-ar-arth from Sir William ap Rice in November 1514. No mention, however, is made of the curate at the time. R. F. Isaacson (ed. and trans.), *The Episcopal Registers of the Diocese of St. David's 1397–1518*, 3 vols (London: The Honourable Society of Cymmrodorion, 1917–1920), II, p. 808.

INTRODUCTION   31

It appears then that Peniarth 182 was not a manuscript commissioned by a patron, but rather a book owned by the scribe himself; it possibly included texts that were of personal interest to Huw Pennant (including some of his own poetry, *Llyfr Theophrastes* (a tract on marriage attributed to Theophrastus),[131] and the genealogies of Welsh saints and princes), as well as texts that may have been useful to him in his role as curate, priest or chaplain. Religious texts include *Hystoria Gweryddon yr Almaen* (pp. 261-300), *Esgyniad Meir i'r nef* (The Assumption of the Blessed Virgin Mary, pp. 179-98), *Ystoria o Wyrthie Mihangel* (The Miracles of the Archangel Michael, pp. 77-142) and *Y Bibyl Ynghymraec* (The Bible in Welsh, pp. 46-47, 170-77, 199-235).[132] One can easily imagine that these texts were read either as part of his private devotion or to the communities he served on the appropriate feast days associated with Ursula and the 11,000 virgins (21 October), the Archangel Michael (29 September) and the Assumption of the Virgin Mary (15 August).

Although Welsh manuscripts regularly provide the names of medieval poets, it is rare for the name of the author of a prose text to be recorded. Nevertheless, at the end of *Hystoria Gweryddon yr Almaen* it is made clear that Syr Huw Pennant was the original author of the Welsh version and that he did not merely copy the text: he was responsible for adapting the text from Latin into Welsh so that it could be understood by his intended audience:

> Ac velly y teruyna Ystoria Gweryddon yr Almaen hyd y medrodd Syr Huw Pennant i thynnu o'r Llading yNghymraec val y gallai rai kerddgar i dyall o'i hiaith e hun.[133]

> [And thus ends *Ystoria Gweryddon yr Almaen* as far as Sir Huw Pennant was able to translate it from Latin into Welsh so that lovers of literature could understand it in their own language.]

Since the manuscript appears to have been in his possession rather than commissioned, this most likely suggests that he intended to transmit the text orally and that he had translated it so that he could read the Life of Ursula and the 11,000 virgins aloud in Welsh to his cultured audience.

Relatively little is known of Huw Pennant. The first extant list of clergy in the diocese of Bangor, compiled in 1504, names Huw Pennant as curate of Dolwyddelan, so it would appear that before he moved to 'Llanfihangel' he was

---

[131] On this text, see T. M. Chotzen, '"La Querrelle des femmes" au pays de Galles', *Revue Celtique*, 48 (1931), 42-93 (pp. 45-50).

[132] *RepMW*, I, Peniarth 182. Despite its misleading name *Y Bibyl Ynghymraec* is not the Bible but a Welsh translation of sections of *Prompuarium Bibliae*, a summary of the history of the world from the creation to the martyrdom of SS Peter and Paul, drawing on the Bible and apocryphal texts.

[133] Pen. 182, p. 299; see edition below, p. 58; *rai kerddgar* literally means 'some poetry lovers' but also implies cultured people generally.

serving in Gwynedd.[134] Huw almost certainly had links to the Augustinians and may even have been an Augustinian canon (unless he was a paid stipendiary), since Dolwyddelan was appropriated to the Augustinian canons of Beddgelert in 1504 when the bishop of Bangor, Thomas Piggott, died. The bishop who preceded him, as well as the bishop who succeeded him, belonged to the Augustinian Order.[135] Three of the Augustinian houses in north Wales were founded on the sites of the old Welsh *clasau* (at Penmon, Bardsey and Beddgelert), and the regular canons, although ordained, led quasi-monastic lifestyles serving their communities and servicing their parish churches.[136]

One of the few facts stated about Huw Pennant in the *Dictionary of Welsh Biography* is that he was the son of Dafydd Pennant of Bychton and the brother of Thomas Pennant, the renowned abbot of Basingwerk (1481–1522).[137] Yet, in the genealogy recorded by Bartrum, no brother named Huw is listed for Thomas Pennant.[138] Instead Thomas's brother Rhys ap Dafydd had a son named Huw Pennant who was married to Jonet ferch Richard and had eleven children by her.[139] This would make Thomas Pennant Huw's uncle, and both men members of the clergy who had large families. Celibacy does not appear to have been a prerequisite for important monastic or clerical roles in late medieval Wales (as elsewhere during this period) and certainly did not prevent Thomas Pennant from becoming a well-respected abbot of the Cistercian house at Basingwerk.[140] Thomas Pennant has been shown to have received his education at the Cistercian house of Valle Crucis, and it is not beyond the realms of possibility that Huw may have been educated at the abbey too. Thomas compiled a series of grammatical treatises, possibly for the purpose of teaching Latin.[141] One can easily imagine that if Huw Pennant was his nephew, Thomas may have

---

[134] A. I. Pryce, *The Diocese of Bangor in the Sixteenth Century* (Bangor: Jarvis & Foster, 1923), p. 82.
[135] Bishop Henry Dean (1495–1500) and Bishop John Perry (1504–1508).
[136] See Monastic Wales <http://www.monasticwales.org> (accessed 5 June 2018).
[137] R. Looker, 'Huw Pennant ('Syr') (*fl*. during the second half of the 15th century), cleric, poet, and antiquary', *The Dictionary of Welsh Biography* (1959) <http://biography.wales/article/s-HUWo-PEN-1450> (accessed 23 April 2019).
[138] Peter C. Bartrum (ed.), *Welsh Genealogies AD 1400–1500*, 18 vols (Aberystwyth: National Library of Wales, 1983), x, Tudur Trefor 11 (C_1).
[139] Bartrum (ed.), *Welsh Genealogies*, x, Tudur 11 (C_2). In the genealogy recorded by John Edward Griffith, 'Hugh' is noted as a brother of Thomas Pennant, but 'Hugh Pennant' is also recorded as his nephew (son of Dafydd ap Pennant as in the version of the genealogy recorded by Bartrum), *Pedigrees of Anglesey and Carnarvonshire Families with their Collateral Branches in Denbighshire, Meirionethshire and Other Parts* (Horncastle: W. K. Morton, 1914), p. 214.
[140] His son Nicholas Pennant was the last abbot of Basingwerk. See Bartrum (ed.), *Welsh Genealogies*, x, Tudur Trefor 11 (C_1).
[141] D. Thompson, 'Cistercians and Schools in Later Medieval Wales', *Cambridge Medieval Celtic Studies*, 3 (1982), 76–80 (p. 77).

been keen to mentor his protégé and encourage his religious and scholarly pursuits. Daniel Huws has suggested that Thomas Pennant's hand is present in the margins of the Black Book of Basingwerk that was produced at Valle Crucis, a manuscript that contains a Welsh version of Geoffrey of Monmouth's *Historia regum Britanniae*.[142] Thomas sponsored some of the eminent Welsh poets of his day, including Gutun Owain (the second scribe of the Black Book of Basingwerk), Tudur Aled and Siôn ap Hywel ap Llywelyn Fychan. In a poem by Tudur Aled he is accredited with either erecting or renovating the well chapel at Holywell — a building that includes on its vaulted ceiling the coat of arms of William Stanley (Margaret Beaufort's brother-in-law who lived in Holt, Wrexham) and Katherine of Aragon.[143]

These Tudor connections are interesting when considering possible sources for the Welsh Life of Ursula and the image of St Ursula that was current and being promulgated at that time. In 1501 when Katherine of Aragon arrived in Britain for her marriage to Henry VII's eldest son Arthur, she was welcomed by a lavish pageant and greeted on London Bridge by figures dressed as St Katherine and St Ursula. Ursula, in most versions of her legend, was deemed to be British, but in the pageant she was claimed to be of Lancastrian heritage and was said to share her royal blood and lineage with the future queen:

> Madam Kateryn, because that I [Ursula] and ye
> Be come of noble blod of this land
> Of Lancastre, which is not oonly of amyte
> The cause, but also a ferme band
> Betweene you and this realme to stonde […]
> As Arthure, your spouse, than the secunde nowe
> Succedith the furst Arthure in dignite,
> So in lyke wise, Madame Kateryn, yow
> As secunde Ursula shall succeed me.[144]

Ursula claimed descent from King Arthur in a celebration that represented the successful culmination of the Tudor dynasty. Katherine of Aragon was cast as a second Ursula and Arthur Tudor as a second King Arthur, in a celebration that echoed and distorted both the hagiographical legend of Ursula and Geoffrey of Monmouth's *Historia regum Britanniae*. No mention was made, of course, to the fact that in the hagiographical legend Ursula's betrothal is not a cause for celebration but rather an unwelcome marriage to which she is reluctantly forced to agree.

Huw Pennant was clearly a supporter of the Tudors, and pro-Tudor

---

[142] *RepWM*, Black Book of Basingwerk.
[143] Jones (ed.), *Gwaith Tudur Aled*, II, p. 526. William Stanley was one of Henry VII's chief supporters at the Battle of Bosworth.
[144] Gordon Kipling (ed.), *The Receyt of the Ladie Kateryne*, EETS o.s. 296 (Oxford: Oxford University Press, 1990), p. 15.

vaticinatory verse is found in his work.¹⁴⁵ In one poem he laments the fact that Richard III has incarcerated the princes in the Tower of London and 'predicts' that before the feast of St Anne the raven Richard will have his feathers plucked and Henry VII, the red rose of Somerset, will be crowned king. He also copied a list of kings, starting with Brutus and ending with Henry VIII *brenin Lloegr a Chymry*, 'king of England and Wales', in Peniarth 182.¹⁴⁶ Thus, although the Life of Ursula is set at a time when the tyrannical 'English' king is an adversary of the Britons, elsewhere in the manuscript he suggests that contemporary England and Wales are united under the Tudor king.

As well as composing his own political poetry in the fifteenth century, by the early sixteenth century Huw Pennant was producing his own versions of Welsh hagiographical texts that provide an important insight into popular religious devotion in Wales during this period. The Welsh Life of Sylvester preserved in Llanstephan 34 (1580 x 1600), a recusant manuscript discussed above in the section on Welsh hagiography, states that the text was a copy of an earlier Life composed by Huw Pennant.¹⁴⁷ Unfortunately, the original, in Huw Pennant's hand, is no longer extant and one wonders whether he may have adapted other international saints' Lives into Welsh too. His version of the Miracles of the Archangel Michael contains a formula very similar to the one found at the end of *Hystoria Gweryddon yr Almaen*:

> Ag velly y tervyna buchedd Mihangel hyd y medrodd Syr Huch Pennant i dyall a'i thynnv yNghymraeg o'r Llading yn ol y Llithion Euraid o vuchedd y saint.¹⁴⁸

> [And thus ends the Life of Michael as far as Sir Huw Pennant was able to understand it and translate it into Welsh from Latin according to the Golden Legend of saints' Lives.]

Given that Huw Pennant specifically notes that his source for *Ystoria o Wyrthie Mihangel* was the *Legenda aurea*, one might have suspected that this would also have been his source for *Hystoria Gweryddon yr Almaen*, but surprisingly this does not seem to have been the case.¹⁴⁹

The Welsh Life of Ursula contains a relatively brief account of the Life and

---

¹⁴⁵ Bangor University MS 1267, fol. 34v. On this poetry, see Gruffydd Aled Williams, 'The Bardic Road to Bosworth', *Transactions of the Honourable Society of Cymmrodorion* (1986), 7–31 (pp. 23–24).
¹⁴⁶ Pen. 182, p. 44.
¹⁴⁷ Aberystwyth, NLW, MS Llanstephan 34, p. 365.
¹⁴⁸ Pen. 182, p. 142.
¹⁴⁹ An edition and discussion of *Ystoria o Wyrthie Mihangel* will be made available by Olga Vanherle, '*Ystoria o Wyrthie Mihangel*: Trawsysgrifiad a Golygiad (Peniarth 182) gyda Nodiadau, Geirfa a Chyfieithiad, Cyd-destunoli'r Testun a Golwg ar Dystiolaeth Farddonol a Llenyddol, Materol a Chelfyddydol Cwlt Mihangel yng Nghymru'r Oesoedd Canol' (unpublished PhD thesis, University of Wales Trinity Saint David, forthcoming).

passion of St Ursula and the 11,000 virgins that provides many of the details found in the standard narrative (best exemplified perhaps by the *Legenda aurea*), including the following: (i) Ursula is the beautiful daughter of a Christian British king; (ii) her father is torn between protecting his devout daughter and defending his kingdom when he is threatened by the pagan king of England who wishes his son to marry Ursula; (iii) Ursula is instructed by an angel to ask for a three-year period of respite while she gathers 11,000 virgins; (iv) it is prophesied that they will be martyred in Cologne and they are instructed to go on pilgrimage to Rome; (v) Ursula and the virgins prepare their ships, practise nautical manoeuvres and sail to Basel; (vi) they are greeted in Rome by the British pope Cyriacus (Kiric) who returns with them to Cologne; (vii) Cologne is besieged by pagans who slaughter the virgins, and the leader of the pagans offers to make Ursula his wife; (viii) Ursula despises him and refuses so he shoots her with an arrow; (ix) she is martyred and gloriously crowned in heaven; (xi) no one else's bones can be buried in the same place as the virgins and a prince's body is repeatedly expelled from the grave when his father attempts to bury him among the martyrs; (xii) Cordula, who hid on the ship because she was afraid, is martyred on the day after the virgins and when she appears in a vision to a nun, a feast is allocated to her on 22 October; (xiii) a sick monk who is particularly devoted to the virgins sees one of the 11,000 in a vision and is told to pray — he excitedly tells his abbot and then immediately dies and is made welcome in heaven by the virgins.

While much of this is similar to the account in the *Legenda aurea*, certain details and characters are missing in the Welsh version: for example, Gerasina, queen of Sicily, who orchestrates the virgins in *Legenda aurea*, is absent, and no mention is made of Africanus and Maximus, the Roman commanders who send messengers to the Huns. Indeed, the perpetrators of the slaughter are not specifically named or noted as Huns in the *Hystoria*.[150] They are referred to merely as a *pla baganieid*, 'plague of pagans'. The Welsh Life differs from the 'standard' Lives found in *Passio II: Regnante Domino* and *Legenda aurea* in certain key respects, including the following: (i) it is set during the time of Constantine son of Maxen and begins with a Welsh genealogy; (ii) almost one third of the text is devoted to a list of the companions who were martyred with Ursula (including bishops, kings, princes and their wives and children); (iii) among those martyred were children and unborn babies; (iv) Cordula spits in the eyes of her pagan oppressors; (v) it describes some of the relics of the martyrs in Cologne as still having arrows in their mouths, blood on their necks and blood-matted hair. Some of these characteristics, as we shall see, can be traced to texts that were circulating in the late fifteenth and early sixteenth

[150] Cf. *LA*, II, pp. 256–60.

centuries, at the time that Huw Pennant was adapting the Life into Welsh.[151]

Hystoria Gweryddon yr Almaen opens with a Welsh saintly genealogy; this is not Ursula's genealogy but the genealogy of St Peblig, a local native saint associated with Llanbeblig near Caernarfon. No attempt is made to claim that Ursula was related to Peblig, but Huw Pennant draws on his knowledge of specifically Welsh narrative traditions at the start of the Life of Ursula to set the scene, and this naturally has the effect of associating Ursula's homeland with what is now Wales. In most versions of the Life Ursula's father is one of the many kings of Britain, whereas the Welsh *Hystoria* is set during the reign of Constantine son of Maxen and Elen daughter of Eudaf, and Ursula's father is a descendant of the ancient Britons and one of the kings of *Ynys y Kedyrn*, 'The Island of the Mighty' (that is, the Britain of native medieval myth described in the Mabinogi whose kings and their lineage are the subject of Geoffrey of Monmouth's *Historia regum Britanniae*). Huw Pennant avoids giving Ursula's father a Latin name at this point (in most of the other versions of the Life he is called Nothus, stemming from Deonotus in *Passio II: Regnante Domino*).[152] Huw Pennant's Welsh audience may have naturally assumed that Ursula's ethnic affiliations were Welsh, given that her father's kingdom is threatened and his Christian conscience is pitted against the oppressive forces of the pagan king of nearby *Lloegyr*, 'England'. Huw did not have a Welsh genealogy that he could provide for Ursula, but we know that he was familiar with *Bonedd y Saint*, a list of saintly genealogies that referred to St Peblig as the son of Maxen and Elen ferch Eudaf, because he copied this elsewhere in the manuscript.[153] Perhaps he deemed this appropriate because of Maxen's association with the *Brut* version of the Ursula legend. I also believe that he was familiar with a tractate known as *Y Pedwar Brenin ar Hugain a Farnwyd yn Gadarnaf*, 'The Twenty-Four Kings Judged to be the Mightiest', and that it is possibly from this tractate that he drew his title for the Life of Ursula, *Hystoria Gweryddon yr Almaen*. Like *Bonedd y Saint*, *Y Pedwar Brenin ar Hugain* notes that Maxen and Elen had three children, Peblig, Custennin and Owain, the same as those named at the start of *Hystoria Gweryddon yr Almaen*. The text provides a brief synopsis of the most important kings mentioned in *Brut y Brenhinedd*, the Welsh adaptation of *Historia regum Britanniae*, paying particular attention to the cities they founded. In Geoffrey's *Historia* Maximianus son of Loelinus marries

---

[151] For a preliminary discussion of the Welsh Life and its sources, see Jane Cartwright, 'The Middle Welsh Life of St Ursula and the 11,000 Virgins', in *The Cult of St Ursula and the 11,000 Virgins*, ed. by Cartwright, pp. 163–86.

[152] Later in the Life Huw Pennant notes that his name is Nothus, in the long list of Latinized names of companions who accompany Ursula.

[153] Pen. 182, p. 39. Barry Lewis has prepared a new edition of *Bonedd y Saint* based on all known versions which will supersede the one found in Peter C. Batrum (ed.), *Early Welsh Genealogical Tracts* (Cardiff: University of Wales Press, 1966).

the unnamed daughter of Octavius, and in the Welsh *Brut y Brenhinedd* Maxen ap Llywelyn marries Eudaf Hen's daughter. Although she is not named in the Latin texts or the Welsh *Brut Dingestow* version, she is called Elen ferch Eudaf in both the Black Book of Basingwerk version of the *Brut* and this tractate.[154] *Y Pedwar Brenin ar Hugain* proceeds with a summary of the legend of the 11,000 virgins who were sent to Brittany but were martyred in Cologne:

> Ac yr Maxen hwnnw o Elen i bv dri mab, Peblic a Chustenin ac Ywain vinddv. [Ywain] a vv varchoc vrddol, a Chustenin a vv dywyssoc yMhrydain a chyff kenedl i bawb yno, a Ffeblic sydd sant anrrydeddus. Ac yn yr amser hwnnw y gollyngwyd i Lydaw o ynys Brydain c mil o lavvrwyr a xxx mil o varchogion vrddolion, a l mil o verched gwyr kyffredin, ac xj mil o verched boneddigion, a rrai hyny a aethant i Gwlen [yn] yr Almaen, ac a verthyrwyd yno yn enw gwir Dduw, a rrai hyny yw Gweryddon yr Almaen.

> [Macsen had three sons by Elen, Peblig, Custennin and Owain Blacklip. [*Owain*] was a noble knight, Custennin was prince in Britain and ancestor of all [the princes] there, and Peblig was an honourable saint. At that time a hundred thousand labourers and thirty thousand noble knights, fifty thousand daughters of common men and eleven thousand daughters of nobles were sent from the island of Britain to Armorica. They went to Cologne in Germany, and were martyred there in the name of the true God. They are the Virgins of Germany.][155]

In none of the many extant versions of the Life of Ursula is the title 'the Virgins of Germany' suggested, and it is certainly plausible that Huw Pennant derived his title for the Welsh Life of Ursula, *Hystoria Gweryddon yr Almaen* (literally 'The Story of the Virgins of Germany'), from this tractate. The earliest extant version of *Y Pedwar Brenin ar Hugain* seems to be the text in Aberystwyth, NLW MS Llanstephan 28 by Gutun Owain,[156] the scholar and scribe largely responsible for the Black Book of Basingwerk who, as we have seen, composed poetry for Huw's uncle Thomas Pennant. It is certainly likely that Huw was familiar with his work and he may have had access to the same sources.[157] Another copy of *Y Pedwar Brenin ar Hugain* can also be traced directly to Huw's family for, in 1604, John Jones of Gellilyfdy transcribed a version of *Y Pedwar*

---

[154] She is also named Elen in the Cotton Cleopatra version; see John Jay Parry (ed.), *Brut y Brenhinedd Cotton Cleopatra Version* (Cambridge, Mass.: The Medieval Academy of America, 1937), p. 97.

[155] Peter C. Bartrum, 'Y Pedwar Brenin ar Hugain a Farnwyd yn Gadarnaf', *Études Celtiques*, 12 (1968–1971), 157–94 (p. 172 (edition), p. 181 (translation)).

[156] For a list of the extant manuscripts, see Bartrum, 'Y Pedwar Brenin ar Hugain', pp. 160–63.

[157] Ben David Guy has suggested that Huw Pennant and Gutun Owain derived their saintly genealogies, either directly or indirectly, from Hengwrt 33, a lost manuscript associated with Valle Crucis: Guy, 'A Lost Medieval Manuscript from North Wales: Hengwrt 33, the Hanesyn Hên', *Studia Celtica*, 50 (2016), 69–105.

Brenin ar Hugain in Peniarth MS 215 and noted that his source was the Book of Thomas ap Rhys ap Hywel ap Ieuan Fychan, which was written in 1517.[158] The genealogies reveal that this Thomas ap Rhys was Huw Pennant's brother-in-law, the brother of Jonet,[159] and the text was produced around the same time that Huw was working on *Hystoria Gweryddon yr Almaen*. Thus, it seems that Huw Pennant was well educated and well connected, and that he was both related to and part of the significant literary and ecclesiastical circles traditionally associated with Basingwerk and Valle Crucis, even if he had moved south by the time he composed his Welsh Life of Ursula.

The brief summarized version of the Ursula legend in *Y Pedwar Brenin ar Hugain* is based on Geoffrey of Monmouth's account, but it differs from his narrative in two key respects. Geoffrey of Monmouth does not mention Cologne, but in the Welsh tractate the virgins are killed in Cologne en route to Brittany. In Geoffrey's secular account, the women are murdered, but in the Welsh tractate they are martyred in the name of God (*a verthyrwyd yno yn enw y gwir Dduw*), as in the hagiographical Life. Wace in his Norman French *Roman de Brut* (1155) was the first to introduce Cologne to the secular version of the legend and, as noted by Bryan, the two versions of the Ursula legend pressured each other until the secular version was eventually adapted to accommodate some of the details in the *vita*, as here in *Y Pedwar Brenin ar Hugain*.[160] Names that are repeatedly connected with the legend of the 11,000, Constantine/Custennin, Maxentius/Maxen and Helen/Elen,[161] are borrowed from the secular narrative and employed at the beginning of *Hystoria Gweryddon yr Almaen* for their saintly Welsh connections as an appropriate way to introduce the legend of St Ursula. The effect of setting the legend of St Ursula at a very specific time and verifying this with detailed genealogical information is to create an air of authenticity. This is also the effect of the very long list of companions who accompanied Ursula.

Elizabeth of Schönau was the first to explain the identity of the men, women and children in Ursula's wider entourage, and, as we have seen, her evidence was used to authenticate the 'relics' that were uncovered in twelfth-century Cologne. The details she provided were used to verify the supposed historical accuracy of the legend. Yet the names provided in the Welsh list do not reflect those given by Elizabeth in the main. Although more than 145 manuscript copies of her *Liber revelationum* are extant, the Welsh list bears closer resemblance to the *Epistola ad vergines christi uniuersas super historia nova undecim milium virginium* attributed by the Bollandists to Hermann Joseph.[162] Born in Cologne

---

[158] Aberystwyth, NLW, Peniarth MS 215, pp. 121–37.
[159] Bartrum (ed.), *Welsh Genealogies*, x, Tudur Trefor 13 (C₂).
[160] Bryan, 'Ursula in the British History Tradition', pp. 132–33.
[161] See Notes 2, 3, 4, pp. 60–63 below.
[162] *AS Octobris*, pp. 173–201.

in the twelfth century, he was Elizabeth of Schönau's successor and continued to have mystical visions. A Premonstratensian from the Abbey of Steinfeld, he himself was made a saint and his biography was recorded by the prior of Steinfeld.[163] Levison queried Hermann's authorship, and the text has also been attributed to an English Premonstratensian friar named Richard.[164] The fact that the text that follows *Hystoria Gweryddon yr Almaen* in Peniarth 182 is a hymn by Hermann Joseph also supports the suggestion that the Welsh Life is derived from the Hermann Joseph recension of the Ursula legend. The hymn, *O vernantes Christi Rosae*, 'O springtime roses of Christ', refers to the virgins as 'darling doves of Christ', which is characteristic of the imagery habitually used by Hermann Joseph.[165] Huw Pennant made no attempt to translate the hymn into Welsh but instead copied this in Latin, preserving the alliteration and rhyme in the original text.[166] Furthermore, in the *Hystoria* Huw twice addresses Cologne using the vocative particle:

> O santaidd Gwlen, gwyn dy vyd, kanys kynnullaist gnawd ac esgyrn y santaidd verthyri a chanys kleddaist ag ymgeleddaist hwynt.[167]
>
> [Oh holy Cologne, blessed are you, for you have collected the flesh and bones of the holy martyrs and you have buried and treasured them.]

The emphasis on the importance of Cologne as a pilgrimage site and religious centre for men and women suggests that Huw's text was drawn, at least in part, from texts originally produced in Cologne or in close association with Cologne.

In the late fifteenth century, early printed editions began to appear of *Epistola ad virgines christi*, the Latin version attributed to Hermann Joseph that included the long list of companions. The first was printed in Cologne by Arnold ter Hoernen in 1482, while others were printed by Johann Guldenschaff (1490 and 1494) and Hermann Bumgart (1500 and 1503), and a related text was published in Cologne by Martin von Werden (1500, 1504, 1507 and 1509; reprinted in 1512).[168] In Britain the Latin version attributed to Hermann Joseph was included in the *Nova Legenda Anglie* printed by Wynkyn de Worde in

---

[163] François Petit, *Spirituality of the Premonstratensians: The Twelfth and Thirteenth Centuries*, trans. by Victor Szczurek, ed. by Carol Neel (Collegeville, Minnesota: Liturgical Press, 2011), pp. 118–36. He acquired the surname 'Joseph' because he was renowned for his devotion to the Virgin Mary.

[164] Mrs T. F. (Mary) Tout, 'The Legend of St Ursula and the Eleven Thousand Virgins', in *Historical Essays by Members of the Owens College, Manchester: Published on Commemoration of its Jubilee (1851–1901)*, ed. by T. F. Tout and J. Tait (London: Longmans, Green, and Co., 1902), pp. 17–56 (pp. 32–33).

[165] Petit, *Spirituality of the Premonstratensians*, p. 128.

[166] Pen. 182, pp. 301–12.

[167] Pen. 182, p. 275; see edition below, p. 54, lines 108–09.

[168] See Catherine Sanok, *New Legends of England: Forms of Community in Late Medieval Saints' Lives* (Philadelphia: University of Pennsylvania Press, 2018), p. 317 n. 65.

London in 1516, and Margaret Beaufort sponsored a Middle English version of the *Lyf of Saynt Vrsula* attributed to Edmund Hatfield, a monk of Rochester, which also included the long list of companions. It is undated but thought to have been printed in 1509 by Wynkyn de Worde.[169]

Hystoria Gweryddon yr Almaen contains a very similar list of the principal virgins who accompanied Ursula, the ten leaders who each sailed with a fleet of 1,000 virgins (thus making 11,000 when added to Ursula and her fleet of 1,000), the bishops and kings who accompanied Ursula's betrothed Etherius, as well as the various kings, princes, dukes and earls from overseas who were also martyred alongside the virgins. The list stresses not only the loyalty of Ursula's followers but also their familial relationships; many were said to be related to either Ursula or Etherius, and this echoes the biblical idea of holy kinship. Whilst the list might appear mundane to a modern audience, this was obviously not perceived to be the case by Huw Pennant as he adapted it for his Welsh audience and chose not to abbreviate this section (comprising 1071 words or 28% of the entire text). Clearly to Huw Pennant this performed an important function: 16,000 martyrs are claimed and although not all are named, enough detail is provided to make the list of martyrs sound convincing: they are no longer 'numbers' but named individuals. Perhaps when read aloud the list performed a similar function to the very long list of Arthurian companions listed in *Culhwch ac Olwen*,[170] or perhaps it functioned in a similar way to the lists of Welsh genealogies and kings recorded elsewhere in Peniarth 182 by Huw Pennant. His Welsh audience would have been familiar with the use of Welsh genealogies as a means of legitimizing both power and sanctity.

Sanok examines Hatfield's *Lyf of Saynt Vrsula* in the context of the emergence of an 'archipelagic' idea of Britain and notes that:

> Hatfield's legend insists on the *aggregate*; the virgins, along with the kings and bishops who accompany them, hail from different kingdoms and different lineages — singular, finite communities within an England recognized as an aggregate of local places and identities [...] We might suspect that the appeal of the Cologne version of the Ursula legend at this moment, when England was being reimagined as an island within an archipelago, lies precisely in its shift away from the generic identity of the 11,000 virgins to their individuation within an aggregate community.[171]

It is interesting, therefore, in the Welsh context, that Huw Pennant chose to adapt a text affiliated to this particular version of the Life of Ursula into Welsh. The strong emphasis on Cologne remains, and the *Hystoria*'s list of kings from Ireland, Normandy, Flanders, Brabant and Frisia renders the legend truly

---

[169] Edmund Hatfield, *Lyf of Saynt Vrsula* (London: Wynkyn de Worde, 1509?).
[170] Rachel Bromwich and Simon D. Evans (eds), *Culhwch ac Olwen* (Caerdydd: Gwasg Prifysgol Cymru, 1988), pp. 7-15.
[171] Sanok, *New Legends*, pp. 259, 261.

international in scope. Yet many of the martyrs are described as *hwn a hanoedd o vrenhinawl waed a char i Wrsla*, 'who was descended of royal blood and a relative of Ursula', and the fact that Ursula and Cyriacus are given Welsh names (Wrsla and Kiric, *hwn a elwid Kiric yNghymraec, yn Llading Ciriacus*), along with the opening genealogy of St Peblig, suggests some attempt to localize the legend and make it relevant to a Welsh audience. As Sanok suggests, versions of the legend that include the long list of companions posit a model for 'retaining a discrete identity within a larger composite'.[172]

Towards the end of the list of kings, Huw Pennant explains that there were many kings at that time ruling over small regions:

> Y rhain oll brenhinedd oeddynt o gywoeth, gallu ac anrhydedd, kanys yn y kyfamser hwn yr oeddynt amdler o vrenhinedd ar vychodedd o gyfoeth, val y dywedir yn Llyfr y Brenhinedd, nid amgen no bod devddeng mrenin ar hugain y mewn maes yn erbyn tri brenin.[173]

> [All of these were kings of wealth, power and honour, since at that time there were numerous kings with small amounts of wealth, as is stated in the Book of Kings, namely there were no less than thirty-two kings against three kings on the battlefield.]

Once again, his source for this can clearly be seen to have been affiliated to the Latin version attributed to Hermann Joseph that is found also in *Nova Legenda Anglie*:

> Erantenim tunc temporis regum regna modica, sicut in libro regum legitur, quod triginta duo reges contra tres ad bellum venerant praeparati; et etiam filii regum reges, et ducum duces, et comitum comites appellari solent.[174]

> [For at that time, the realms of the king were modest, as it is said in the Book of Kings, thirty-two kings came prepared for war against three; and even the sons of kings used to be called kings, and the sons of dukes, dukes, and the sons of counts, counts.]

It is tempting to see this as a reference to Geoffrey of Monmouth's renowned text tracing kingship, *Historia regum Britanniae*, which the author may have been reminded of when listing kings who accompanied Ursula, but there is no reference to thirty-two kings waging war against three kings in Geoffrey's *Historia*.[175] Scriptural references and spiritual imagery would perhaps be

---

[172] Sanok, *New Legends*, p. 261.
[173] Pen. 182, p. 290; see edition below, p. 57, lines 209–12.
[174] *AS Octobris*, p. 177.
[175] The Middle English prose *Brut* and the Anglo-Norman prose *Brut* refer to thirty-three (not thirty-two) kings ruling Britain before the coming of the Romans, but this does not fit the allusion: Friedrich W. D. Brie (ed.), *The Brut, or The Chronicles of England*, EETS o.s. 131 and 136 (1906, 1908; repr. as one volume, Woodbridge: Boydell & Brewer, 2000), I, pp. 30ff; Julia Marvin (ed. and trans.), *The Oldest Anglo-Norman Prose Brut Chronicle: An Edition and Translation*, Medieval Chronicles, 4 (Woodbridge: Boydell Press, 2006), pp. 106–07.

anticipated in the work of Hermann Joseph, but it does not appear that this is a reference to the biblical Book of Kings either. Although Huw Pennant's allusion may be traced to Hermann Joseph's work, the meaning of the reference remains opaque.

Between the list of martyrs and the description of relics in Cologne, Huw Pennant refers to the large numbers of babies and children (even unborn children) who were murdered alongside Ursula. While most texts refer to the fact that children were slaughtered with the virgins, they do not elaborate on this in such detail; Huw notes the ages of the foetuses and highlights the cruelty perpetrated as newly conceived babies are martyred in the womb. In Hermann Joseph's Latin text (*Epistola ad vergines christi*), as in the Welsh, some of the babies are so young that it is barely three months since the day they were conceived.[176] *Hystoria Gweryddon yr Almaen*, however, omits the detail that the children who accompanied the 11,000 were miraculously fed by sucking on the thumbs of the virgins.[177]

The Welsh Life then continues with an account of the bodies and skulls found at Cologne, complete with gory details such as the fact that the fragments of Clemencia's broken skull were matted together with dried blood; Katrin had an arrow in her head and Sophia an arrow in her mouth as though she had been struck as she prayed to God; Cristina's neck was still covered in fresh blood, as though it has just been severed; Benigna's whole body was preserved with hair as beautiful as when she was alive; another virgin's body remained shapely although the flesh had been pressing on her bones for years. This section is quite peculiar and it is not found in the 'Hermann Joseph' recension. It appears to stem from a relic list cataloguing and describing the relics, rather than any of the extant narrative Lives. Whilst the relics are often described as showing signs of the saints' suffering (such as an axe mark in the skull), they are usually dry bones rather than fleshy and blood-spattered with voluminous hair.

In the thirteenth century Elizabeth of Spalbeek (*fl.* 1246–1304), a stigmatized mystic from Spalbeek in the diocese of Liège, approximately a hundred miles west of Cologne, became involved in the distribution and interpretation of the relics of Ursula's entourage when she was consulted as a clairvoyant. A list of relics compiled in the thirteenth century, but preserved in a sixteenth-century manuscript, contains the names of over 150 Ursuline martyrs, followed by short notes describing the violent nature of their deaths and elaborating on their familial relationships.[178] Walter Simons, who is editing the relic list, suggests

---

[176] *AS Octobris*, p. 184; *NLA*, image 342.
[177] Cf. *AS Octobris*, pp. 178–79.
[178] Liège, Bibliothèque de l'Université, MS 366, fols 15r–27r; Walter Simons, personal communication, 25 March 2019. I am grateful to Walter Simons for sharing his work on Elizabeth of Spalbeek and the Sint-Truiden relics with me prior to the publication of his edition of the relic list and his forthcoming volume on Elizabeth. On Elizabeth of

that many of the comments may have been made by Elizabeth of Spalbeek, who was consulted by Abbot William of Sint-Truiden, while others may have been written on *schedulae* attached to the relics in Cologne. Some of the same saints' names occur in both Huw Pennant's list and the Latin list, although the precise details are different. While in the *Hystoria* Benigna's whole body survives, in the Liège list she is described as having been struck by a sword in the face so that her eyes and brain melted. While in the Welsh text Katrin has an arrow in her head, there are eight saints named Katerina in the Liège list, all of whom are decapitated except one whose heart was pierced by a sword. Cristina in the *Hystoria* has blood around her neck, while two girls named Christina in the Liège relic list are decapitated. Clemencia's head is crushed with a club in Welsh, whereas Jacobus's head is crushed in the Liège list; in Welsh Iago's (i.e. Jacobus's) head and eyes are described as being full of blood. The stock descriptions of the martyrdom — decapitations, sword through the heart, blow to the head — might be applied to different individuals, but the existence of the Liège relic list suggests that other lists no doubt existed and that Huw Pennant may have derived this section from a similar text elaborating on the suffering of the virgins. The names of the virgins and their martyred companions recur in many different contexts and, by the seventeenth century, Crombach was able to identify 9816 of the company.[179] While many of the relics of the 11,000 virgins and Ursula's companions were removed from Cologne and distributed across Europe, Huw Pennant's description of the relics suggests that they were still *in situ* in Cologne, complete with arrow heads and the trappings of martyrdom, rather than encased in silver reliquaries and elaborate busts.[180] No attempt is made to suggest that any of the relics found their way to Wales, and he appears to provide just a few select examples from his source.

Spalbeek, see also Sean L. Field and Walter Simons, 'A Prophecy Fulfilled? An Annotated Translation of the Sources on the Death of the Crown Prince Louis of France (1276) and the Interrogations of Elizabeth of Spalbeek (1276–78)', *The Medieval Low Countries*, 5 (2018), 35–92.

[179] Hermann Crombach, *S. Ursula vindicate. Vita et martyrium S. Ursulae et sociarum undecim millium virginium* (Cologne: Hermann Mylii Birckmann, 1647). In 1182, Caesarius of Heisterbach recorded that the monastery of Altenberg near Cologne received 1,000 bodies of the company: Caesarius of Heisterbach, *Dialogue on Miracles*, trans. by H. von E. Scott and C. C. Swinton Bland, 2 vols (New York: Harcourt, Brace and Company, 1929), I, p. 91. For an extensive list of the saints' relics venerated in Cologne in the medieval period, see Hans-Joachim Kracht and Jakob Torsy, *Reliquiarium Coloniense* (Siegburg: Verlag Franz Schmitt, 2003).

[180] Brief modern references to the 'head of St. Christina stained all over in blood', the dinted head of Pantulus, the youthful Artimia and a small rock-crystal reliquary containing the hair of one of the virgins clotted in blood, preserved among the 'curiosities' at Cologne, suggest that the description of the relics was not Huw's invention: see Albert Gereon Stein, *The Church of Saint Ursula and her Companions in Cologne: Its Memorials, Monuments and Curiosities* (Cologne: H. Theissing, 1896), pp. 25, 27–28.

Before proceeding with an example of how the virgins assisted a sick devotee and speeded his passage to heaven (a miracle found in many versions of the Life), Huw emphasizes the spiritual rewards of praying to the virgins. It is worth noting here that he adds devotion to God, Mary and Michael (the patron of his church and presumably of his parishioners) to the instruction:

> Pwy ddyn bynnac arvero o weddiaw Duw a'r gweryddon bendigedic hyn a'i kymydeithion verthyri val y maent yn gorphowys yn yr vrddedic ddinas Cwlen yn yr Almaen, drwy roddi i vryd ar Dduw a Mair i vam, Mihangel a'r gweryddon, ni bydd ef h[e]b help pan vo rheitia wrtho.[181]

> [Whosoever habitually prays to God and these blessed virgins and their martyred companions as they rest in the noble city of Cologne in Germany, setting his heart on God and Mary his mother, Michael and the virgins, will not be denied help when he needs it most.]

This highlights the direct relevance of the Life to his audience: the relics may rest in Cologne, but veneration of the virgins yields spiritual benefits to all their devotees. The style of other sections of the *Hystoria* also gives the impression that the text may have been adapted for use in church, possibly as a sermon or a reading providing praise for the virgins on their feast day: for example, the dramatic use of rhetorical questions[182] and further religious instructions on how to pray:

> Pwy bynnac a vynno kwplav y pyderav hyn kaned bevnydd drwy'r vlwyddyn ddevddec pater ar hugain ac Aue Maria gida phob pater. A hyn a gwplae rhyf y gweryddon.[183]

> [Whosoever wishes to complete these prayers let him sing daily throughout the year the thirty-two prayers and with each prayer a Hail Mary. And this completes the virgins' praise.]

Unlike native Welsh medieval prose, there is very little direct speech in *Hystoria Gweryddon yr Almaen*: only on three occasions do we hear the characters speak and rather than interactive dialogue between characters, this involves one character addressing another.[184] As a result, there are fewer examples of idiomatic Middle Welsh expressions for oaths and exclamations

---

[181] Pen. 182, p. 142; see edition below, p. 58, lines 248–51. On omission of the particle *a*, see Notes 38, pp. 69–70 below.

[182] *Pwy o Gristion allai vod mor galed gallon pan welai y rhyw gynulleidua o vendigedic saint y sydd yno gwedy i hanffurvo o'r wedd hon gan y melldigedic kwn, gelynion Crist, hyd nad wylai y dwfr hallt pe bai ddwyfron o bres a chalon o vaen?*, 'What Christian could be so hard of heart that when he sees such a company of blessed saints that are there deformed in this way by the cursed dogs, enemies of Christ, that he would not cry salty tears even if he had a chest of brass and a heart of stone?'.

[183] Pen. 182, p. 299; see edition below, p. 58, lines 272–74.

[184] Direct speech occurs when (i) the angel addresses Ursula, (ii) the pagan addresses Ursula and (iii) one of the virgins addresses the sick monk.

than commonly occur in the native narrative corpus.[185] The use of rhetorical questions, as well as personifying Cologne and addressing the city in the second person singular, adds to the dramatic delivery of the narrative. Common Middle Welsh narrative conventions that occur here include periphrasis with a verbal noun as the object of the preterite form of *gwneuthur*, the narrative verbal noun, frequent use of the various constructions with *sef*, and the use of *llyma* and *nachaf* to express the unexpected.

The fragmented nature of the Welsh Life suggests that Huw Pennant was drawing on more than one source and that he was willing to adapt his sources in order to weave as much information as possible into his *Hystoria*. We have a genealogy from Welsh sources, the main Life, the list of companions that acts as a lengthy aside and follows the *passio* in Welsh, the unusual description of the relics, one further miracle performed by the virgins, and an appendix on the number of religious institutions in Cologne. As we have seen, it is highly likely that his work was influenced by the early printed books appearing in the late fifteenth and early sixteenth centuries that included a version of the legend that elaborated on the identity of the virgins and the wider entourage that accompanied Ursula. It is also plausible that his *Hystoria* was still in progress when Wynkyn de Worde's publications publicized this version of the Life, and he may have been familiar with the Middle English *Lyf* sponsored by Margaret Beaufort. However, since he specifically notes that his source was a Latin text, we have no reason to doubt this. Several English loan words appear in the *Hystoria* (e.g. *certaen*, *sampyl*, *ystaciwn*); however, rather than betraying his sources, this probably serves only to demonstrate the kind of Welsh vocabulary that was familiar to Huw Pennant in this period. He uses similar English loan words in his Welsh version of *Ystoria o Wyrthie Mihangel* (e.g. *sampyl*, *dragwn*), which he specifically notes is a translation of *y Llithion Euraid* (the *Legenda aurea*). It is most likely that his main source of inspiration for his *Hystoria* was *Nova Legenda Anglie* (or its source — Edmund Hatfield refers to having used a lost Latin sermon for his English *Lyf*). Nevertheless, he was also keen to incorporate Welsh material drawing on *Bonedd y Saint* and *Y Pedwar Brenin ar Hugain*. Perhaps he deliberately avoided naming a source at the end of the Life of Ursula because he was conscious of drawing material from more than one text.

Although Ursula is not specifically noted as being Welsh, this is at least inferred in the *Hystoria* and, some seventy years after the Welsh Life was composed, it was confidently asserted in an important recusant text, *Y Drych*

---

[185] Elsewhere these are also found in translated texts such as Erich Poppe and Regine Reck (eds), *Selections from Ystorya Bown o Hamtwn* (Cardiff, University of Wales Press, 2009), p. xvi. The individual branches that make up *Pedeir Keinc y Mabinogi* contain between 42% and 50% direct speech: Sioned Davies, *Pedeir Keinc y Mabinogi* (Caernarfon: Gwasg Pantycelyn, 1989), p. 43, and on linguistic formulae, see pp. 31–45.

Kristnogawl, the first book thought to have been printed in Wales. *Y Drych* is essentially a treatise on the Four Last Things (*De Quatore Hominis Novissmis*). Part of the text is believed to have been printed secretly in a cave near Llandudno in 1587 and the rest copied from a manuscript in 1600. The work, which is generally assumed to have been by Robert Gwyn, leader of the Catholic Mission in Wales, naturally emphasizes the importance and abundance of Welsh saints:

> Beth a ddywedwn am Vrsula Santes a Chymbraes, a hitheu yn ferch i Frenhin y Cymbry a ddioddefodd farwolaeth er cadw ei morwyndod ag vnmil ar ddeg o forynion yn santesol yn dioddef gyda hi? A'r cwbl a ddoethant o wlad y Cymbry.[186]

> [What shall we say about Ursula — saint and Welsh woman — the daughter of a king of the Welsh people who suffered martyrdom in order to preserve her virginity and the 11,000 saintly virgins who suffered with her? And they all came from the land of the Welsh.]

An interesting Welsh Ursuline historiography ensued: by the seventeenth century Cyriacus had become conflated with St Curig and, in 1903, the Unitarian minister and antiquarian George Eyre Evans claimed not only that Ursula and the 11,000 virgins were Welsh, but also that they were martyred in Ceredigion.[187] It is not known for how long the church at Llangwyryfon in Ceredigion has been dedicated to St Ursula and whether a smaller group of native female saints may have become associated with Ursula's *gwyryfon*, 'virgins', when the tales about them fell into obscurity, or whether the current dedication has an unbroken history: the site itself is certainly of some antiquity.[188] The cult of the virgins proliferated to other minor churches and chapels, such as the now extinct Capel Santesau between Llanwenog and Llanybydder which, according to Edward Lhuyd in the seventeenth century, was dedicated to Ursula's virgin martyrs, and Capel Betws Leucu, dedicated to Lleucu (or Lucia), claimed to be one of Ursula's companions.[189] One late medieval Welsh calendar (NLW MS Cwrtmawr 44) lists the feast of St Wrw on the same day as *Gŵyl y Gweryddon*

---

[186] Geraint Bowen (ed.), *Y Drych Kristnogawl* (Cardiff: University of Wales Press, 1996), p. 4. See also Geraint Bowen, '*Y Drych Cristianogawl*: Astudiaeth', *The Journal of Welsh Ecclesiastical History*, 5, supplementary volume (1988), 1–66.

[187] See Notes 77, pp. 75–76 on Kiric, below; George Eyre Evans, *Cardiganshire* (Aberystwyth: The Welsh Gazette, 1903), pp. 256–57.

[188] An early Christian stone with an incised cross, drawn by Samuel Rush Meyrick, has been dated by Nancy Edwards to the ninth century: Edwards, *A Corpus of Early Medieval Inscribed Stone Sculpture in Wales Vol II: South-West Wales* (Cardiff: University of Wales Press, 2007), p. 174. For a more detailed discussion of the cult of St Ursula and the 11,000 virgins in Ceredigion, see Cartwright, 'The Middle Welsh Life', pp. 177–82.

[189] Edward Lhuyd, *Archaeologia Cambrensis: Parochialia*, 3 parts (London: Cambrian Archaeological Society, 1909–1911), Part III, p. 89; Jane Cartwright, 'Santesau Ceredigion', *Ceredigion*, 14 (2001), 1–36.

(the feast of the virgins, 21 October).[190] At Eglwyswrw in Pembrokeshire (possibly under the influence of the Ursula legend) it is claimed that the local people refused to bury corpses in the chantry chapel that contained the local saint's tomb because they would be miraculously ejected overnight, in much the same way as an imposter's bones would be expelled from the relics of the virgins in Cologne.[191]

Editorial Methodology

Editorial interference has been kept to a minimum. Punctuation and paragraphing have inevitably required some interpretation, and the same rules governing modern punctuation have been applied to the edition. Personal names and place names have been capitalized, but no attempt has been made to alter these to standard forms: thus, Wrsula, Wrsla and Vrsla all occur at different points in the text for Ursula. Where the Welsh names differ from their equivalents in other texts, standard forms have been provided in the Index of Personal Names and the character's wider literary context discussed, where necessary, in the Notes. As far as it was practical to do so, the original orthography has been preserved and no attempt has been made to standardize spelling where variant forms occur: for example, *gorffowys, gorffywys, gorphowys* vn. 'to rest, lie'. Only where scribal errors have been perceived have missing words or letters been inserted, and any editorial insertions have been clearly noted in square brackets. On the rare occasions were words or letters have been removed, for example where repetition of letters or words occur at the end and beginning of lines, these have been corrected in the edition and any emendations explained in the Notes.

Huw Pennant uses a mark similar to two dots above the grapheme <u> to distinguish between <u> and <n> and he generally uses a fine stroke over <i>: since neither of these are particularly significant, they have not been reproduced here. He also uses <R> to represent <Rh> and <rh> and this occurs in the middle of a sentence (e.g. Pen. 182, p. 262, lines 14–15, *Ai hymddygiad Rinweddawl*) as well as in the middle of a word (e.g. Pen. 182, p. 286, line 6, *er AnRydedd igrist*). These have been altered to <Rh> and <rh> as necessary in the edition: for example, *a'i hymddygiad rhinweddawl*, 'and her impeccable behaviour', and *er anrhydedd i Grist*, 'in honour of Christ'. Huw Pennant generally uses <r> to represent both <r> and <R>, and whilst on most occasions this is employed correctly, it is occasionally problematic when both a capital letter and lenition is required, as in the following examples: Pen. 182, p. 285, line

---

[190] Aberystwyth, NLW, MS Cwrtmawr 44, p. 6. St Llŷr's feast is also listed on the same day.
[191] B. G. Charles, 'The Second Book of George Owen's Description of Penbrokeshire', *National Library of Wales Journal*, 5, part iv (1948), 265–85 (p. 278).

1, *i Rüfain*, 'to Rome', and p. 286, line 1, *o Rüfain*, 'from Rome', since he uses <R> to represent <Rh> elsewhere. These inconsistencies have been corrected in the edition and lenition noted after the prepositions: *i Rufain* and *o Rufain*, 'to Rome' and 'from Rome'. Both <a> and an enlarged <a> occur in Pen. 182; the edited text complies with the rules that govern modern capitalization. Where standard medieval abbreviations have been used in the manuscript, these have been extended in the edition without drawing attention to them: so, for example, *vz* has been rendered *verch*, 'daughter', and *Ewgen'* *Ewgenius*. Only where letters are missing and no abbreviation noted have these been inserted in square brackets. A certain amount of interpretation has also been applied to the joining of words (e.g. *o naddunt > onaddunt, y roedd > yr oedd*), as well as word separation (e.g. *vnvedarddec > vnved ar ddec, addysgyssai > a ddysgyssai*), with the aim of making the text more accessible to a modern audience and students of Middle Welsh in particular. In the manuscript the following forms are frequently, but not consistently, joined to the following words, but these have been separated in the edition: the affirmative relative pronoun *a* (e.g. *aelwid > a elwid*); the preverbal particle *a* (*aoedd > a oedd*); the conjunction *a / ac* (*Acval > Ac val*); the definite article *y* (*ynefoedd > y nefoedd*); the preverbal particle *y* (*ydanvones > y danvones*); and numerals (*tairblynedd > tair blynedd, vnvilarddec > vn vil ar ddec*).

In the *Hystoria* nasalization of <p> after the preposition *yn* is consistently spelt <-m p-> and in these cases I have separated the preposition from the noun, e.g. *ympob > ym pob* and *ymprydyn > ym Prydyn*. There are no cases of <-mh-> in this text. Where nasalization of <b> has occurred, e.g. *y medrod* (yn + <b> > m), rather than adding an additional <m> (*y[m] medrod*), the preposition has been joined to the noun, e.g. *ymedrod* and *ymoliav*. In compound prepositions the nazalisation of the nominal element is not shown, e.g. *ymplith*. No examples occur in the text where nasalization of <t> would be expected, e.g. following the preposition *yn* or the possessive pronoun 1 sg. *vy*. There is only one example of nasalization of <c, k> after *vy*, *vynghariad*, and I have separated the possessive pronoun from the noun, *vy nghariad*.[192] When the nasalization of <c, k> after the preposition *yn* is spelt <-ngh-> these words have not been separated, although capitalization has been inserted in proper nouns, e.g. *ynghyfenw > ynghyfenw, ynghymraec > yNghymraec*. There is also one example where the mutation of the initial consonant of the dependant noun is not shown, *yngkolen > yng Kolen*.[193] In this instance the two words have been separated and capitalization applied. Nasalization is also shown in compound prepositions with <c, k>, e.g. *ynghyd*. There are also examples of *ynghwaneg* and *ynghwanegu* (Modern Welsh *ychwaneg* and *ychwanegu*).

---

[192] See edition below, p. 53, line 95.
[193] See edition below, p. 52, lines 53–54.

The spirant mutation is regularly shown; examples include: following the conjunction *a* (*a chanys, a chaffael, a Chwlen*); following the negative particle *ni* (*ni chwplae*); following the conjunction *no* (*no chynt*); following the possessive pronoun 3 singular feminine *i* (*i thad*); following the infixed possessive pronoun '*w* (*y'w thad, a'i tharaw*).

Lenition is noted consistently in the Middle Welsh text; some examples include: following prepositions (*ar vychydoedd, dan law, o vrenhinoedd*); following adjectives (*trwm veddwl*); following the relative particle *a* (*a elwid*); following the possessive pronoun 3 singular masculine (*a'i vab*); singular feminine nouns following the definite article lenite (*y vrenhines*); adjectives that follow singular feminine nouns lenite (*y vrenhines rinweddawl*); singular feminine nouns lenite after the numeral *vn* (*vn vil*); nouns lenite after the numeral *dav* (*dav dywyssawc*). Where lenition and aspiration are expected these are indicated in the Glossary even if they are not realized in the text.

TEXT

§1

Hystoria Gweryddon yr Almaen

Yn yr amser yr oedd Gustennin vab Maxen o Elen verch Eudaf o Gaer Sallawc
i vam yn vrenin ym Prydyn ac Ywain i vrawd, hwn a elwid Ywain Vinddu,
yn varchoc vrddol a'r trydydd brawd oedd Beblic Sant: yn [y] kyfamser hyn
yr oeddynt amraevael vrenhinedd yn Ynys y Kedyrn. Eithyr ymplith eraill   5
o vrenhinoedd y deyrnas hon yr oedd gwr sanctaidd, teilwng yn vrenin ar
i duedd, yr hwn a hanoedd o vrenhinawl waed yr hen Vrytanieid. A'i wraic
yntev oedd ddwywawl a santaidd. Ac val y byddynt y brenin teylwnc hwn a'i
vrenhines yn gweddiaw Duw o vniawnvryd kalon gan veddyliaw kaffael etifedd
o vab, yr hwn a gadwai y bywyd yn ol i dad, sef y danvones Duw vddunt etifedd   10
o verch. Hon a vedyddiwyd ac a elwid Wrsla. Eisioes o'r pan vedrai hi dywedud
gyntaf, i rhoddi dan law athro a wnaethont i mam a'i thad val y dysgai hithav y
ffydd Gatholic a chadw gorchymyn Duw. A phan vyddai y verch hon yn oedran
gwra, kyn decked a chyn addwyned oedd hi a'i hymddygiad rhinweddawl a'i
harveroedd val y kerddai son o'i hurddas hi drwy'r tyrnassoedd.   15

§2

Sef yn y kyfamser hwnnw yr oedd pygan yn vrenin yn Lloegyr a mab oedd
i hwnnw yn oedran gwreika. Ac oherwydd klywed mor ardderchawc a
rhinweddawl oedd Vrsla, ac o vrenhinawl waed — eithyr mwy o gywoeth ag
o allu bydawl oedd [gan] y pygan no thad Wrsla, y pagan hwn gwrthwyneb i
rinweddav da oedd ef, eithyr y vrenhines rinweddawl oedd hithav, ac nid oedd   20
gwbwl ganmoladwy genthi ymddygiad y brenin — val kynt, anvon kennadav o
vnoliaeth a wnaethont i geisiaw Wrsla i'r mab hwn yn briawd. Y mab hwn tec ac
arverol oedd oherwydd y ddeddyf a ddysgyssai ef. A gwedy dyfod y kennadav
a gofyn y verch yn briawd i'r mab hwn, drwy addaw kelenigion y'w mam ac
y'w thad os y verch a roddid i'r mab; os hithav nis rhoddid, bygwth dinustyr i   25
vrenhiniaeth. Eithyr val yr oedd y brenin santaidd, hwn oedd dad i Wrsula, yn
sefyll mewn trwm veddwl ac nid heb achos kanys os rhoddi i verch, yr hon oedd
gredadun i bod yn Gristynoges, a wnelai ef i'r pygan anffyddlon, ofnus oedd
y sorrai Dduw. Os yntav ni chwplae ewyllys y pygan, peregil oedd am i vywyd
pressennol. Ac val yr oedd y brenin yn gweddio y goruchel Dduw, yr hwn a   30
ddengys kynhorthwy y'w ffyddlawn bobyl ym pob kaledi, nachaf angel o'r nef

yn ymddiddan ac Wrsla, yr hwn a archai iddi hi gyttunaw a'r kenadav ac addaw priodas. Eithyr erchi a wnai yr angel iddi hi ofyn vn vil ar ddec o vorynion, a chaffel tair blynedd o yspas, a chaffael y rhain o verched boneddigion val y gallai hi, drwy gydymddeithas y rhai hyn, ddysgu priodi erbyn y dydd y sydd yn dyvod. 'A hyn a ryng bodd i'r brenin a'i vab ac a ddiovala dy dad tithav.' Sef yna, llawenhav a oruc Wrsla a'i thad a'i mam ac vfyddhav wrth gyngor yr angel. Yn ol yr ateb hwn y kennadav adref aethont.

§3

A gwedy bodlonhav y brenin o'r atteb hwn a'i vab, peri a wnaethont keisiaw drwy'r tyrnassoedd y rhai teckaf ac addwynaf o verched brenhinedd, a thywyssogion, a dugieid, ac ieirll, ac arglwyddi, a marchogion vrddolion. A gwedy keffid y rhai hyn ynghyd, i hanvon yn drwssiedic a wnaid att Wrsla. Kymaint hefyd ac allai i thad i dwyn ynghyd, ef a'i rhoe at Wrsla. Hithav yn llawen, gan ddiolch i'r goruchel Dduw, a'i derbyniai hwynt yn groessawys val bai o'r nefoedd y delynt. A'i dysgu hwynt a wnai hithav yn y ffydd Gatholic. A mynych yr anvonid engylion o'r nefoedd attaddunt y'w dysgu ac y'w kadarnhav hwynt yn ffydd Grist. Ac oherwydd maint kynvigen yr hen Sattan, mynych iawn y devynt engylion y tywyllwc i geisiaw i twyllaw i bechodav: weithiav o geisiaw ganthunt briodi meibion brenhinedd ac arglwyddi; weithiav eraill i ordderch ac ymrafael bechodav; eraill y kymellynt hwy yn ol ewyllys y knawd. Eithyr o ras Duw, ac annoc yr engylion da, wellwell y kynhelynt weryddawl grefydd a phob dydd yn rhagorawl rhag i gilidd.

§4

Dros ben hynny engylion nef a brophwydynt ac a hysbyssynt i Wrsla, pan yw yng Kolen yn yr Almaen, yr ynillynt hi a'i chymydeithion weryddon ev koroni yn y nefoedd gidac engylion o ddioddef ev merthyrv dros y ffydd Gatholic. Hithav, y vendigedic Wrsla, mynegi a wnai y gyhafal weledigaeth a phregethu vddunt o gariad perffaith, yr hwn a ddyly tyrnassu rhwng Duw a dyn, val nad ofynheynt hwy angav korphorawl, yr hwn a ynillai i'r enaid y bywyd tragywyddawl. Kanys val y keffir yn esgrifenedic: 'P[er]fecta caritas fo[r]as mittit timore[m].' Sef yw hynny, 'Kariad perffaith a ddilea gofal'. Ag o'r wedd hon, drwy lan rybydd, y deffroe hi i chydymddeithion i garu Duw ac y'w ofni ymlaen dim. Hwyntav oll, i chyd-weryddon, parod vddynt ev klustiav i warandaw geiriav i tywyssoges ac o vnoliaeth ysbrydawl veddwl ac o ewyllys ev kalonnav, kyfodi ev dwylaw a'i golwc parth a'r nefoedd a orugant a rhoddi ev gognwd yn hollawl ar gadw ev krefydd a'r llw a'r evdduned a roessynt hwy i Grist, vab Duw. Ac er i vwyn ef a chariad ar yr Arglwyddes Vair Vorwyn, vam Iessu, tyngu o vnoliaeth a wneynt hwy ar ddioddef angav kynt noc y gedewynt ffydd Grist.

§5

Eissioes gwedy kwplav tair blynedd a chaffael o bawb onaddunt wybod bod hwylwynt a'r mor yn barod, wedy vddynt baratoi ev llongav a biteiliaw, kyrchu y kefnvor a orugant a lledu hwyliav. Sef y gyhafal wareav a wneynt: weithiev y gwelid hwynt yn ffo; weithiev yn ymlid; weithiev yn wyneb i helynt; weithiev yn gwrthwyneb val pe baent yn ymladd. Ac o'r wedd hon, pan weles Duw o'i ras, ydd aethont i Gwlen yn yr Almaen, yn y lle maent i kyrff kyssegredic yn gorffowys. Sef angel Duw a'i rhybuddiai hwynt i vyned i bererindod Rufain. Oddyno kyfodi hwyliav ac i ddinas Basil y tirynt ag yno y gedewynt y llongav. Oddyno ar i traed yr aethont Rvfain. Sef yn y kyfamser hyn, yr oedd pab yn Rhufain ac ef a hanoedd o'r Brytanieid: Kiric oedd i henw. Eithyr pan wybydd ef o ddyfodiad Wrsla a'i chymedeithion, ac o'r ynys yr hanoeddynt, i kroesawy yn llawen a wnaeth y pab. A gwedy vddynt gerdded y'r ystaciwn a chaffael bendith y pab, ymchwelud a orugant parth a Chwlen yn yr Almaen.

§6

Eithyr val y byddynt yn dynessav y dywededic ddinas, nychaf pygan ysgymvn ac aneirif lu gantav o'r ymelldigedic elynion Krist i gyd ac ef. Gwedy iddo ef enill y dref a dunystyr y Kristynogion oeddynt drigianwyr yn y dinas bonheddic a ddywetpwyd vry, a gwedy iddo ef gaffael ysbi o ddyfodiad y gweryddon bendigedic i'r dinas, gellwng a oruc ef y bla byganieid, dan gri, am ben morynion Duw, mal bleiddiav am ben devaid. Ac o'r wedd hon lladd a dunvstyr y gwmpeini saint a santesav oeddynt yno yn angristynogawl, hyd pan ddoethant i'r lle yr oedd y santaidd vorwyn Wrsula yn gweddiaw Duw, ac arglwyddes y morynion a'i brenhines ar na allai ofn knowdol dros vrevawl vuchedd y byd hwn ddilev i chydymddeithion weryddon o'r llywenydd eneidiol a bery byth. Eithyr pan ganvu yr emelldigedic bygan hwn oedd dwyssoc y pyganieid mor ardderchawc oedd Wrsula, dechrav ymddiddan a orug ef o'r wedd hon: 'A vorwyn,' eb ef, 'dy osgedd a vynaic pan hanwyd o rieni addwyn. Bai buassai ymi dy weled kynt no hyn, ni laddyssid dy gydymddeithion mal i lleasswyd mwy no chynt, vy nghariad,' eb ef, 'Kymer gyssur da, kanys wyd teilwng. Ti a geffi yn briawd y nebun, yr hwn yr ergrynant amerodreth Rhufain rhacddaw ef a'i allu.' Sef a orug morwyn Grist, kyfodi i golwc parth a'r nefoedd gan roddi i gognwd ar yr Iessu a Mair i vam, y neb y kedwis hi i morwyndawd er i mwyn o'r amser y ganyssid hyd yr awr hon, a ffieiddiaw a oruc y santaidd Wrsla yr emelldigedic bygan hwn a'i weithredoedd a'i allu. A phan wybu y melldigedic bygan hwn i Wrsla i vingamv ef, dodi saeth yn y llinyn a saethu y vorwyn santaidd, a'i tharaw a saeth yn anghevawl. Ac o'r wedd hon y syrthiodd yn y maes hwn ymysc teilwng gydymddeithion. Ac o'r wedd hon, val maen gwyrthuawr, y talai hi deilwng enaid i Dduw drwy ynill i choroni yn y nefoedd, yn ol gorvod yn y maes hwn.

§7

Pwy o ddyn knowdol allai a'i galon veddylied nev draethu a'i dafawd y gyhafal gerddav a dawns a vu yna gan y saint a'r engylion o weled ynghwanegu graddav y llywenydd? O santaidd Gwlen, gwyn dy vyd, kanys kynnullaist gnawd ac esgyrn y santaidd verthyri a chanys kleddaist ag ymgeleddaist hwynt. Gorvuost ar dy elynion, a thi a ynillaist rydd-deb o'th hir gaethiwed.

§8

Eithyr o vewn yr amgylch y kladdwyd y santaidd verthyry hyn, ni lyfesir kladdu neb rhyw ddyn daearol. Ac yn sampyl ar hynny, yr oedd gynt vrenin yn ynys Brydain a mab iefanc oedd i'r brenin hwn, yr hwn yr oedd vryd i dad arno ac a garai yn vawr. Eithyr, val y mynnodd Duw, y mab hwn a vu varw ac, val yr oedd gariad y brenin a'i ognwd ar Wrsla a'r gweryddon, peri a wnaeth y brenin hwn myned a'r korff i Gwlen a'i gladdu ymedrod y saint. Eithyr gwedy myned ac ef i eglwys y gweryddon, a'i gladdu ymysc y saint, y bore drannoeth yr oedd y korph hwn ar wyneb y bedd. Ac o'r wedd hon, val y kleddid ef y naill dydd, erbyn tranoeth y bydd ef ar wyneb dayar. Eithyr o'r diwedd y korph hwn a gyfodes vwchben y bedd yn gyfywch a chubed, val y gwelir heddiw val y dydd kyntaf, er dangos sampyl na ddyleir kladdu korph pechadur ymysc y kyssegredic verthyri hyn.

§9

O santaidd Gwlen, bendicka di Dduw kanys ef a gadarnhaodd kloav dy byrth, ac ef a heddychodd dy randiredd. Ac o ddyfodiad y santaidd verthyri y bendigawdd Duw dy blant, y sawl a drigant ynod ti. E[i]thyr yr oedd merch iefanck ymysc y saint a'r santessav pan ddoethant i Gwlen, hon a elwid Cordula. Pan weles y vorwyn hon grevlondeb y pyganieid melldigedic yn rhwygo knawd tyner y boneddigion saint a santessav yn amgylchyn y dinas, sef a wnaeth hi, ymguddiaw y mewn vn o'r llongev hyd trannoeth. A'r bore drannoeth meddyliaw a oruc y vendigedic vorwyn hon nad oedd deilwnc iddi golli coron dragywydd yn y nef gida'r gynifer saint a santessav y buassai yn i kwmpeniaeth er certaen o amser. Ac ar vrys dyfod a oruc hi ymysc i gelynion, a ffoeri yn i llygaid, a'i hangreistio hwynt o hanffyddlonder, a chymryd i marvolaeth dros y ffydd Gatholic o ewyllys i challon. A phan weles Duw, o'i drugaredd, gyfodi gwyl yn enw y santaidd verthyri ynghyfenw y dydd y merthyrwyd hwynt ag nad oedd weddi i'r verch hon, oherwydd na ddioddefodd hi yn y dydd kyntaf, ymddangos a oruc Cordula i vynaches a oedd mewn krefydd, ac erchi a oruc hi kyfodi gwyl iddi dranoeth yn ol gwyl y gweryddon. Ac velly y gwnaethbwyd.

§10

Yma weithion y dywedir o henwav certaen o saint a santessav o vrenhinawl waed a dugiaid ac ieirll a marchogion vrddolion. Kyntaf a ffennaf tywyssoges o'r vn vil ar ddec weryddon: Wrsla verch Nothus, brenin o'r Brytanieid; arall oedd Pynnosa, merch i dduc bonheddic, hwn oedd ewyrth vrawd tad i Wrsla; arall oedd Cordula, merch iarll; y bedwaredd dywyssoges oedd Elevtheria, kefnitherw i Wrsula, merch i dduc bonheddic; y bymed dywyssoges oedd Fflorencia, merch i vrenin a chares i Wrsla; y pvm merched hyn oeddynt bennaf o'r vn vil ar ddec weryddon.

§11

Ar ol hyn yr oeddynt vn ar ddec o verched brenhinedd ac arglwyddi, y rhain oeddynt doethion a bucheddawl, a mil o verched gida phob vn onaddunt. Henwav y merched hyn: vn oedd Iota, merch brenin ardderchawc, hon oedd gymen a doeth, ardderchawc a chyflawn o rinweddav da ac iddi ddwy chwioredd gyda hi. Y rhain oeddynt garessav i Wrsla — y naill onaddunt a elwid Genimiana, arall oedd Iusticia; yr ail dywyssoges a elwid Benigna, merch i dduc, a chida hi yr oeddynt bedair chwioredd, a'i henwav — vn onaddunt oedd Sibilia, arall oedd Mobilia, arall oedd Ewffrofnia, y [iiij] oedd Ewstachia; y drydedd dywyssoges hon a elwid Clemencia, merch iarll kadarn a dwy chwioredd iddi gida hi — vn a elwid Silian, arall Iuductam; y iiij dywyssoges merch i dwyssoc vrddedic, kefnither i Wrsla, hon oedd a dwy chwioredd iddi gida hi — y rhain a elwid Ewlalia a Serena; y v. oedd merch iarll bonheddic, Carpophora, a dwy chwioredd gyda hi — Ewtropiam oedd y naill onaddunt, Paladoram oedd y llall; y chweched oedd merch i vrenin, Colwmba oedd i henw ac vn chwaer iddi gida hi — Cordula oedd i henw; y vij tywyssoges Benedicta y gelwid hi, merch i dwyssoc vrddedic o wr dwywol santaidd, a phedair merched oeddynt gyda hi — y rhain oeddynt pedair chwioredd: y rhain a elwid Cornula, Prudencia, Sapiencia ac Illwstris; yr wythved tywyssoges hon a elwid Odilia, merch iarll a'i dwy chwioredd gyda hi — Silian ac Wrsia y gelwid hwynt; y nawed a elwid Celindys, merch i iarll, hon oedd deg ac ardderchawc ac vn chwaer oedd iddi gyda hi — Virgilia oedd i henw; y x oedd Sibilia, merch i vrenin kadarn, a thair chwioredd oeddynt y'w dylyn — y rhain a elwid Iulia, Lucia ac Ewgeina; yr vnved ar ddec oedd Lucia vorwyn, hon oedd ddoeth a chymen, merch brenin a chares oedd i wr priod Wrsla, ac vn chwaer iddi gida hi — Placida y gelwid hon. Yr vn verch ar ddec hyn oeddynt tywyssogion ar yr vn vil ar ddec weryddon, kanys pob vn onaddunt a dywyssai vil o verched dan i llaw a'i llywodraeth ac a'i dysgai ac a'i llywodraethai yn ol hyn y dywedir o'r gynvlleidua.

§12

Esgyb a verthyrwyd yno: y kyntaf oedd pab Rhufain, hwn a elwid Kiric yNghymraec, yn Llading Ciriacus. Y pab hwn ef a dderbyniodd y merched kyssegredic hyn i Rufain, ac ef a'i bedyddiodd hwynt ac a'i bendigawdd, ac ef a edewis y dinas o anvodd y kardinaliaid, ac ef a wrthodes vod yn bab yn Rhufain ac yn amerodyr. Ac i Gwlen yn yr Almaen y doeth ef. Ac yno yr ymroes ef i vod yn verthyr kyssegredic a chidac ef dav gardinal — vn onaddunt a elwid Poncius, arall oedd Petrus; hefyd dav ddiagon — y naill onaddunt oedd Calixtus, arall oedd Kilianus; hefyd tri arvollwr vn a elwid Ambrosius, arall oedd Iustinus, y trydydd a elwid Cristianus; archdiacon o Rufain, hwn a elwid Fflorentius; hefyd dav dywyssawc a ddilynynt y pab — vn oedd Ewgenius, arall oedd Nicostrastus. Pawb onaddunt yn barawd i offrwm teilwng eneidiav er anrhydedd i Grist yno; hefyd y doeth esgob Basil, gwr santaidd teilwng, Pantulus oedd i henw; hefyd esgob o wlad Antiochia, Iacobus oedd i henw, gwr teilwng santaidd; hefyd esgob Melden, ewythyr vrawd i mam i Wrsla.

§13

Weithiau y dywedir henwav yr esgyb oeddynt gida mab y brenin, gwr priod Wrsla: y kyntaf oedd Wiliam Esgob, gwr doeth kymen, hwn a hanoedd o vrenhinawl waed a char i Wrsla; yr ail oedd Colu[m]banus, esgob vrddedic, kefynderw i Wrsla; y trydydd gwr doeth vrddedig, Eleutherius oedd i henw; y pedwerydd Lotarius i gelwid, gwr ffyddlon, santaidd, diwair, ewythyr i vab y brenin gwr priod Wrsla; y v. Mawricius, esgob Levitan; y vi Ffolarius, esgob Luws; y vii Sulpicius, esgob Raben.

§14

Weithion y treithir o'r brenhinoedd a'r arglwyddi, dugieid, ieirll, a boneddigion vchelwaed: kyntaf oedd Etherius, mab brenin o Loegr, gwr priod Wrsla, hwn oedd chwe blwydd ar hugain a thri mis o oedran. Y mab hwn aeth drwy'r mor yn erbyn Wrsla hyd mewn tref a elwir Magwnsia. Yno y bedyddiodd Kiric Bab ef ac y troes i henw ef ac a'i gelwis ef Etherius, yr hwn a elwid gynt Oloffernes, hwn a verthyrwyd rhwng dwylaw Wrsla i briawd; ail oedd Olifer, brenin vrddedic; y trydydd oedd Crophorus; y pedwerydd brenin Luctus y gelwid; y v. Clodonius, brenin kadarn a'i wraic — a['r] wraic hon a elwid Blandina; y vi brenin a elwid Canutus a'i wraic, Balbina oedd i henw; y vij. brenin Pupinus y gelwid a'i wraic, hon a elwid Margaret, kares i Wrsla; yr wythued brennin Aldwlff y gelwid a'i wraic hon a elwid Dronisia; y nawed brenin Amic y gelwir, gwr da kanmoladwy, a'r ddwy verched gidac ef — y rhain a elwid Columba

oedd y naill, Cordula oedd y llall; y x brenin Syrianus oedd i henw, a'i wraic a
elwid Sibli, a'i thair chwioredd gida hi; y xi o'r brenhinoedd Reffridus y gelwid
ef, hwn a droes i ffydd Grist o gyngor i wraic. Y rhain oll brenhinedd oeddynt
o gywoeth, gallu ac anrhydedd, kanys yn y kyfamser hwn yr oeddynt amdler o 210
vrenhinedd ar vychodedd o gyfoeth, val y dywedir yn Llyfr y Brenhinedd, nid
amgen no bod devddeng mrenin ar hugain y mewn maes yn erbyn tri brenin.

§15

Dros ben hyn yr oeddynt ymravael vrenhinedd a thywyssogion o ymravael
wledydd o'r tu draw i voroedd, a dugieid, ac ieirll, ac arglwyddi a marchogion
vrddolion: rhai o Iewerddon, rhai o Normandi, rhai o Fflandrys, rhai o wledydd 215
Braban; eraill o wledydd Ffrisia. Ef a las yn y maes o blant bychain mwy no
phum cant, heb gyfrif y rhai oeddynt ymoliav i mammav. Val y maent i heskyrn
heddyw y'w dangos: rhai ohonvnt kyn bychaned val y tybygir nad oeddynt tri
misyriad ymoliav i mamav pan las hwynt.

§16

Wrth hynny y maent yn nombyr y merthyri hyn oll ynghwaneg i vn vil ar 220
bymtheg. Rhwng mawr a bychan y maent heddiw y'w dangos yn eglwys y
gweryddon yn y dywededic ddinas Kwlen certaen o gyrff y morynion hyn. O'r
rhai hyn, dwy a henynt o wledydd Cesilia a'r rhai hyn y maent kyn decked i
gwallt ar i pennav heddyw a'r dydd y merthyrwyd hwynt, eithyr bod y gwaed
yn i rhwymo'r gwallt ynghyd ar i pennav, a'i kyrff yn ffurfaidd heddyw, eithyr 225
bod y knawd yn gwasgu wrth yr esgyrn gwedy i bod yn gorffwys ynghwaneg
i d[e]c o vlynyddoedd. Vn o'r merched hyn a elwid Barthimia; arall oedd i
henw Arthimia. Hefyd y mae korff merch yn gyfan yn i ddangos a'r gwallt kyn
decked a phan yttoedd yn vyw: Benigna oedd henw y verch hon a hanoedd o
wledydd Maritene. Hefyd y mae korff gwr santaidd yn gorffwys yno mewn 230
golwc: Pantulus oedd i henw, rhyw amser esgob Basil, a'r dyrnod ar y pen
heddyw yn dangos hyd pan dorres kwbwl o ffiolen y pen. Morwyn hefyd hon a
elwid Cristina a'r gwaed heddyw ynghylch i mynwgl val pe bai ynewydd dorri;
morwyn hefyd hon a elwid Clemencia, hon a ddrylliesid i phen a chnwpae,
eithyr bod y gwaed gwedy ysgrowlingo y gwallt yn kynnal yr esgyrn ynghyd: 235
merch oedd hi i iarll bonheddic; hefyd merch arall, Katrin y gelwid, a'r saeth
yn i phen a gwallt mawr ar i phen; morwyn hefyd a elwid Sophia a'r saeth yn
i genav a'i genav yn egored val y byddai yn gweddiaw Duw pan drewid a'r
saeth. Yno hefyd y mae korph esgob y'w ddangos: hwn a hannoedd o wledydd
Antioetsia, hwn a elwid Iago, hwn y mae i ben a'i lygaid yn llawn gwaed 240
heddyw y'w ddangos val y dydd kyntaf. Hefyd y maent yno esgyrn y pennav,

a'r chwarelav a'r pennav saethav ynddunt heddyw y'w dangos: rhai onaddunt y maent hysbyssol i henwav yn y byd hwn; eraill ger bron Duw ni hebyrgofir yn y lle yr adnabyddir pawb oherwydd i weithred. Pwy o Gristion allai vod mor galed gallon pan welai y rhyw gynulleidua o vendigedic saint y sydd yno gwedy i hanffurvo o'r wedd hon gan y melldigedic kwn, gelynion Crist, hyd nad wylai y dwfr hallt pe bai ddwyfron o bres a chalon o vaen?

§17

Pwy ddyn bynnac arvero o weddiaw Duw a'r gweryddon bendigedic hyn a'i kymydeithion verthyri val y maent yn gorphowys yn yr vrddedic ddinas Cwlen yn yr Almaen, drwy roddi i vryd ar Dduw a Mair i vam, Mihangel a'r gweryddon, ni bydd ef h[e]b help pan vo rheitia wrtho. Yn sampyl ar hyn val yr oedd gynt gwr o grefydd yn arver o weddiaw Duw a gweryddon yr Almaen, nychaf y syrthiodd ef mewn trwm glefyd val y byddai ef anobeithiol o'r byd. Eithyr, mwy no chynt, nid aent o'i gof y bendigedic weryddon ac, val y byddai ef yn dwyn i glefyd o'r wedd hon, sef y gwelsai ef vorwyn ddisglair yn sefyll ger i vron. Hon a ofynnai iddo adwyniad ef y neb a safai yn gynhyrchol ger i vron. Sef ydd atebai gan ddywedud nad oedd ef cyfadnabyddus ar y gyhaval vorwyn. Sef yna yr atebai hithav, 'Vn wyf i,' heb hi, 'o'r merched yr wyd ti yn i gweddiaw ac yn i karv. Ac val y mynech di gaffael diolch genym ni, dywaid vn vil ar ddec o bederev ac Aue Maria gida phob pader a thi a gai dy iechyd. A phan el dy enaid o'th gorph ni a ddown i'th dderbyn i'r nefoedd.' Ar hyn, diflannv a wnai'r santes. A'r gwr hwn a gyfodes yn iach i vyny a, chynta ac y gallodd, kanv a wnai ef y sertaen byderev a ddywetpwyd vchod a, phan weles Duw vod yn amser, klyfychu a oruc y gwr hwn o'r klefyd a'i duc o'r byd hwn i'r dragywyddol vuchedd. Eithyr val y byddai yr abad a certaen o'r kwfaint vwchben y dywedic vynach, erchi yn gyffrous a wnai y mynach arloesi ffordd i'r gweryddon. A phan vydd yr abad yn rhyfeddu beth oedd y gair hwn, y mynach a hysbyssai o'r weledigaeth a gair y santes ac val yr helpant y santaidd weryddon y sawl a'i gweddio hwynt o lan veddwl. Ac ar hyn y tervynai y santaidd vynach a chida'r gweryddon val y bai ef gyfrannoc o'r wledd a bery byth i'r lle y delom oll drwy weddiaw y glan weryddon. Amen.

§18

Pwy bynnac a vynno kwplav y pyderav hyn kaned bevnydd drwy'r vlwyddyn ddevddec pater ar hugain ac Aue Maria gida phob pater. A hyn a gwplae rhyf y gweryddon. Ac velly y teruyna Ystoria Gweryddon yr Almaen hyd y medrodd Syr Huw Pennant i thynnv o'r Llading yNghymraec val y gallai rhai kerddgar i dyall o'i hiaith e hun.

§19

Y maent yn y dinas vrddedic Kolen xj o Eglwyssi Coleds; hefyd y maent devddec o vynachlogoedd gwyr o ymrafael grefydd; hefyd deng mynachlog merched o ymravael grefydd; hefyd amyn vn vgain o eglwyssi plwyf; y maent hefyd yn y dinas bonheddic Colen ynghwanec a chant o gapeloedd ag aneirif o gyrff saint 280 a santessav, ac aneirif o bardynav gwedy i ymrafael baboedd i rhoddi. Pwy bynnac a vai tan not o'r pardynav hyn, ef allai gaffael gras yn y byd hwn ac yn y byd a bery byth i'r lle y delom oll a Christynogion da'r byd. Amen.

NOTES

§1

1 **Hystoria Gweryddon yr Almaen** 'The Story of the German Virgins': the title also occurs on p. 299 on Pen. 182 without the initial <H>: *Ystoria Gweryddon yr Almaen*. The title Huw Pennant provides at the start of the Life has been adopted here for the volume's title. However, both *Hystoria* and *Ystoria* were used in MW and Huw Pennant uses *Ystoria* earlier in the manuscript for the title of his Welsh translation of the Miracles of the Archangel Michael. It is used elsewhere in the titles of a number of texts that are translations into MW (e.g. *Ystorya Bown o Hamtwn, Hystoria Lucidar, Ystorya Adaf*). On the possible origin of the title *Hystoria Gweryddon yr Almaen*, see Introduction. For abbreviations of grammatical terms used in the Notes, see Glossary.

2 **Yn yr amser yr oedd** 'during the time that [...] was', Pen. 182, p. 261 *yn yr amser yr amser oedd*; repetition of *yr amser* has been deleted in the edition.

2 **Gustennin vab Maxen** As noted in the Introduction, according to the tractate *Y Pedwar Brenin ar Hugain a Farnwyd yn Gadarnaf* Maxen had three sons, all mentioned here in the Welsh version of the Life of St Ursula, Custennin (Constantine), Owain and Peblig (Bartrum, 'Y Pedwar Brenin ar Hugain', p. 172). The historical Maxen (Magnus Maximus), a native of Spain, came to Britain and usurped Gratian's throne in 383, becoming emperor until 388 when he was slain by Theodosius I in Italy. Historical sources mention only his son Victor (Prosper of Aquitaine, *Chronica Minora*, ed. by Th. Mommsen, Monvmenta Germaniae Historica, 11 vols (Berlin: Weidmannos, 1892), III, p. 169; *TYP*, p. 466). Although Gildas (d. *c*. 570) in his *De excidio Britannie* was critical of Maxen for denuding Britain of its troops during his campaign in Gaul, he became known as 'the founding figure of independent post-Roman Britain' (D. N. Dumville, 'Sub-Roman Britain: History and Legend', *History*, 62 (1977), 173–92 (p. 180)). According to *Breudwyt Maxen*, Maxen married Elen ferch Eudaf (see note below) and she became conflated, via the epithet Luyddog ascribed to her in the *Breudwyt*, with Elen Luyddog or Elen ferch Coel, wife of Constantius and mother of Constantine the Great, whose eldest son Constantine (Custennin in Welsh) was emperor from 337 to 340. The Harley version of *Historia Brittonum* refers to the latter Constantine's burial at Caer Saint (Segontium, see below); numerous Roman coins bearing either his name or his mother Helena's name were discovered at Caernarfon. In the

thirteenth century a tomb reputedly containing his body was discovered at Caernarfon and his relics were translated to a nearby church (Peter C. Bartrum, *A Welsh Classical Dictionary: People in History and Legend up to about A.D. 1000* (Aberystwyth: National Library of Wales, 1993), pp. 156–157). Antonina Harbus notes that Constantine was a popular name in Britain and that because 'both Constantine and Magnus Maximus were associated with Caernarfon in medieval tradition, the two naturally intermingled, especially with respect to their relationship with Helena [...] the native Elen acquired the attributes of St Helena at some stage before Maximus and Helena were paired' (*Helena of Britain in Medieval Legend* (Cambridge: D. S. Brewer, 2002), pp. 59–60). Like Constantine the Great who married Helena, Maxen who married Elen is also ascribed a son called Custennin/Constantine who had links with Caernarfon. It is significant that Huw Pennant has chosen to set his version of the Life of Ursula during the reign of Custennin fab Maxen, progenitor of an important saintly lineage associated with Caernarfon in a Life in which numerous Continental kings, earls and nobles are listed. This is unique to the Welsh Life of Ursula.

2 **Elen verch Eudaf** In *Breudwyt Maxen Wledic* the emperor Maxen sees a woman of outstanding beauty in his dreams and he cannot rest until he finds her. He eventually discovers her at Caer Aber Saint (see note on Gaer Sallawc below) and marries her. She is known as Elen ferch Eudaf and the *Breudwyt* describes how her brother Cynan conquers Brittany and cuts out the tongues of the native women so that their language does not corrupt the language of the British settlers. In the *Breudwyt* Maxen's wife Elen is said to have been associated with the Roman road Sarn Helen and it is claimed that this is why she was known as Elen Luyddog (Elen of the Hosts) (Brynley F. Roberts (ed.), *Breudwyt Maxen Wledic* (Dublin: School of Celtic Studies, Dublin Institute for Advanced Studies, 2005), pp. lxv–lxvii). In the *Brut* tradition Maxen is a descendant of Elen Luyddog (not her husband) and his unnamed bride (daughter of Octavious/Eudaf) is never confused with Elen Luyddog or Elen ferch Coel, finder of the true cross. The Cleopatra version of *Brut y Brenhinedd* explains that Elen ferch Coel acquired the epithet Luyddog after finding the true cross: *Ac o'r achos hynny y elwyd hi o hynny allan yn elen luhydawc. Ac oy rinwedawl ethrylith ay dysc y cavas hi pren y groc yr hwn y diodefawd iessu grist arney* (Parry (ed.), *Brut y Brenhinedd*, p. 95) ('And for that reason she was called Elen Luyddog from then onwards. And because of her virtuous genius and learning she discovered the wood from the cross upon which Jesus Christ had suffered'). Benjamin David Guy suggests that 'St Helena is deliberately merged with Geoffrey's invented daughter of Eudaf, creating the Breudwyt Maxen's Elen Luyddog' ('Constantine, Helena, Maximus: On the Appropriation

of Roman History in Medieval Wales, *c.* 800–1250', *Journal of Medieval History*, 44 (2018), 381–405 (p. 404)). On the *Brut* version of the Life of Ursula see the Introduction.

2 **Gaer Sallawc** In the medieval period Caer Sallawc was another form of the name Caer Saint (Segontium, i.e. Caernarfon). Although in ModW Caersallog is used for Salisbury in Wiltshire, it is clear from the context here that Huw Pennant is referring to Caernarfon in north Wales. Peter C. Bartrum traces a series of mistakes which he suggests gave rise to the later Salisbury ('Some Studies in Early Welsh History', *Transactions of the Honourable Society of Cymmrodorion* (1949), 279–302 (pp. 301–02)). As noted above, in *Breudwyt Maxen* Maxen discovers Elen at Caer Aber Saint in Arfon and dedicates three strongholds to her at Caer Saint, Caerllion (Caerleon) and Caerfyrddin (Carmarthen). The element *Saint* (Segontia) reflects the name of the river that flows into the Menai Straits at Caernarfon and does not appear to have any particular association with saints. Cair Segeint is referred to in *Historia Brittonum* (p. 27) and Kaer Seint yn [in] Aruon in *Branwen* (Ifor Williams (ed.), *Pedeir Keinc y Mabinogi* (Caerdydd: Gwasg Prifysgol Cymru, 1930), p. 232). The poet Cynddelw Brydydd Mawr also refers to a battle that took place at Aber Seint in his elegy to Owain Gwynedd (d. 1170) (Nerys Ann Jones and Ann Parry Owen (eds), *Gwaith Cynddelw Brydydd Mawr*, II (Caerdydd: Gwasg Prifysgol Cymru, 1995), poem 4, p. 48). Roberts suggests that the site of Eudaf's court may reflect continued use or recognition of the site of the Roman fort Segontium on a hill about one kilometre from the Menai Straits that was later replaced by the more prestigious Caernarfon (Roberts (ed.), *Breudwyt Maxen*, pp. 40–41). The fact that Huw Pennant uses Caer Sallawc here rather than the more commonly used Caer Saint appears to suggest that he was either drawing on the tract *Y Pedwar Brenin ar Hugain* or the same source as used by its author (i.e. Gutun Owain in the case of the earliest extant copy in NLW, MS Llanstephan 28). It is noticeable that in this tract Maxen founded a stronghold at Kaer Sallawc (not Caer Saint) and that this is explained as being *Kaer Sallawc y[w r] Gaer yn Arvon*, 'Caer Sallog is Caernarfon' (Bartrum, 'Y Pedwar Brenin', pp. 172, 181). See the Introduction for a discussion of the tractate and its relevance to *Hystoria Gweryddon yr Almaen*.

3 **Ywain Vinddu** In addition to *Y Pedwar Brenin ar Hugain*, Owain Finddu (Blacklip) is also said to have been one of Maxen's sons in the genealogy of St Cadog, where it is claimed that he accompanied his mother to Jerusalem when she found the true cross (Bartrum (ed.), *Early Welsh*, p. 24; Benjamin David Guy, 'Medieval Welsh Genealogy: Texts, Context and Transmission', 2 vols (unpublished DPhil thesis, University of Cambridge, 2016), II, pp. 56–59).

According to the Triads, Owain son of Maxen was one of the *Tri Chynweissyat Enys Prydein*, 'Three Chief Officers of the Island of Britain', who guarded Britain against invasion (*TYP*, p. 25). Edward Lhuyd recounts a tale *c.* 1698 in which Owain son of Maxen fought a giant near Dinas Emrys, Gwynedd: having hurled metal balls and shot arrows at each other, neither of them survived and Owain declared that he should be buried where one of his arrows landed (*TYP*, pp. 466–67; see also Taliesin Williams (ed.), *Iolo Manuscripts: A Selection of Ancient Welsh Manuscripts* (Llandovery: William Rees, 1848), pp. 81–82). The poet Rhys Goch Eryri referred to Gwynedd as *tir mab Macsen*, 'the land of Macsen's son', which is taken by Bromwich as an indication of the antiquity of the legend (*TYP*, p. 467).

4   **yn varchoc vrddol** 'a dubbed knight'; *vrddol* (and *vrddedic* used below) can also mean 'noble'. The plural form of the adjective *vrddolion* is used on three occasions below to describe knights.

4   **Beblic Sant** According to *Bonedd y Saint* and *Y Pedwar Breinin ar Hugain*, St Peblig was the son of Maxen Wledig and Elen ferch Eudaf. Huw Pennant had copied the reference to Peblig's parentage earlier in the same manuscript in his version of *Bonedd y Saint* (Pen. 182, p. 39). No Life of St Peblig is extant, but it is likely that he is the saint depicted in the Llanbeblig Hours (*c.* 1400) on fol. 3v, in close proximity to his father Maxen (fol. 3r): see NLW MS 17520A, available on the National Library of Wales website, <https://www.llyfrgell. cymru/?id=258&L=1> (accessed 23 April 2019). The parish church at Llanbeblig is dedicated to him near the ruins of the Roman fort Segontium (see the note on Gaer Sallawc above), and his feast day on 3 July is noted in the liturgical calendar in the Llanbeblig Hours, along with the dedication of the church at Llanbeblig on 6 June. Although Elen ferch Eudaf does not display any saintly characteristics in *Breudwyt Maxen Wledic*, it is likely that her association with St Helena made her a suitable candidate for becoming the mother of a local Caernarvonshire saint such as Peblig. As noted by Guy, the idea of St Peblig's parentage 'was probably a product of Llanbeblig's proximity to Caernarfon where Eudaf's court is located in *Breudwyt Maxen*' and the court was deliberately located there by its author to convey the importance of Gwynedd in the legendary past (Guy, 'Constantine', pp. 403–04).

4   **yn [y] kyfamser hyn** 'at that time', Pen. 182, p. 161 *yn kyfamser hyn*. While it is also possible that a nasal mutation was intended here, i.e. *yng kyfamser hyn* (cf. *yng Kolen*, §4), it is assumed that this is a scribal error and *y* has been inserted: cf. *yn y kyfamser hyn*, §5, and *yn y kyfamser hwnnw*, §2, which uses the sg. masculine demonstrative pronoun rather than the neuter sg. *hyn*. See also

the discussion of nasal mutation in the section on 'Editorial Methodology' in the Introduction.

5   **Ynys y Kedyrn** 'the Island of the Mighty', that is, Britain. *Kedyrn* is a pl. form of the adjective *kadarn*, 'strong, mighty', and refers to the men of the island, Ynys y [Gwyr] Kedyrn; on the adjective, see *GMW*, §35. The term occurs in the Second and Third Branches of the Mabinogi (see, for example, Ian Hughes (ed.), *Bendigeiduran Uab Llyr* (Aberystwyth: CAA, Prifysgol Aberystwyth, 2017), p. 20 n. 36). In the Welsh version of the *Holy Greal, Y Seint Greal*, Britain is described as *Ynys y Kedyrn*, although this does not occur in the French source; Robert Williams (ed. and trans.), *Y Seint Greal: The Holy Greal* (Gwynedd, 1897; repr. Pwllheli: Jones, 1987), p. 192; William A. Nitze and T. Atkinson Jenkins (eds), *Le Haut Livre du Graal: Perlesvaus* (Chicago: University of Chicago Press, 1932).

7   **yr hwn** 'the one who': the demonstratives *yr hwn, yr hon* are often used as the antecedent of a non-defining relative clause, particularly in translated works; see *GMW*, §74. Both *hwn* and *yr hwn* are used as overt markers to introduce relative clauses in this text. Cf. *hwn a elwid Ywain Vinddu*, 'he/the one called Owain Blacklip', in the same paragraph.

7   **yr hen Vrytanieid** 'the ancient Britons': In *Passio II: Regnante Domino*, Ursula's father is King Deonotus who lived 'in the lands of Britain' (Sheingorn and Thiébaux (trans.), *The Passion*, p. 15), and in the *Legenda aurea* he is known as Nothus or Maurus (*LA*, II, p. 256). In the Welsh Life he is a descendant of the ancient Britons and is not named as Nothus, king of the Britons, until later in the Life when the virgins and other companions who accompanied Ursula are listed: see §10.

10   **yr hwn a gadwai y bywyd yn ol i dad** 'who would outlive his father': lit. 'the one who would keep the life after his father'. An alternative meaning could be 'who would live life in the same manner as his father': see GPC Online, s.v. *ol* (v), 'in accordance with'.

10–11   **sef y danvones Duw vddunt etifedd o verch** 'God sent to them a daughter as an heir': *sef*, which consists of *ys*, 'it is', + *ef*, occurs frequently in MW and refers to something which follows. It is used adverbially here. On the uses of *sef* see *GMW*, §55 (f); Emrys Evans, 'Cystrawennau "sef" mewn Cymraeg Canol', *BBCS*, 18 (1958–1960), 38–54; T. Arwyn Watkins, 'The *sef* [...] Realization of the Welsh Identifactory Copula Sentence', in *Dán do Oide: Essays in Memory of Conn R. Ó Cléirigh*, ed. by A. Ahlqvist and V. Capková (Dublin: Institiúid Teangeolaíochta Éireann, 1997), pp. 579–93.

11–12 **o'r pan vedrai hi dywedud gyntaf** lit. 'from when she could say first', that is, 'from the [moment] when she could first speak; as soon as she was able to speak'.

12 **i rhoddi dan law athro a wnaethont i mam a'i thad** 'her mother and father placed her under the tutelage of a teacher': lit. under the hand of a teacher. The education of the female saint is usually not recounted in as much detail as that of the male saint, but many are allocated a tutor — although we do not learn the name of Ursula's tutor; cf. St Winefride being placed under the tutelage of St Beuno (Cartwright (ed. and trans.), *Buchedd Gwenfrewy*). The construction vn. + *a* + *wnaeth* + subject is common in MW; while in ModW the 3. sg. of *gwneud* would be expected (*gwnaeth ei mam a'i thad*), in MW the 3 pl. is common.

13–14 **oedran gwra** 'marriageable age', lit. 'the age to seek a man/husband'. The Lives of many female saints begin when they reach puberty, and a common hagiographical pattern is that conflict arises with secular authority when the female saint refuses to marry. On the biographical patterning of the female saint, see Cartwright, *Feminine Sanctity*, pp. 85–87.

14 **kyn decked a chyn addwyned oedd hi** 'she was so pretty and so gentle': two adjectives in the equative degree describe Ursula. The same adjectives *tec* and *addwyn* used in the superlative are used to describe the 11,000 virgins in §3. On the equative followed by a clause expressing result, see *GMW*, §44.

§2

16 **Sef yn y kyfamser hwnnw** 'Now at that time', that is, 'at the same time'; the use of *sef* is unusual here according to Evans's classification because he does not include *sef* followed by another adverb; see *GMW*, §55 (f 3) and lines 16, 37, 76, and 258 in *Hystoria Gweryddon yr Almaen*.

16 **Lloegyr** 'England': if the legend is set in ancient Britain, one would not expect reference to England. While Geoffrey of Monmouth in his secular version of the legend was keen not to confuse Celtic Britain with what later became known as 'England', many of the later versions of the legend conflate the two. There is a Latin gloss near the start of the Latin Life of Ursula attributed to Hermann Joseph in the *Acta sanctorum* that sarcastically comments that 'Blessed Hermann' assumed that there were English people living in Britain in the year 238 and that this would certainly not please the Welsh (*AS Octobris*, p. 178). Unfortunately, the Bollandists do not state their manuscript sources for the Life or the notes.

17 **oedran gwreika** 'marriageable age', lit. 'the age to seek a woman/wife'. The verbal noun *gwreicka* or *greyckao*, based on the noun *gwreic*, is attested from the thirteenth century; see GPC Online, s.v. *gwreica*.

17–22 **Ac oherwydd klywed … yn briawd** This particularly long sentence is cumbersome and difficult to punctuate: the pagan is contrasted with Ursula's father, but he is also contrasted with his own queen. In addition, Ursula's father's worldly wealth is compared to that of the more affluent pagan. The meaning is perhaps rendered: 'And since he heard how excellent and virtuous Ursula was, and of royal blood — only that this pagan had greater wealth and earthly power than Ursula's father, that pagan was the complete antithesis of virtuous characteristics; but the queen was virtuous and she did not entirely approve of the king's behaviour — as before, they sent messengers in solidarity to attempt to secure Ursula as a wife for this son.'

18–19 **mwy o gywoeth ag o allu bydawl oedd [gan] y pygan** 'the pagan [had] greater wealth and earthly power': the preposition denoting possession was missing here, so this has been inserted in square brackets.

21 **genthi** 3 sg. f. preposition *gan*, 3 sg. m. *gantav* and 3 pl. *ganthvnt* are also used in *Hystoria Gweryddon yr Almaen*. Peter Wynn Thomas has suggested that these are northern forms ('Middle Welsh Dialects: Problems and Perspectives', *BBCS*, 40 (1993), 17–50).

21–22 **anvon kennadav … a wnaethont** In MW narrative the construction vn. + *a* + *wnaeth* / *oruc* + subj. (stated or understood) is very common; see *GMW*, §180 (3), and Peter Wynn Thomas, '(GWNAETH): Newidyn Arddulliol yn y Cyfnod Canol', in *Cyfoeth y Testun: Ysgrifau ar Lenyddiaeth Gymraeg yr Oesedd Canol*, ed. by Iestyn Daniel et al. (Caerdydd: Gwasg Prifysgol Cymru, 2003), pp. 252–80. Cf. also *llawenhav a oruc Wrsla a'i thad a'i mam*, 'Ursula and her mother and father rejoiced', §2, below.

23 **arverol** 'accustomed'. The pagan king's son is described in positive terms from the outset in the Welsh text. The suggestion here appears to be that although he was a pagan, he was fair and accustomed to following the law. In the *Legenda aurea* Ursula insists that he must be baptised before she will agree to marry him (*LA*, II, p. 256). In the *Hystoria* she requests a three-year respite and 11,000 virginal companions but does not include her suitor's baptism as one of the conditions.

24–25 **addaw kelenigion y'w mam ac y'w thad** 'promising gifts for her mother and her father', *y* (prep. ModW *i*) + '*w* infixed possessive pronoun 3 sg. f. that causes aspiration. On unstressed possessive pronouns in MW, see *GMW*, §56; Sims-Williams (ed.), *Buchedd Beuno*, pp. 116–19. Huw Pennant generally uses *i* for the prep. 'to, from', rather than *y* (e.g. *i'r pygan*), but when this is followed by an infixed pronoun, he prefers *y* > *y'w* (rather than *i'w*); there are ten other examples of *y'w* in the text where '*w* occurs as 3 sg. m, 3 sg. f. and 3 pl.

27   **mewn trwm veddwl** 'in deep thought'. An attributive adjective normally follows the noun, but there are numerous examples in the *Hystoria* of adjectives preceding nouns (e.g. *ffyddlawn bobyl*, 'faithful people'; *goruchel Dduw*, 'almighty God').

26–29   **Eithyr val yr oedd … ac nid heb achos kanys os rhoddi i verch, yr hon oedd gredadun i bod yn Gristynoges, a wnelai ef i'r pygan anffyddlon, ofnus oedd y sorrai Dduw.** 'But as the pious king, who was Ursula's father, was standing deep in contemplation, and not without cause since if he gave his daughter, who believed she was a Christian, to this unfaithful pagan, he was afraid that he would offend God.' The syntax of this sentence is made complex by the insertion of the relative clause *yr hon oedd gredadun i bod yn Gristynoges*, which qualifies *i verch*, into the conditional clause *os rhoddi i verch a wnelai ef i'r pygan anffyddlon*. This clause has a bipartite structure, with *os*, 'if it is', followed by a relative clause (compare *GMW*, §272 (b.1), lit. 'if it is giving his daughter which he would do to the unbelieving pagan'), and is itself inserted into the *kanys*-clause, *kanys ofnus oedd y sorrai Dduw*, 'because he was afraid that he would offend God'.

29   **Os yntav ni chwplae ewyllys y pygan** 'If he did not fulfil the pagan's wish': *ni chwplae*, lit. 'were not to complete', *ni* (negative particle), + imperfect 3 sg. *kwplav*, 'to complete'.

31   **ym pob kaledi** 'in every hardship': nasalization of <p> is not marked in the text; see the section on 'Editorial Methodology' in the Introduction on word separation.

31–32   **nachaf angel o'r nef yn ymddiddan ac Wrsla** 'lo an angel from heaven was talking to Ursula'. The use of the interjection *nachaf* makes the scene more dramatic. As noted by Ned Sturzer, MW is one of the languages which use a special grammatical construct to express the unexpected (i.e. adverbial phrase + *llyma* or *nachaf* + clause): see 'How Middle Welsh Expresses the Unexpected', *Cambrian Medieval Celtic Studies*, 41 (2001), 37–53. On other common interjections in MW, see *GMW*, §279–80. In the *Legenda aurea* and the Middle English version attributed to Edmund Hatfield, Ursula provides her answer acting on divine inspiration (*LA*, II, p. 256; cf. Hatfield, *Lyf of*

Saynt Vrsula, p. 76), although the texts do not specifically describe the angel's visitation. Marx argues that the compiler of the *South English Legendary*, who introduced an angel into this scene to dictate the terms of Ursula's betrothal, 'created a dramatic situation that changes the emphasis of the narrative [...] this episode is conceived as part of an emotional drama' (Marx, 'Saint Ursula', p. 147). Parallels are also found in the Life attributed to Hermann Joseph and the *Nova legenda Anglie* (*AS Octobris*, p. 174; Horstmann (ed.), *Nova Legenda*, II, p. 473).

34–35 **y rhain o verched ... y rhai hyn** Pen. 182, p. 265 *yr Rain o verched ... yr Rai hyn*. As noted in the Introduction, Huw Pennant uses <R> to represent <Rh> and <rh>. These have been altered to *Rh* or *rh* in this edition. One would expect the definite article *yr* to be used before a vowel, although it also occasionally occurs in MW before a consonant where the preceding word ends in a vowel (see *GMW*, §27). In these two examples Pennant uses *yr* before *Rain* and *Rai* (and there are two further examples of *yr Rain* in Pen. 182, p. 281) although the preceding word does not end in a vowel. However, in the vast majority of cases he uses the definite article *y* before *R* (i.e. *Rh/rh*), e.g. Pen. 182, pp. 266, 282, 289, 290, 291, 295. In this edition *yr Rain* (i.e. *yr rhain*) has been altered to *y rhain* on the four occasions where this occurs.

36 **'A hyn a ryng bodd i'r brenin a'i vab ac a ddiovala dy dad tithav.'** 'And this will please the king and his son and your father will be relieved.' The use of direct speech is unexpected here. As noted in the Introduction, almost the whole of the *Hystoria* is narrated in the third person with very little direct speech; the only other examples of dialogue occur in §6 when the pagan who murders the virgins addresses Ursula, and in §17 when one of the virgins appears to a sick monk and offers him advice. The switch from narrative to brief direct speech in the episode above, in which the angel offers Ursula advice, strikes the reader as peculiar, but the only alternative here would mean altering the possessive pronoun to *i thad hithav*, 'her father'. The possessive pronoun used by Huw Pennant, therefore, indicates that punctuation for direct speech is needed here. There are no tags introducing direct speech and denoting who is speaking as are often found in MW prose (e.g. *heb ef*); for an analysis of direct speech in *Pedeir Keinc y Mabinogi*, see Davies, *Pedeir Keinc*, pp. 24–27, and on the phenomenon known as 'slipping', i.e. when indirect discourse abruptly shifts to direct discourse, see J. Kerling, 'A Case of "Slipping": Direct and Indirect Speech in Old English Prose', *Neophilogus*, 66 (1982), 286–90; G. Richman, 'Artful Slipping in Old English', *Neophilogus*, 70 (1986), 279–91; and Erich Poppe, 'Slipping in Some Medieval Welsh Texts: A Preliminary Survey', in *Le slipping dans les langues médiévales*, ed. by Jürg Rainer Schwyter, Erich

Poppe and Sandrine Onillon (Lausanne: Université de Lausanne, Faculté des Lettres, 2005), pp. 119–51. Poppe provides a detailed survey of slipping in several medieval Welsh texts (both native and translated) and notes that although these instances do not occur frequently, they are often introduced semantically by a general verb of saying: in this example *erchi*, 'to ask'. He also notes that in some translated texts the Latin construction *dicere quia* used to introduce direct quotation 'often supplies in the subsequent context a conflicting trigger to make the Welsh redactor slip into direct quotation from the indirect one which was suggested to him by *quia*' (Poppe, 'Slipping', p. 150). In Pen. 182, p. 265, in the phrase *A hyn a Ryng bodd*, the <R> indicates that Huw Pennant has not marked lenition following the preverbal particle. This has been corrected in this edition.

38   **Yn ol yr ateb hwn y kennadav adref aethont.** 'In accordance with this answer the messengers went home.' The preverbal particle *a* is omitted here before the verb *aethont*, 'they went'; it would appear that this is not a scribal error but a deliberate omission before the verb with initial <a> and it has, therefore, not been replaced in this edition (e.g. *y kennadav adref [a] aethont*). Huw Pennant demonstrates a tendency to omit both preverbal and relative particles before verbs beginning with <a>. There are three further examples of this below where the particle *a* is omitted before *allai* (twice) and *arvero*; see Notes 106–08, pp. 79–80; 244–46, p. 94; 248, p. 94 below. Comparison with other texts adapted into Welsh by Huw Pennant yields further examples of this tendency in his work: cf. *Ystoria o Wyrthie Mihangel*, Pen. 182, p. 77, *Mihangel anvones y dialaethav ar blant yr Aifft*, 'Michael wreaked vengeance [lit. sent the punishments] on the children of Egypt'. There are other examples in his work in which he omits the relative particle before verbs beginning with the vowel <y>: *hwn ymkanodd kyfodi korff Moesen o'r bed*, 'he who intended to raise Moses's body from the grave' (*ymkanodd* is a variant of *amkanodd*, 'he intended', Pen. 182, p. 77; Vanherle, '*Ystoria*'), and on other occasions he retains the preverbal particle *a* but omits the initial <y>: *Mihangel, ynghweryl y Tad o'r nef, a 'mladdodd a'r dragwn* (transcription Pen 182, p. 77, *amladdodd ar dragwn*), 'Michael, on behalf of the Father in heaven, fought the dragon'. Emrys Evans, 'Cystrawen y Rhagenw Personol yn Rhyddiaith Gymraeg y Cyfnod Canol' (unpublished MA thesis, University of Wales, Swansea, 1958), pp. 24–25, notes several examples of the particle *a* being omitted before verbs beginning with <a>, including in J. Gwenogvryn Evans (ed.), *The White Book Mabinogion: Welsh Tales & Romances Reproduced from the Peniarth Manuscripts* (Pwllheli: privately printed, 1907), p. 145, Stephen J. Williams (ed.), *Ystorya de Carolo Magno* (Caerdydd: Gwasg Prifysgol Cymru, 1968), p. 110, and John Morris-Jones and John Rhŷs (eds), *The Elucidarium and Other Tracts in Welsh From Llyvyr Agkyr Llandewivrevi A.D. 1346 (Jesus College MS. 119)* (Oxford: Clarendon

Press, 1894), pp. 32 and 58. David W. E. Willis, *Syntactic Change in Welsh* (Oxford: Oxford University Press, 1998), pp. 138–41, suggests that by the late sixteenth century omission of the particle was common in all contexts. The particle is no longer used in spoken ModW and Willis suggests that it is to the late sixteenth century that we should date its disappearance.

§3

40–41   **y rhai teckaf ac addwynaf o verched brenhinedd, a thywyssogion, a dugieid, ac ieirll, ac arglwyddi, a marchogion vrddolion** 'the prettiest and most gentle daughters of kings, princes, dukes, earls, lords and noble knights'. As one might expect, superlative forms of the adjectives *tec*, 'pretty', and *addwyn*, 'gentle', are used to describe the virgins who accompany Ursula on her final pilgrimage. On use of the preposition *o* with the superlative when a degree of comparison is expressed, see *GMW*, §47. Female saints are inevitably described as being the most beautiful of all women (cf. St Gwenfrewy, *A morwyn deccaf yn y byt oed honno*, 'And she was the prettiest maiden in the world', Sims-Williams (ed.), *Buchedd Beuno*, p. 146), and they are almost without exception of high status. The social ranking of the principal virgins selected for Ursula's journey is of utmost importance in this particular version of the hagiographic Life. In Geoffrey of Monmouth's *Historia regum Britanniae* and *Brut y Brenhinedd* Ursula is accompanied not only by 11,000 noblewomen but also by 60,000 commoner women as she sails to Brittany to meet her betrothed Conanus Meiriadocus (Geoffrey of Monmouth, *The History of the Kings of Britain*, pp. 106–07).

41   **marchogion vrddolion** 'noble knights' or 'dubbed knights': *vrddolion* is the plural form of the adjective *vrddol*, which can mean either 'dubbed' or 'noble', both of which make sense in this context.

42   **yn drwssiedic** 'well dressed' or 'adorned'. In most versions the virgins are carefully selected according to their status and beauty. In *Passio II: Regnante Domino* the well-born and beautiful maidens 'received feminine ornaments to increase their royal splendour' as they prepare to accompany Ursula on her pilgrimage (Sheingorn and Thiébaux (trans.), *The Passion*, p. 21).

43   **ef a'i rhoe at Wrsla** 'he would give them to Wrsla': *rhoe* imperfect 3 sg. of *rhoddi* which is more commonly followed by the prep. *i*; on *rho(dd)i at*, see GPC Online, s.v. *rhoddaf*; cf. also *deffroe* in §6 imperfect 3. singular of *deffroi*, 'to awaken', and *cwplae/kwplae* §2 imperfect 3 sg. of *kwplav*, 'to finish, complete', both ending in <e> rather than <ei>. The meaning here is that Ursula's father is contributing girls from his kingdom in addition to those collected by the pagan king and his son.

44–45   **val bai o'r nefoedd y delynt** 'as if they had come from heaven': *delynt* is imperfect subjunctive 3 pl. *dyvod*. On the subjunctive, see *GMW*, §123.

46–47   **y'w dysgu ac y'w kadarnhav hwynt** 'to teach and to confirm them': two examples of the infixed possessive 3 pl. pronoun *'w*; cf. above where *y'w* is used in the 3 sg. On *'w*, see *GMW* §56, N2 and also §24a.

47   **Sattan** 'Satan, the devil' and his angels of darkness attempt to pollute the virgins' faith by trying to persuade them to marry (*o geisiaw ganthunt briodi*), lust after men (*i ordderch*) and give way to the temptations of the flesh (*kymhellynt hwy yn ol ewyllys y knawd*). Sexual deviancy is the sin that is regularly selected in the Lives of female saints as the most appropriate means of derailing women's devotion to the Christian faith.

49   **weithiav eraill** 'at other times' or 'on other occasions'.

51–52   **Eithyr o ras Duw, ac annoc yr engylion da, wellwell y kynhelynt weryddawl grefydd a phob dydd yn rhagorawl rhag i gilidd.** 'Nevertheless, by God's grace, and the encouragement of the good angels, they maintained their virginal faith increasingly better and better and every day was more excellent than the previous one.': *rhag i gilidd* (lit. 'from each other'). The female saints' education often focuses primarily on how to avoid lust and marriage. St Gwenfrewy, for example, is encouraged by her parents to receive instruction from Beuno that centres on maintaining her virginity: *y gymryd dysc y ymoglyd rhac gordderchiad y'w chadw yn lan, a hitheu gan y hannoc o warder Duw yn tyfu beunydd wellwell o fryd a doethineb yn gyflawn o'r Yspryd Glan*, 'to take instruction on how to avoid lust and keep herself pure, and she encouraged by God's compassion grew every day better and better in mind and wisdom full of the Holy Spirit' (Cartwright (ed. and trans.), *Buchedd Gwenfrewy*).

51   **wellwell** 'better and better': a composite adjective formed by repeating the comparative form of the adjective *da* attested from the fourteenth century, see GPC Online, s.v. *gwellwell*.

§4

53–54   **yng Kolen** 'in Cologne': for editorial practice regarding the marking of nasal mutation, see Introduction. The text uses *Kolen/Colen* and *Cwlen* for Cologne, although *Cwlen* occurs more frequently.

54   **chymydeithion weryddon** 'virginal companions' is the sense here: *chydymdeithion* is a pl. adjective rather than a noun, so a more lit. translation would be 'companionable virgins'. Cf. also §17 *kymydeithion verthyri*, 'martyred

companions' (lit. 'companionable martyrs'), below. Lenition follows the adjective because Huw Pennant has chosen to position the adjective before the noun.

55 **o ddioddef ev merthyrv dros y ffydd Gatholic** 'as a result of their suffering martyrdom for the Catholic faith': on *o* meaning 'as a result or consequence of', see GPC Online, s.v. *o* 14a. One of the main indications of sanctity was the saints' willingness to die for their faith. As noted by Thomas F. X. Noble and Thomas Head, 'Saints were those persons who had been judged by God to be worthy of entrance to the kingdom of heaven immediately after death' (*Soldiers of Christ: Saints and Saints' Lives from Late Antiquity and the Early Middle Ages* (London: Sheed & Ward, 1995), p. xiv). Ursula and the virgins' sanctity is assured by the angels, who forewarn them that, following their martyrdom, they will be crowned immediately in heaven.

56 **y gyhafal weledigaeth** 'the same vision'. Adjectives normally follow the noun, but may precede it, in which case the initial consonant of the noun is lenited; for other examples of *cyhafal* preceding the noun, see GPC Online, s.v. *cyhafal*. Another example occurs in *Hystoria Gweryddon yr Almaen*, §17: *y gyhafal vorwyn*, 'the same virgin' or 'the said virgin'; *cyhafal* has a similar meaning to *dywedic*, which also precedes nouns, e.g. §17 *y dywededic vynach*, 'the said/aforementioned monk'.

59–60 **'P[er]fecta caritas fo[r]as mittit timore[m].' Sef yw hynny, 'Kariad perffaith a ddilea gofal'** 'That is "Perfect love casts out fear"': In Pen. 182, p. 268, the Latin quotation is abbreviated. According to 1 John 4. 18: 'There is no fear in love, but perfect love casts out fear; for fear has to do with punishment, and whoever fears has not reached perfection in love.' Ursula's exhortation to her virginal companions, as she learns of their imminent martyrdom, reflects John's first letter, in which he emphasizes that those who love God need have no fear on the Day of Judgment for they can boldly face the future. The theological significance here is that since Ursula has fully awoken her companions to God's love, they can boldly and confidently face martyrdom in Cologne.

62 **parod vddynt ev klustiav i warandaw** lit. 'ready for them their ears to listen'. In other words, all of the virgins were eager to listen to Ursula; [*oeddynt*] could be inserted following *klustiav* in this sentence. It is possible that *vddynt* is a scribal error here and that Huw Pennant may have intended to write *oeddynt*.

62 **i tywyssoges** 'their princess'. Since lenition is not noted, *i* is taken as the possessive pronoun 3 pl. rather than the definite article here.

NOTES

63 **o vnoliaeth ysbrydawl veddwl** 'in mental, spiritual unity' (lit. 'of unity of spiritual mind'): *vnoliaeth* is used twice in this section to emphasize that the virgins are united in their faith and determination to suffer martyrdom. The corporate unity of the 11,000 virgins is one of the distinctive features of their cult; see Montgomery, *St. Ursula*, pp. 38, 180.

64 **gognwd** 'trust, mind, faith'. There are no recorded examples of the word *gognwd* used in this context in other medieval texts. It is possible that *goglyd*, 'trust, mind, faith', was meant here: see GPC Online, s.v. *gognwd* and *goglyd*². However, it would appear that Huw Pennant did not merely make a careless scribal error, as he used the same word again on two further occasions in the text: e.g. *gan roddi i gognwd ar yr Iessu a Mair i vam*, 'putting her trust in Jesus and Mary his mother' (and also §9), which suggests that he clearly intended to use *gognwd* in this particular context.

66–67 **tyngu o vnoliaeth a wneynt hwy ar ddioddef angav kynt noc y gedewynt ffydd Grist** 'they vowed together that they would suffer death before they would relinquish Christ's faith' (lit. they took a vow of unity). Ursula is depicted as the leader of a fleet. Almost like a military general, she prepares the virgins for combat. In the *Legenda aurea* and many other versions of the tale, Gerasina, queen of Sicily and Ursula's aunt, plays an important role in preparing the virgins for battle, although she is not mentioned in the Welsh text. Jacobus de Voragine in his *Legenda aurea* refers to the virgins as 'her fellow soldiers' and they 'all took the oath of this new knighthood' (*LA*, II, p. 257). Helen Nicholson has argued that Ursula and the virgins had a particular relevance to the military religious orders since one of their roles was to defend Christian pilgrims from attack by the 'infidel': 'there was an obvious parallel with a religious order whose members travelled around Christendom and might well have to face danger, suffering and death together' ('St Ursula and the Military Religious Orders', p. 42).

§5

68–70 **Eissioes gwedy kwplav tair blynedd … wedy vddynt baratoi ev llongav … kyrchu y kefnvor a orugant** 'Three years later … having prepared their ships … they set sail' (lit. 'Already after completing three years … after they prepared their ships … seeking the ocean they did'). Chronological order is important in the narrative and Huw Pennant often uses *gwedy* + vn … vn. + *a* + *orugant* …, 'having done… they did…'. In this sentence there are two clauses beginning *gwedy*.

69 **hwylwynt** 'a favourable sailing wind': linked compound noun.

69 **biteiliaw** vn. lit. 'to victual, supply with provisions': detailed preparations are made for the journey over a period of three years and the probable meaning here is that the ships were stocked with food and provisions.

70–72 **weithiev y gwelid hwynt yn ffo; weithiev yn ymlid; weithiev yn wyneb i helynt; weithiev yn gwrthwyneb val pe baent yn ymladd** 'on some occasions they could be seen fleeing; at other times in pursuit; occasionally facing danger; sometimes they were retaliating as though they were fighting'. It is likely that the parallelism between *yn wyneb i helynt*, 'facing danger', and *yn gwrthwyneb*, 'retaliating', is intentional. In most versions of the legend, the virgins practise military manoeuvres as though they are preparing for battle at sea. Ironically, since their martyrdom in Cologne has been pre-ordained, they have no intention of retaliating against their murderers and welcome death as a release from the constraints of corporeal existence. Sam Riches argues that Ursula is a figure of complex gender identity, noting that she established 'what amounts to a female chivalric order in the form of an elite grouping of women sailors, and led her female companions in preparation for the possibility of a sea-borne attack during their voyaging' ('Male Martyrs, Female Models? St Ursula and St Acacius as Leaders and Victims', in *The Cult of St Ursula and the 11,000 Virgins*, ed. by Cartwright, pp. 245–61 (p. 245)). At the end of *Passio II: Regnante Domino* revenge is enacted when, following the martyrdom, the virgins (who have all been slaughtered) reappear in a vision on the battlefield and drive out the Huns from Cologne. They are depicted on the city walls defending Cologne in thirteenth-century sculpture depicting the defence of Cologne (see below, Notes 108, p. 80 and 123–34, p. 82), as well as in late fifteenth-century woodcuts in early printed books; see Montgomery, *St. Ursula*, Figures 24 and 27.

73–74 **yn y lle maent i kyrff kyssegredic yn gorffowys** 'in the place where their sacred bodies rest'. In ModW *mae*, the present 3 sg. form of the verb *bod*, would be required in this context; however, in MW the pl. subject *kyrff*, 'bodies', requires the present 3 pl. form *maent*. This is one of the areas in which the narrative appears disjointed, since Huw Pennant refers to their bodies in Cologne before he has described their martyrdom.

75 **i ddinas Basil y tirynt** 'they landed in the city of Basel'. Basel is the furthest navigable point of the Rhine, so they leave their ships there and travel on foot to Rome. Given the importance of Basel in the legend, it is little wonder that Ursuline relics were acquired by Basel cathedral. In 1270 Heinrich von Neuenberg, bishop of Basel, was given the sacred head of St Pantulus, first bishop of Basel, who is named later in the Welsh Life as one of Ursula's

companions. An elaborate reliquary bust was made for Pantulus's head and this was displayed, along with a reliquary bust of St Ursula, on the feast of the virgins in Basel (Montgomery, 'St Ursula', pp. 140–50).

76 **Oddyno ar i traed yr aethont Rvfain.** 'From there they went on foot [to] Rome.' One would expect to see the prep. *i*, 'to', before *Rvfain*, 'Rome' (cf. *aethont i Gwlen*, §5). However, it is possible that Huw Pennant lenited *Rvfain* here because he was treating the noun as the direct object of the concise verb *aethont*: he would appear to deliberately use <r> here to represent <R> rather than his usual <R>, which he employs for <Rh> (transcription of Pen. 182, p. 271 *oddyno Ar i traed yrAethont rvfain*).

76 **Sef yn y kyfamser hyn** 'Now at that time'. The use of the neuter sg. is unusual here (lit. 'in the meantime of this'). See also Notes 4, p. 63 above, *yn [y] kyfamser hyn*.

77 **Kiric** Pope Cyriacus, the fictional pope who welcomes Ursula and her companions to Rome and later is martyred alongside the virgins in Cologne. In most versions of the legend Cyriacus is British and provides a particularly warm welcome to Ursula, since he considers her and her companions to be his fellow countrymen and women. Huw Pennant's phraseology here, *ac ef a hanoedd o'r Brytanieid*, 'and he was descended from the Britons', reflects his earlier description of Ursula's father in §1, *a hanoedd o vrenhinawl waed yr hen Vrytanieid*, 'who was descended from the royal blood of the ancient Britons', suggesting that they are of the same ethnic group. He does not draw any specific parallels between St Cyriacus and the Welsh St Curig, although he later notes that he has both a Welsh (*Kiric*) and a Latin name (*Ciriacus*). By the late seventeenth century Cyriacus and Curig had become conflated; Thomas Price claimed that 'Ciricius (erroneously sayd by some to have beene pope) is sayd to have come with S. Ursula from Rome, he hath many churches in Wales dedicated to him by the name Cyric ferthyr' (Aberystwyth, NLW, MS 3108B, fol. 11[r]). Elizabeth of Schönau, as we saw in the Introduction, was tasked with explaining why Cyriacus's gravestone was found in Cologne among the virgins' graves. Her visions suggested that Ursula was accompanied by many holy bishops and great men, but that Cyriacus was held in disdain because he had refused to remain in high office (Elizabeth of Schönau, *The Complete Works*, p. 218). Jacobus de Voragine adds that Cyriacus was related to a number of the British virgins, and explains that the reason no pope named Cyriacus is listed among the popes of Rome is that his name was expunged from the list because the cardinals 'thought that he must be out of his wits to abandon the glory of

the pontificate and go off with a lot of silly women' (*LA*, II, p. 158). This Cyriacus should not be confused with St Cyriacus who was one of the twenty-seven martyrs (d. *c*. 303) who were put to death during the Diocletian persecutions.

79 **ystaciwn** One of the stational churches in Rome, presumably the *statio* where mass would be said. Pilgrims visiting Rome would travel to the various stational churches (originally approximately twenty-five in all), where the bishop of Rome would join them and lead them in prayer. Gregory the Great (d. 604) established the order in which the churches should be visited, as well as the liturgy to be recited, and designated this a Lenten custom. The word *statio* originally referred to fast days but came to mean the place within which the pilgrims would process; see H. Leclercq, 'Station Days', *CE*, XIV, pp. 268–69.

§6

81 **Eithyr val y byddynt yn dynessav y dywededic ddinas, nychaf…** 'However, as they were approaching the aforementioned city, behold …'. The switch of tense here (consuetudinal imperfect 3 pl.) combined with the use of the interjection *nychaf* enhances the drama of the scene as the martyrdom is about to begin.

81 **pygan ysgymvn** 'a villainous pagan'. In most versions of the tale the Huns are specifically named as the perpetrators responsible for slaughtering the virgins and their entourage, but the Welsh version does not mention the Huns or their leader Julius; cf. *LA*, II, p. 258. On the association between the Huns and Hungarians and Ursula's popularity in Hungary, see Tüskés, 'The Cult of St Ursula in Hungary'.

82 **i gyd ac ef** 'with him' is superfluous here, since *ganthav*, 'he had' (preposition with suffixed personal pronoun 3 sg. m.), denoting possession, occurs earlier in the sentence.

87 **santesav** 'female saints': Pen. 182 has *santtesav*. However, since the word is split across the line-break, *sant|tesav*, it is plausible that Huw Pennant made a mistake here when he repeated the letter *t* at the beginning of line 11 on p. 272. This has, therefore, been altered to *santesav* in the edition, although *santtesav* is also acceptable. *Santessav* occurs on five occasions in the text but there are no further examples of *santtesav*. Cf. *y santaidd verthyri* §7 below, in which *sant|taidd* is also split across a line-break (Pen. 182, p. 275, lines 11–12), although *santaidd* occurs on sixteen other occasions.

89   **a'i brenhines** 'and their queen': *'i* is possessive pronoun 3 pl. here, not 3 sg.

86–91   **Ac o'r wedd hon lladd a dunvstyr y gwmpeini saint a santesav oeddynt yno yn angristynogawl, hyd pan ddoethant i'r lle yr oedd y santaidd vorwyn Wrsula yn gweddiaw Duw, ac arglwyddes y morynion a'i brenhines ar na allai ofn knowdol dros vrevawl vuchedd y byd hwn ddilev i chydymddeithion weryddon o'r llywenydd eneidiol a bery byth.** 'And in this unchristian fashion killed and destroyed the company of male and female saints who were there, until he came to the place where the holy virgin Ursula was praying to God, and the lady and their queen [the one] whose companions' earthly fear of the fragile life of this world could not remove from the joy of the soul that lasts forever.' This is one possible interpretation of this very awkward sentence; *ar* here is a demonstrative pronoun rather than a preposition (*GMW*, §75). It often serves as an antecedent to a relative clause (see Morris-Jones, *A Welsh Grammar*, pp. 298–99), but in this instance it is not entirely clear which of the elements in this sentence refer to *ar* as an antecedent, nor how *ac arglwyddes y morynion a'i brenhines*, 'and the lady and their queen', relates to the preceding context. This suggests that something went awry as this section was translated or adapted into Welsh.

90   **chydymddeithion weryddon** 'virginal companions' is the sense here, although *weryddon* is the main noun and *chydymddeithion* is an attributive noun describing the virgins (lit. 'companionable virgins' or virgins travelling together). Cf. also §17, *kymydeithion verthyri*, 'martyred companions' (lit. 'companionable martyrs' or martyrs travelling together). Lenition is not expected after a pl. noun but since *chydymddeithion* is used adjectivally here and precedes the noun *weryddon*, this has caused lenition.

92–93   **dechrav ymddiddan a orug ef o'r wedd hon: 'A vorwyn,' eb ef** 'he began conversing with her in this fashion: "Hey virgin," he said'. Unlike in the previous example of direct speech (cf. §2), here Huw Pennant introduces the pagan's dialogue clearly by referring to it as *ymddiddan*, 'conversation, talk', addressing Ursula using the vocative particle *a* and providing a tag to clarify who is speaking.

94–95   **Bai buassai y mi dy weled kynt no hyn, ni laddyssid dy gydymddeithion mal i lleasswyd mwy no chynt, vy nghariad** 'If I had seen you earlier, your companions would not have been killed as they were killed earlier, my love'. On uses of *bai*, see GPC Online, s.v. *pe*. Morgan notes that *bei/bai* and *pei* were felt to be basic forms of the conjunction meaning 'if', and one would not necessarily expect to see *pai* at the beginning of a sentence as one would in ModW (T. J. Morgan, *Y Treigladau a'u Cystrawen* (Caerdydd: Gwasg Prifysgol Cymru, 1952),

p. 328; see also Poppe and Reck (eds), *Selections*, p. 49 n. 119). On the origin of the conjunction *bei/bai* as imperfect subjunctive 3 sg. of *bot*, see Morris-Jones, *A Welsh Grammar*, p. 349: it later developed as a conjunction, 'if', and was used before a verb in the imperfect subjunctive or pluperfect as it is here (*GMW*, §274). *Ni laddyssid* is pluperfect impersonal and *lleasswyd* is preterite impersonal.

96-97 **Ti a geffi yn briawd y nebun, yr hwn yr ergrynant amerodreth Rhufain rhacddaw ef a'i allu.** lit. 'You may have, as a husband, him, [i.e.] he of whom and his host the Roman empire quakes in fear.' The sentence is awkward because of the juxtaposition of the pronoun *nebun* and the demonstrative pronoun sg. m. *hwn*. Cf. 'for I find you deserving of me — the victor over all Europe, the man before whom even the Roman Empire quakes with fear — as a husband' — this description of the Hun is first introduced in *Passio II: Regnante Domino* (Sheingorn and Thiébaux (trans.), *The Passion*, p. 28). One would not generally expect the sg. noun *amerodreth*, 'empire', to take a pl. verb *ergrynant*, and it is possible that it is here acting semantically as a pl. noun (in much the same way as the sg. noun *pobyl*, 'people', is often construed as pl.: see GPC Online, s.v. *pobl* (b) and the examples given there). The affixed pronoun *ef* is redundant here and may indicate that Huw Pennant is translating. A common topos in the Lives of female saints is that the saint must avoid an unwanted marriage. Having successfully postponed one marriage proposal, Ursula is again accosted by an unwanted suitor, only on this occasion her robust refusal leads to her martyrdom. On the patterning and traditions found in the Lives of female saints, see Cartwright, *Feminine Sanctity*, pp. 67-94.

97 **Sef a orug morwyn Grist, kyfodi i golwc parth a'r nefoedd** 'This is what Christ's virgin did, [she] raised her gaze to heaven': for the syntax of *sef*, see *GMW*, §55 f, Watkins, 'The *sef*', and Borsley et al. (eds), *Syntax of Welsh*, pp. 317-18; this is the substantival use here, often realized as *sef* + *a* + *gorug/gwnaeth* + subj. + vn. It is usually equivalent in meaning to the simple preterite, but the cataphoric emphasis on the vn. is difficult to convey in English.

98 **gognwd** See Notes 64, p. 73 above.

98-99 **y neb y kedwis hi i morwyndawd er i mwyn** 'she [i.e. Mary] for whom she [i.e. Ursula] had kept her virginity'. In this relative clause *y neb* (lit. 'the one for whom') could refer to either Jesus or Mary, and one would generally expect the female saint (Christ's bride) to preserve her virginity for Christ. However, since there is no lenition after the possessive pronoun (*er i mwyn*), the text currently suggests that she had maintained her virginity in honour of the Virgin Mary, and the edition would need to be altered to *er i vwyn* in order for this to mean that she had preserved her virginity for Christ from the time she was born. Cf.

Buchedd Fargred, the Welsh Life of Margaret, *Mi a gredaf y Duw hollgyuoethawc ac yn Iessu Grist y vab ef, yn Harglwyd ny, y gwr a gettwis vy gwyrdaut [hyt] hynn,* 'I believe in almighty God and Jesus Christ his son, our Lord, the man who has guarded my virginity until now' (Melville Richards (ed.), 'Buchedd Fargred', *BBCS*, 11 (1939), 324–34 (p. 327)).

102   **a'i tharaw a saeth yn anghevawl** 'and mortally wounded her with the arrow', lit. 'and hit her with an arrow mortally'. Unlike many other martyrs (such as Katherine of Alexandria and Margaret of Antioch, whose Lives were also translated into MW) Ursula is not beheaded but pierced with an arrow. This became her iconographic emblem and she is depicted in a modern stained-glass window in her church at Llangwyryfon in Ceredigion holding an arrow and sheltering the virgins under her cloak; see Cartwright, 'Santesau Ceredigion', p. 21, Plate 5.

103–04   **val maen gwyrthuawr** 'like a precious stone'. Zechariah 9. 16–17 describes how God's people will sparkle in heaven like precious jewels in a crown. Ursula is compared to a precious gem as she yields her soul and is crowned in heaven.

105   **yn ol gorvod** 'in accordance with the triumph': *gorvod* is a m. noun rather than the more frequently used verbal noun.

105   **yn y maes hwn** 'in this field': i.e. the *ager Ursulanus*, the field in which it was believed that Ursula and her companions were martyred. In 1106 an abundance of skeletons was found on the north side of the city during the construction of the new city walls. These were assumed to be the remains of Ursuline martyrs, since the location of their martyrdom was believed to be outside the northern walls of Roman Colonia; Scott B. Montgomery, 'What's in a Name? Navigating Nomenclature in the Cult of St Ursula and the Eleven Thousand Virgins', in *The Cult of St Ursula and the 11,000 Virgins*, ed. by Cartwright, pp. 10–28 (p. 16). Excavation of the Roman cemetery between 1155 and 1164 was carried out by Abbot Gerlach of Deutz and recorded by his sacristan Theodorich. On the excavations of the *ager Ursulanus* see Monica Sinderhauf, *Die Abtei Deutz und ihre innere Erneuerung: Klostergeschichte im Spiegel des verschollenen Codex Thioderici* (Vierow: SH-Verlag, 1996), pp. 36, 42–59, 248, and Introduction above.

§7

106–08   **Pwy o ddyn knowdol allai a'i galon veddylied nev draethu a'i dafawd y gyhafal gerddav a dawns a vu yna gan y saint a'r engylion o weled**

ynghwanegu graddav y llywenydd? 'What carnal man can consider with his heart or describe with his tongue such songs and dance as took place among the saints and angels as they saw the dignity of their joy increase?': *graddav* (pl. noun) is here interpreted as 'dignity' or 'worth': for this meaning, see GPC Online, s.v. *gradd* 3(b). However, the meaning is ambiguous in this context and it could also refer to the saints and angels rejoicing as their ranks increase, i.e. as they are joined by Ursula and her martyred companions: see GPC Online, s.v. *gradd* 3(a), and cf. *Passio II: Regnante Domino*: 'Oh, what dancing there was in heaven on this day, and what a gathering of the citizenry of the skies! And what rejoicing of the apostles! How harmonious the glory of the martyrs and holy virgins exulting in the increase of their order!' (Sheingorn and Thiébaux (trans.), *The Passion*, p. 29). The preverbal particle *a* is omitted here before *allai*; see Notes 38, p. 69.

108   **O santaidd Gwlen** 'Oh holy Cologne': *Sancta Colonia*. Huw Pennant regularly positions the adjective *santaidd* before the noun (cf. *santaidd verthyri* below), which causes lenition. Here, and in §9 below, *Gwlen* is preceded by a vocative particle which adds to the dramatic effect of the narrative (*GMW*, §19; Morgan, *Y Treigladau*, pp. 415–24). Cologne is personified and the city is seen to have been delivered of its attackers by Ursula and her companions via their martyrdom. The virgins became civic patrons and protectors of the city of Cologne: their relics, found in all of the churches within the city walls, were seen to offer protection to the city and make its walls impenetrable. *Passio II: Regnante Domino* describes how the citizens of Cologne, freed from their long incarceration, emerged through the city gates and buried the virgins honourably (Sheingorn and Thiébaux (trans.), *The Passion*, p. 31).

109   **y santaidd verthyri** 'the holy martyrs': Pen. 182 has *y santtaidd verthyri*. However, since the word is split across the line-break *sant|taidd* it is plausible that Huw Pennant made a mistake here when he repeated the letter *t* at the beginning of line 12 on p. 275. This has, therefore, been altered to *santaidd* in the edition, although *santtaidd* is also acceptable. *Santaidd* occurs elsewhere in the text on sixteen occasions (spelt consistently with one *t*); cf. *santesav* §6 above.

§8

111–12   **Eithyr o vewn yr amgylch y kladdwyd y santaidd verthyry hyn, ni lyfesir kladdu neb rhyw ddyn daearol** 'However, in the vicinity of where these saintly martyrs were buried, no one dares bury any earthly man': *ni lyfesir kladdu* negative particle + present impersonal + vn. One of the peculiarities of the virgins' relics is that no imposter's bones could be buried alongside them

NOTES 81

or mixed in with them because they would be automatically expelled. This hagiographical topos is also found at Eglwys Wrw in Wales, where the bones of anyone buried in the chantry chapel alongside St Wrw's relics were said to be miraculously ejected overnight as a punishment for disrespecting the sacred space reserved for St Wrw: see Cartwright, 'The Middle Welsh Life', p. 171. The Clematius Inscription (thought to be fifth century) is the earliest extant reference to a group of martyred virgins associated with Cologne. It records that Clematius built a basilica to honour the site of their martyrdom and that if anyone's bones other than those of the holy virgins were buried there, they would be punished 'by eternal hellfire' (Montgomery, 'What's in a Name?', p. 14). On the Clematius Inscription, see also Introduction and Militzer, 'The Church'.

112   **Ac yn sampyl ar hynny** 'As an example of this': a variant of *siampl* or *sampl*, 'example, instance', that derives from Middle English; see GPC Online, s.v. *siampl*. The word occurs three times in the text. Huw Pennant uses the word in the same context in *Ystoria o Wyrthie Mihangel* (Pen. 182, p. 106: *Gellir kaffael dyall drwy sampyl*, i.e. 'One could understand by means of an example').

113-14   **yr hwn yr oedd vryd i dad arno** 'who was dear to his father' (lit. 'of the one on whom his father's mind was'): lenition after the imperfect tense was commonplace in MW: thus *bryd > vryd*. The mutation is important here because *bryd* (< *pryd*, 'face, countenance') would have provided a completely different meaning, i.e. 'who resembled his father' (lit. 'he whose father's countenance was upon him').

115   **ognwd** see Notes 64, p. 73 above.

119-20   **Eithyr o'r diwedd y korph hwn a gyfodes vwchben y bedd yn gyfywch a chubed** 'Eventually his corpse rose above the grave as high as a cubit': Pen. 182, p. 277 *achubed* has been separated > *a chubed*, 'as a cubit'; *cubed* is a variant form of *cubyd* which is here mutated. See GPC Online, s.v. *cufydd*.

121-22   **er dangos sampyl na ddyleir kladdu korph pechadur ymysc y kyssegredic verthyri hyn** 'in order to show by example that a sinner's body should not be buried among these blessed martyrs'. On this topos, see Notes 111-12, pp. 80-81 above. The Cistercian Caesarius of Heisterbach (1180-*c*. 1240) recounts a tale of how the bones of a horse were immediately ejected from among the relics when they accidentally became mixed with the 11,000 virgins' bones (Caesarius of Heisterbach, *Dialogue*, II, pp. 91-92). Montgomery reads this as an example of how the 11,000 virgins are often treated as a single entity, and suggests that the relics serve 'as manifestations of the corporate body of the Eleven Thousand Virgins of Cologne' (Montgomery, *St. Ursula*, p. 1).

§9

123–24   **O santaidd Gwlen, bendicka di Dduw kanys ef a gadarnhaodd kloav dy byrth, ac ef a heddychodd dy randiredd** 'Oh holy Cologne, bless God since he secured the locks on your gateways and he brought peace to your regions'. The author continues to address Cologne in the second person sg. and the aggrandisement of the city of Cologne here (and later in the text) suggests that the original exemplar for this particular version of the Life was either produced in Cologne or was closely associated with Cologne, as noted in the Introduction. Medieval Cologne was a heavily fortified city protected by massive circuit walls and gates such as the Ulrepforte. The only occasion when the city walls were breached was in 1268, when Archbishop Englebert II von Falkenstein broke through the walls near the Ulrepforte gate during a siege of the city. His army of approximately 5,000 troops, however, was not victorious, since it was believed that Ursula and her entourage appeared and successfully defended the city. The siege was commemorated in a plaque *c*. 1378 and various other medieval images including woodcuts that depicted the virgins as an army atop the city walls (Montgomery, *St. Ursula*, Figures 24 and 27 and discussion pp. 99–115; on medieval Cologne, see Leonard Ennen and Gottfried Eckertz, *Quellen zur Geschichte der Stadt Köln*, 6 vols (Cologne: M. DuMont-Schauberg, 1860–1879), and on the siege, see Michael Toch, 'The Medieval German City under Siege', in *The Medieval City under Siege*, ed. by Ivy A. Corfis and Michael Wolfe (Woodbridge: Boydell Press, 1999), pp. 35–48 (pp. 42–44)). The virgins and their impenetrable virginity became synonymous with the impenetrable city walls.

125–26   **merch iefanck** 'a young girl': *iefanck* is a variant of *ieuanc* (cf. *mab iefanc*, §8); see GPC Online, s.v. *ieuanc*.

126   **Cordula** One of the principal virgins in the Life and perhaps the saint with whom many readers would have identified, since she initially showed weakness and was afraid when confronted with the cruelty and ferocity of the pagans as they ripped the virgins' flesh to shreds. She is highlighted alongside Ursula and Pinnosa in liturgical offices from the tenth century onwards (Hoefener, 'From St Pinnosa to St Ursula', pp. 72–73), and she makes her first appearance in *Passio I: Fuit tempore pervetusto* (written 960–976). Her feast day is celebrated on 22 October, since, as indicated in the Life, she was martyred on the day after the other virgins. Cordula became a popular figure, perhaps because her vulnerability made her memorable. She is depicted in the ship alongside Ursula and Cyriacus in an image kept at the Germanic National Museum in

Nuremberg (by the Master of the Pursed Lips): the image, dated 1510, belongs to the same period in which Huw Pennant was composing *Hystoria Gweryddon yr Almaen*; see <https://commons.wikimedia.org/wiki/File%3A1510_Martyrium_der_hl._Ursula_anagoria.JPG> (accessed 20 January 2018).

128–29 **sef a wnaeth hi, ymguddiaw y mewn vn o'r llongev hyd trannoeth** lit. 'this is what she did, she hid on one of the ships until the next day': for the syntax of *sef*, see *GMW*, §55 f; this is the substantival use here, often realized as *sef* + *goruc/gwnaeth* + subj. + vn; cf. also Notes 97, p. 78 above and Borsley et al. (eds), *Syntax of Welsh*, pp. 317–18.

131–32 **gida'r gynifer saint a santessav y buassai yn i kwmpeniaeth er certaen o amser** 'with so many male and female saints in whose company she had been for a certain period of time': *i* here is a possessive pronoun 3 pl. rather than 3 sg, since aspiration would be noted if the sentence referred to saints in *her* company; *certaen*, 'certain', is derived from Middle English or borrowed directly from Old French. The spelling indicates English influence and the word occurs four times in Huw Pennant's text; see GPC Online, s.v. *sertaen*.

132–33 **a ffoeri yn i llygaid** 'and spat in their eyes'. In almost all other versions of the Life of Ursula, having hidden timidly on the ship, Cordula emerges defiant the following day and suffers martyrdom gladly. Only in the Welsh version does she spit in the pagans' eyes, suggesting even greater defiance than in the other versions of the tale. Huw Pennant appears to heighten the drama in this particular scene by adding this detail and also the verbal noun *rhwygo* above, creating a vivid picture of the ripping of the virgins' flesh not found in *Passio II: Regnante Domino* or *LA*.

133 **a'i hangreistio hwynt o hanffyddlonder** 'and rebuked them for [their] infidelity': Sandi *h* is expected following the infixed pronoun 3 pl. *'i*, but not following the prep. *o*. Huw Pennant appears to have deliberately inserted this between two vowels in order to make this easier to pronounce.

137 **ymddangos a oruc Cordula i vynaches a oedd mewn krefydd** 'Cordula appeared to a nun who was in religious orders', lit. 'who was in religion'. In the Welsh version the nun is not named, but in *Passio II: Regnante Domino* she is Helmdrude of Heerse (Sheingorn and Thiébaux (trans.), *The Passion*, pp. 34–36).

137–38 **ac erchi a oruc hi kyfodi gwyl iddi dranoeth yn ol gwyl y gweryddon** 'and asked her to establish a feast in her honour on the day following the feast of the virgins': *yn ol* here means 'after, following'; see *GMW*, §245 (q).

138 **Ac velly y gwnaethpwyd** 'And thus it was done': has the effect of drawing this section to a close (i.e. this is the end of the *passio*) before proceeding with the long section naming the companions who travelled with Ursula. One wonders whether Huw Pennant is switching sources here: see the discussion in the Introduction.

§10

140 **Kyntaf a ffennaf tywyssoges** 'the first and foremost princess': two adjectives in the superlative degree used attributively precede the noun.

141 **vn vil ar ddec weryddon** 'eleven thousand virgins': cf. §2, *vn vil ar ddec o vorynion*, 'eleven maidens', and §17, *vn vil ar ddec o bederev*, 'eleven thousand prayers'. Nasalization is expected after *dec*, 'ten' (see Morgan, *Y Treigladau*, pp. 138–40), or lenition after the prep. *o*, 'of'. The normal construction of eleven thousand is *vn vil ar ddec o* + pl. noun. However, on lenition of pl. nouns following numerals, see *GMW*, §20, and on numerals used as substantives or as adjectives, see *GMW*, §51.

141 **Wrsla verch Nothus, brenin o'r Brytanieid** 'Ursula daughter of Nothus, king of the Britons': Pen. 182, p. 280 *Wrsla vz Nothus*: *vz* is a common abbreviation of *verch*, 'daughter', which has been expanded here. Only in the list of Latinized names is Ursula's father named in *Hystoria Gweryddon yr Almaen*: when he is first introduced his lineage as an ancient Briton and one of the kings of the Isle of the Mighty takes precedence over his name. Huw Pennant reminds us again here of his ethnicity. In *Legenda aurea* he is 'a most Christian king named Notus or Maurus' (*LA*, II, p. 256). On the development of her father's name, see Introduction.

142 **Pynnosa** As noted in the Introduction, Ursula did not become the main protagonist in the legend associated with the martyred virgins until the late tenth century, after Pinnosa's relics had been translated from Cologne to Essen. The anonymous *Sermo in Natali SS. Virginum XII Millium* was a sermon written in 922 for the nuns of the convent of the 11,000 virgins at Cologne. It was intended to commemorate the virgins on their feast day and prevent the memory of their heroic martyrdom from being lost (Sheingorn and Thiébaux (trans.), *The Passion*, p. 47). In this sermon Pinnosa is cast in the role of the British king's daughter who led the virgins to Cologne. *Sermo in natali* also adds the detail that her British name was Winnosa 'while we call her Pinnosa' (Sheingorn and Thiébaux (trans.), *The Passion*, p. 53). For the Latin text of the sermon, see *AS Octobris*, pp. 154–57, and J. Klinkenberg, 'Studien zur Geschichte

der Kölner Märterinnen', *Bonner Jahrbücher*, 89 (1890), 118–24. Pinnosa is named in a ninth-century litany from Cologne alongside Brittola, Martha, Saula, Sambatia, Saturnina, Gregoria and Palladia. On the development of the cult's medieval liturgical offices, see Hoefener, 'From St Pinnosa to St Ursula'. Pinnosa is not named in the standard version of the tale found in the *Legenda aurea*. However, as in the Welsh text, she is named second among the principal virgins in the Latin Life attributed to Hermann Joseph, *Nova Legenda Anglie*, and the Middle English version attributed to Edmund Hatfield, where it is also suggested that she is related to Ursula 'of her orygynall' (*AS Octobris*, pp. 176, 188; *NLA*, image 335; Hatfield, *Lyf of Saynt Vrsula*, image 7). On the list of companions who accompanied Ursula, see Introduction.

142   **ewyrth vrawd tad i Wrsla** 'Ursula's uncle on her father's side'.

143   **Cordula** see Notes 126, p. 82 above.

143–44   **Elevtheria, kefnitherw i Wrsula** 'Elevtheria, Ursula's cousin': her cousin Elevtheria is described as her aunt's daughter in both the Latin Life attributed to Hermann Joseph and the Middle English version by Edmund Hatfield (*AS Octobris*, p. 176; Hatfield, *Lyf of Saynt Vrsula*, image 7).

145   **Fflorencia, merch i vrenin a chares i Wrsla** 'Fflorencia [Florencia], daughter of a king and one of Ursula's relatives'. While the Welsh and Middle English texts only mention that Florencia is the daughter of a king, the Latin text attributed to Hermann Joseph specifies: *quae filia erat regis Ægidii, qui consobrinus fuit patris beatae Ursulae* (*AS Octobris*, p. 176), 'who was the daughter of King Aegidi[us], who was the cousin of the father of blessed Ursula'.

145   **pvm merched** 'five girls': a sg. noun generally follows the numeral, but in MW there are many examples of a pl. noun following the numeral. Huw Pennant seems to favour the use of the pl.; cf. §11, *ddwy chwiorydd*, and §14, *ddwy verched*, below.

§11

147   **vn ar ddec o verched brenhinedd ac arglwyddi** 'eleven daughters of kings and lords': Pen. 182, p. 281 *vn ar ddec o verched brenhinedd ar arglwyddi*; *ar* here is taken to be a scribal error and this has been altered to *ac* in this edition.

147–48   **y rhain oeddynt doethion a bucheddawl** 'who [lit. these] were wise and devout': Pen. 182, p. 281 *yr Rain oeddynt doethion a bucheddawl*. As noted in the Introduction, Huw Pennant uses <R> for <rh> or <Rh>, and this is sometimes preceded by the definite article *yr* rather than *y*: since one would expect *yr* only before a vowel, *yr Rain* has been rendered *y rhain* in the edition.

149–50   **hon oedd gymen a doeth** '[she] who was accomplished and wise'. Here there is another example of lenition after the imperfect tense, which was commonplace in MW.

150–51   **ddwy chwioredd** 'two sisters'. A sg. noun generally follows the numeral, but in MW there are many examples of a pl. noun following the numeral; cf. §14, *ddwy verched*, below.

151   **onaddunt** Huw Pennant's preferred form of the 3 pl. preposition *o*. He uses *onaddunt* nine times and *ohonvnt* only once.

152   **Benigna** named second in the list of eleven virgins who each guided 1,000 virgins to Cologne in both Hermann Joseph's Latin list and Edmund Hatfield's Middle English list of companions (*AS Octobris*, p. 176; Hatfield, *Lyf of Saynt Vrsula*, image 7). The name Benigna occurs again in the Welsh text, since her whole body is said to have been preserved at Cologne: this is unique to the Welsh text (see §16 and also Introduction).

153–54   **a chida hi yr oeddynt bedair chwioredd, a'i henwav — vn onaddunt oedd Sibilia, arall oedd Mobilia, arall oedd Ewffrofnia, y [iiij] oedd Ewstachia** 'and with her were four sisters, and their names — one of them was Sibilia, another Mobilia, another Ewffrofnia [Euphrosyna], the fourth was Ewstachia [Eustachia]': Pen. 182, p. 281. Huw Pennant makes a mistake here as he lists the names of Benigna's sisters, referring to Ewstachia as the third (iij) rather than the fourth sister. This has been corrected in this edition. He has no doubt became confused, since the next main virgin on the list, Clemencia, is the *third* leader of 1,000 virgins. Here he is counting not only the principal virgins but their sisters that accompanied them too.

156   **y iiij dywyssoges** 'the fourth princess'. She is not named in the Welsh Life but Sapientia is the fourth leader of the virgins, the sister of Eulalia and Serena in Latin and Middle English (*AS Octobris*, p. 176; Hatfield, *Lyf of Saynt Vrsula*, image 8).

157–58   **a dwy chwioredd iddi gida hi** lit. 'and two sisters to her with her': Huw Pennant juxtaposes the two prepositions *i/y* and *gyda* several times in his list of companions and their sisters; he uses the possessive pronoun *i* more frequently in his list of accompanying kings and their wives in §14.

159-60 **Ewtropiam ... Paladoram** Carpophora's two sisters Eutropia and Palladora. Huw Pennant has used the accusative Latin forms of these two sister's names rather than the nominative, although he has used the nominative forms of the other names; cf. *AS Octobris*, p. 189, where they occur in the accusative.

161-62 **Benedicta y gelwid hi** 'She was called Benedicta'. Here rather than the more common *a + elwid +* name (cf. *a elwid Benigna*, 'who was called Benigna', above), the fronted predicative is followed by the particle *y*; cf. *A'r seithuet mab idaw, Peredur y gelwit*, 'and his seventh son was called Peredur' (Glenys Goetinck (ed.), *Historia Peredur Vab Efrawc* (Caerdydd: Gwasg Prifysgol Cymru, 1976), p. 7). In the long list of names, Huw Pennant seems to vary his sentence structure deliberately in order to avoid monotony: *vn a elwid Silian ... Cordula oedd i henw ... Placida y gelwid hon*, 'One who was called Silian ... Cordula was her name ... this one was called Placida'.

164 **Sapiencia** Sapiencia (or Sapientia) is listed as one of Benedicta's sisters in Welsh and Latin but omitted in Middle English (*AS Octobris*, p. 176; Hatfield, *Lyf of Saynt Vrsula*, image 8). This is presumably a different Sapiencia to the one named as the fourth princess and leader of 1,000 virgins in Latin and Middle English, whose name is omitted in the Welsh text; see Notes 156, p. 86 above, *y iiij dywyssoges*.

165 **Silian ac Wrsia** Odilia's two sisters are named Julia and Urstitia in Latin or Juliana and Ursicia in Middle English (*AS Octobris*, p. 176; Hatfield, *Lyf of Saynt Vrsula*, image 8).

165 **nawed** 'ninth'. This is a variant form of the more commonly used form of the ordinal *nawfed*. It is attested from the fifteenth century onwards (GPC Online, s.v. *naw*) and occurs again in this text in §14, *y nawed brenin*, 'the ninth king'.

169 **Lucia vorwyn** Two girls named Lucia are listed here in close proximity: one is the sister of Sibilia and the other the sister of Placida. This *Lucia vorwyn*, 'virgin Lucia', the eleventh leader of the virgins, is presumably the one that gave rise to the notion that a virgin named Lucia (or Lleucu) was one of Ursula's virginal companions who became associated with church dedications in Ceredigion, such as Capel Bettws Leucu, although no information is provided in *Hystoria Gweryddon yr Almaen* that specifically links her to Lleucu; see Introduction.

169-70 **merch brenin a chares oedd i wr priod Wrsla** 'she was the daughter of a king and a relative of Ursula's spouse'. Here *gwr priod Wrsla* translates *sponsi*

Ursulae: although they are not yet married, her betrothal to Etherius is now seen in a more positive light, since he converts to Christianity and joins her on the pilgrimage, suffering martyrdom himself alongside his beloved Ursula and her companions. *cares* (here mutated to *chares*) has a variety of meanings: 'kinswoman, cousin, sister, companion, sweetheart'; see GPC Online, s.v. *cares*. Here it is taken to mean 'kinswoman' or simply that she is a 'relative' of Etherius. In Middle English Lucia is described as 'Ryght nye of kynne to the prynce Ethereus' (Hatfield, *Lyf of Saynt Vrsula*, image 8).

171–73   Yr vn verch ar ddec hyn oeddynt tywyssogion ar yr vn vil ar ddec weryddon, kanys pob vn onaddynt a dywyssai vil o verched dan i llaw a'i llywodraeth ac a'i dysgai ac a'i llywodraethai yn ol hyn y dywedir o'r gynvlleidua. 'These eleven girls were leaders of the eleven thousand virgins, since each one of them led and directed one thousand girls under her guidance and instructed and governed them in accordance with that stated by the congregation.' It is not entirely clear what is meant by *y gynvlleidua*, 'the congregation', but in most versions of the legend Ursula and her virginal companions (although they are not usually named in such detail) practise their military manoeuvres in front of an audience of princes and nobility. Cf. *Passio II: Regnante Domino*, 'The pious king was often present at this spectacle, along with his very venerable senators and all the leading figures of the realm. And even the common people — as always, greedy for new things — put aside their serious business and applauded the young women's manoeuvres' (Sheingorn and Thiébaux (trans.), *The Passion*, p. 23). Huw Pennant uses the same word in *Ystoria o Wyrthie Mihangel* to mean 'a company or group' of pilgrims, *kynulleidua o bererinion* (Pen. 182, p. 90).

§12

174   **Kiric** see Notes 77, p. 75 above.

175   **yNghymraec** 'in Welsh': Pen. 182, p. 299 *ynghymraec*. For editorial practice regarding the marking of nasal mutation, see the section on 'Editorial Methodology' in the Introduction above.

176–77   **ac ef a edewis y dinas o anvodd y kardinaliaid** 'and he left the city against the wishes of the cardinals'. In *Legenda aurea* it is the cardinals in particular who oppose Cyriacus's decision to follow Ursula. These are presumably not the same as the two cardinals who accompany him: here named Poncius and Petrus. The Latin text attributed to Hermann Joseph moves directly from the list of principal virgins to the list of kings and bishops, beginning with Wilhelmus (William); *AS Octobris*, p. 176.

185   **Pantulus** Bishop of Basel, one of the bishops who were supposed to have accompanied Ursula on her pilgrimage. A gilded silver reliquary bust of a mitred bishop was commissioned in the thirteenth century by Heinrich, bishop of Basel, to honour his predecessor's relics. See Notes 75, pp. 74–75 above and Montgomery, *St Ursula*, pp. 139–50, for a discussion of the reliquary.

185–86   **hefyd esgob o wlad Antiochia, Iacobus oedd i henw** 'also a bishop from the country of Antioch, Iacobus [Jacobus/James] was his name'. Iacobus is not named in the Latin text attributed to Hermann Joseph, while in the Middle English text Bishop Jacobus, claimed to be William's brother and Ursula's uncle, replaces Columbanus, although the location of his bishopric is not noted (Hatfield, *Lyf of Saynt Vrsula*, image 13). Iacobus of Antiochia is presumably the same character as Iago of Antioetsia who is mentioned again in the list of relics later in the Welsh text: this gives the impression that Huw Pennant is possibly drawing on more than one source. Elizabeth of Schönau's visions shed some light on this character, since she claims that James, who was originally from Britain, served as bishop of Antioch for seven years and that he left to join Cyriacus in Rome. Some of his nieces were among the 11,000 virgins and amidst the slaughter he chiselled the inscriptions on the virgins' tombstones. Eventually, three days after the virgins were killed, James was murdered by the same tyrant who killed Cordula. However, in his final request James asked that he be allowed to carve his own gravestone before he too was martyred, and this request was granted. Elizabeth claimed that this information was conveyed to her by St Verena and that it explained why not all of the virgins had inscribed gravestones, since James was slain before he had completed the task of inscribing them; on Elizabeth of Schönau's testimony, see Introduction.

§13

190   **Colu[m]banus** Pen. 182, p. 287 *Coluban* abbreviates the name: Columbanus is the son of Ursula's mother's sister in the Latin text attributed to Hermann Joseph, but he is replaced by Jacobus, a brother of the aforementioned William in the Middle English text (*AS Octobris*, p. 176; Hatfield, *Lyf of Saynt Vrsula*, image 13); see also Notes 185–86, p. 89 above on *Iacobus*.

191   **kefynderw i Wrsla** 'Ursula's cousin': Pen. 182, p. 287, line 5 ends *kefynderwi* and line 6 begins *i Wrsla*: this is assumed to be a scribal error in which Huw Pennant has repeated the *i* rather than a variant of *kefynderw*, so the repetition has been deleted in this edition.

191   **y trydydd gwr doeth vrddedig, Eleutherius oedd ei henw** 'the third wise, ordained man, Eleutherius was his name'. The Welsh text omits Iwanus, who

is the third bishop in the Latin and Middle English texts. Eleutherius is named as the fourth bishop in both of these texts (*AS Octobris*, p. 176; Hatfield, *Lyf of Saynt Vrsula*, image 9).

193   **Mawricius, esgob Levitan** 'Mawricius [Maurisius], bishop of Levicana'. The Latin and Middle English lists refer to Bishop Maurisius but omit the place name (*AS Octobris*, p. 177; Hatfield, *Lyf of Saynt Vrsula*, image 14); *Legenda aurea* makes him bishop of Levicana (*LA*, II, p. 258).

193-94   **y vi Ffolarius, esgob Luws** 'the sixth Ffolarius [Follarius], bishop of Loon [or Lucca]'. Here the Welsh text more closely resembles *Legenda aurea* than the Latin text attributed to Hermann Joseph and Hatfield's *Lyf of Saynt Vrsula*, neither of which refer to Follarius or Sulpicius. Jacobus de Voragine makes Follarius bishop of 'Lucca' (*LA*, II, p. 258). The Welsh form of the name *Luws* indicates that this is the county of Loon (from the French *Looz*), an area roughly equivalent to the modern Belgian province of Limburg. See Field and Simons, 'A Prophecy Fulfilled?', pp. 43, 44 Map 1: 'Loon, Liège and the Low Countries 1276-78'.

194   **Sulpicius, esgob Raben** 'Sulpicius, bishop of Ravenna'. He is referred to along with Follarius in *LA*, II, pp. 258.

§14

196-97   **Etherius, mab brenin o Loegr, gwr priod Wrsla, hwn oedd chwe blwydd ar hugain a thri mis o oedran** 'Etherius, the son of a king of England, Ursula's spouse, who was twenty-six years and three months of age'. On *gwr priod*, see Notes 169-70, pp. 87-88 above. In 1156 Abbot Theoderich discovered an inscription from late antiquity noting the burial of a Christian named Etherius who had died aged twenty-five. The medieval mystic Elizabeth of Schönau provided the interpretation that Etherius was Ursula's fiancé. Etherius's age is specified as twenty-six years and three months in this account. On the inscription, see Militzer, 'The Church', pp. 34-35, and Winfried Schmitz, 'Die spätantiken und frühmittelalterlichen Grabinschriften in Köln (4.-7. Jahrhundert n. Chr.)', *Kölner Jahrbuch*, 28 (1995), 643-776 (pp. 709-80).

198   **Magwnsia** Mainz on the Rhine: the *Legenda aurea* is more vague, noting only that Etherius goes to meet Ursula and her companions when they 'were on their way back from Rome' (*LA*, II, p. 258). Hatfield's Middle English Life also refers to the couple meeting in 'mense the ryche cyte', although this does not occur in the corresponding passage listing the kings, but in a slightly later passage building up to the passion (Hatfield, *Lyf of Saynt Vrsula*, image 14).

199   **ac a'i gelwis ef Etherius, yr hwn a elwid gynt Oloffernes** 'and he called him Etherius who was previously called Oloffernes': Ursula's betrothed (Olofernes) changes his name to Etherius, in accordance with Catholic tradition, when he is baptized and converted from paganism to Christianity. On this practice, see H. H. Thurston, 'Names, Christian', *CE*, x, pp. 673–75.

200   **hwn a verthyrwyd rhwng dwylaw Wrsla i briawd** 'who was martyred in his spouse Ursula's arms': Etherius, who dies in the arms of his beloved Ursula, transforms from pagan oppressor to saintly martyr. Having instigated the initial threat of an unwanted marriage, he ironically later falls victim to Ursula's second unwanted suitor and pagan persecutor. He is frequently depicted in medieval art, pierced by the sword, dying in Ursula's arms: see, for example, the image of Etherius in a fifteenth-century German narrative cycle of Ursula now in the Victoria and Albert Museum: Riches, 'Male Martyrs, Female Models?', Figure 15.

202   **a['r] wraic hon a elwid Blandina** 'and this woman was called Blandina': Pen. 182, p. 289 ~~ai wraic~~ *a wraic hon a elwid Blandina*. Lenition shows that Huw Pennant has accidentally omitted a definite article here as he attempted to alter *a'i wraic*, 'and his wife', to *a'r wraic hon a elwid Blandina*, 'and this woman was called Blandina'. This has been corrected in this edition.

205   **Aldwlff ... Dronisia** 'Adulphus ... Dionysia'.

205   **y nawed brenin Amic y gelwir** 'the ninth king was called Amic' (Avitus).

208–09   **y xi o'r brenhinoedd Reffridus y gelwid ef, hwn a droes i ffydd Grist o gyngor i wraic** 'the eleventh king was named Reffridus [Refridus] and he converted to Christ's faith on his wife's advice'. In the Latin and Middle English versions his wife is called Oliva, although she is not named in Welsh. Hatfield's Middle English text adds two more kings, Bonifacius and Laurencius, taking the total number of kings listed here to thirteen (Hatfield, *Lyf of Saynt Vrsula*, image 10).

211   **Llyfr y Brenhinedd** 'The Book of Kings'. The Latin version attributed to Hermann Joseph also refers to the Book of Kings and the tradition that thirty-two kings waged war against three kings: see the discussion of Huw Pennant's sources in Introduction. In *Ystoria o Wyrthie Mihangel*, in the same manuscript, Huw Pennant regularly uses the formula *val y dywedir yn...*, 'as is said in', or *val y kefir yn esgrifenedig*, 'as is written in', to refer to biblical parallels that were presumably mentioned in his Latin source; see, for example, Pen 182, pp. 99, 102.

212   **devddeng mrenin ar hugain** 'thirty-two kings'. Nasalization occurs here after *devddeng*. However, cf. §18 *ddevddec pater ar hugain*, 'thirty-two prayers', below.

§15

216–17   **Ef a las yn y maes o blant bychain mwy no phum cant** 'More than five hundred small children were killed on the field'. On *ef* employed as a preverbal particle, see *GMW*, §191. It is typically used as an expletive pronoun / subject with impersonal forms; see Borsley et al. (eds), *Syntax of Welsh*, pp. 297–98.

218–19   **rhai ohonvnt kyn bychaned val y tybygir nad oeddynt tri misyriad ymoliav i mamav pan las hwynt** 'some of them were so small that it is thought that they could not have been more than three months in their mothers' stomachs when they were killed'. Most versions do not include the detail that unborn children were murdered. Cf. *AS Octobris*, p. 184; *NLA*, image 342; and see the discussion of this section in the Introduction.

218   **kyn bychaned** 'so small': this is the equative degree of the adjective *bychan*, which is irregular. On the equative followed by a clause expressing result, see *GMW*, §44.

§16

220   **ynghwaneg** a variant of *ychwaneg*.

221–22   **Rhwng mawr a bychan y maent heddiw y'w dangos yn eglwys y gweryddon yn y dywededic ddinas Kwlen certaen o gyrff y morynion hyn.** 'Large and small, there are to be seen today in the church of the virgins in the aforementioned city of Cologne certain bodies of these maidens.' For a discussion of this section of the *Hystoria*, which does not appear in other versions of the *vita*, see the Introduction. Once again, it is possible that Huw Pennant is switching sources here, and either he is using a version of the *vita* that describes the relics not found in *Nova Legenda Anglie* and the 'Hermann Joseph' recension printed by the Bollandists, or he is referring to a relic list; cf. Elizabeth of Spalbeek's work discussed in the Introduction. However, unlike the relics in her list, Huw Pennant is describing the relics *in situ* in Cologne (Walter Simons, personal communication, 25 March 2019).

223–24   **a'r rhai hyn y maent kyn decked i gwallt ar i pennav heddyw a'r dydd y merthyrwyd hwynt** 'and the hair of these was as beautiful on their heads as the day they were martyred'. This is an example of fronting in a main clause of a possessive noun phrase, which on the surface looks like a genitival relative clause. The possessive phrase *'r rhai hyn* is fronted from **gwallt yr rhai hyn* and left as a trace of the possessive third plural *i* referring back to the fronted element. According to Willis, *Syntactic Change*, pp. 89–90, this type is unattested in the MW tales and romances. He provides a sixteenth-century example: *Ac er hynny Pompeius a dorred i benn*, 'And despite that Pompeius had his head chopped off'. There is a further example of this construction in the same paragraph here: *rhai onaddunt y maent hysbyssol i henwav yn y byd hwn*, 'the names of some of these are well-known in this world'. The construction is structurally parallel to fronting from the object of a preposition, as seen in *Y prenneu ereill a deuei ffrwyth arnunt* (T. Jones (ed.), *Ystorya Seint Greal* (Caerdydd: Gwasg Prifysgol Cymru, 1992), pp. 4387–88), 'Fruit grew on the other trees' (**ar y prenneu ereill*); for discussion and further examples, see Willis, *Syntactic Change*, pp. 88–90.

225   **yn i rhwymo'r gwallt ynghyd** 'matting the hair together': the third-person possessive pronoun *i* (meaning *eu*) is unnecessary here, since the verb *rhwymo*, 'to bind, to mat', has an object, *gwallt*, 'hair'. Huw Pennant could either have omitted the *i* (*yn rhwymo'r gwallt ynghyd*, 'matting the hair together') or omitted *gwallt* (*yn i rhwymo ynghyd*, 'matting them together'). Perhaps the awkwardness of this phrase is an indication that he is translating.

229   **Benigna** On Benigna, see Notes 152, p. 86 above. Benigna is one of the virgins whose whole body was preserved, according to Huw Pennant.

232–33   **Morwyn hefyd hon a elwid Cristina a'r gwaed heddyw ynghylch i mynwgl val pe bai ynewydd dorri** 'There is also a maiden who was called Cristina and today [there is] blood around her neck as though it has just been severed' (lit. 'and the blood today around her neck'). The adjective *newydd*, 'new', is used before a verbal noun to denote the immediate past and the verbal noun here is passive in meaning; see *GMW*, §251 N, p. 230. The *y* before *newydd dorri* would appear to be the predicative *yn* which is joined to *newydd* in the manuscript (Pen. 182, p. 293 *val pe bai ynewydd dorri*): this has been kept in this edition rather than adding an additional <n> (e.g. *y[n] newydd dorri*).

235   **eithyr bod y gwaed gwedy ysgrowlingo y gwallt yn kynnal yr esgyrn ynghyd** 'only that the blood matted in her hair holds the bones together': *ysgrowlingo*, lit. 'to glue'; see GPC Online, s.v. *ysgrowlingaf*, where this is given as the first occurrence of this word.

237–39   **morwyn hefyd a elwid Sophia a'r saeth yn i genav a'i genav yn egored val y byddai yn gweddiaw Duw pan drewid a'r saeth** 'also a girl was named Sophia and the arrow in her mouth and her mouth open as though she was praying to God when she was struck by the arrow'. The description of the relics provided by Huw Pennant appears to be unique (or at least I have not been able to find a source for this section), and the relics of the martyrdom — such as the arrow in Sophia's mouth — further dramatize the scene. Here Huw Pennant paints a very vivid picture of the relics in Cologne for his audience. Although it is known that Cologne was a popular pilgrimage destination for the Welsh, medieval poetry often gives the impression that the relics sought there were those of the three kings. On pilgrimage, see Hurlock, *Medieval Welsh Pilgrimage*.

241–42   **Hefyd y maent yno esgyrn y pennav, a'r chwarelav a'r pennav saethav ynddunt heddyw y'w dangos** 'Also today there are on display there skulls with arrows and arrow-heads in them': *pennav saethav* refers to the arrow-heads left in the virgins' heads.

244–46   **Pwy o Gristion allai vod mor galed gallon pan welai y rhyw gynulleidua o vendigedic saint y sydd yno gwedy i hanffurvo o'r wedd hon…** 'What Christian could be so hard of heart that when he sees such a company of blessed saints that are there deformed in this way …'. The preverbal particle *a* is omitted here before *allai*; see Notes 38, pp. 69–70.

246   **y melldigedic kwn** 'the cursed dogs'. Adjectives usually follow the nouns that they qualify; however, Huw Pennant often places adjectives before nouns (see, for example, *vrenhinawl waed*, 'royal blood', *weryddawl grefydd*, 'virginal faith', *mor galed gallon*, 'as hard of heart', *vendigedic saint*, 'blessed saints', *trwm glefyd*, 'serious illness', *vrevawl vuchedd*, 'fragile life'). Lenition is expected following the adjective, but this is not marked here, probably due to provection (-g g- > k). *melldigedic* is used by Pennant elsewhere in this text: before the noun causing lenition (e.g. §6 *emelldigedic bygan*, 'the cursed pagan') as well as following the noun (§9, *y pyganieid melldigedic*, 'the cursed pagans').

§17

248   **Pwy ddyn bynnac arvero o weddiaw Duw a'r gweryddon bendigedic hyn** 'Whosoever habitually prays to God and these blessed virgins': *arvero* here is present subjunctive 3 sg. followed by the prep. *o*; cf. *yn arver o*, below. Once again the particle *a* is omitted before a verb with initial <a>.

249   **kymydeithion verthyri** 'martyred companions' is the sense here, although *verthyri* is the main noun and *kymydeithion* is an attributive noun (lit. 'companionable martyrs' or martyrs travelling together). Cf. also §4, *chymydeithion weryddon*, 'virginal companions' (lit. 'companionable virgins' or virgins travelling together). Lenition is not expected after a pl. noun but since

kymydeithion is used adjectivally here, this has caused lenition.

250 **Mihangel** The Archangel Michael, a universally popular saint who was known for supporting souls on Judgement Day. He is often depicted in both MW poetry and art alongside the Virgin Mary as weighing the souls of the dead in his scales and opposing the devil as he and the Virgin attempt to tip the scales in favour of the dead person: see the wall painting formerly at Llandeilo-tal-y-bont (now in the museum at Sain Ffagan) and Andrew Breeze, 'The Virgin's Rosary and St Michael's Scales', *Studia Celtica*, 24 (1989–1990), 91–98. It is particularly significant here that Huw Pennant includes Mihangel alongside Ursula, the Virgin Mary and God in his recommendation to the audience, since as noted in the Introduction he was probably curate of Llanfihangel (possibly Llanfihangel-ar-arth) at the time of the manuscript's composition, and he also translated the Miracles of the Archangel Michael into Welsh. On the cult of Mihangel/Michael in Wales, see Vanherle, '*Ystoria*', and on the development and transmission of his international cult, see John Charles Arnold, *The Footprints of Michael the Archangel: The Formation and Diffusion of a Saintly Cult, c. 300–c. 800* (Basingstoke: Palgrave Macmillan, 2013), and Richard F. Johnson, *Saint Michael the Archangel in Medieval English Literature* (Woodbridge: Boydell Press, 2005).

251–52 **val yr oedd gynt gwr o grefydd yn arver o weddiaw Duw a gweryddon yr Almaen** 'once as a religious man was habitually praying to God and the German virgins'. The verb *arver* used to frequently be followed by the prep. *o* which has caused lenition here; in ModW it is followed by the prep. *â*.

257 **gyfadnabyddus** Pen. 182, p. 297 *gyfadnabydduddus*: this scribal error has been corrected in this edition and *udd* omitted.

269–71 **Ac ar hyn y tervynai y santaidd vynach a chida'r gweryddon val y bai ef gyfrannoc o'r wledd a bery byth i'r lle y delom oll drwy weddiaw y glan weryddon. Amen.** 'And on this the holy monk passed away and joined the virgins so that he could partake in the feast that will last forever in the place to which we will all go via the intercession of the holy virgins. Amen.': *a chida'r gweryddon*, lit. 'and with the virgins'. The miracle in which the monk is relieved of his physical suffering and ascends into heaven is made directly relevant to the audience, as Huw Pennant uses the present subjunctive 1 pl. *delom*.

§18

272 **Pwy bynnac a vynno kwplav y pyderav hyn** 'Whosoever wishes to complete these prayers': Pen. 182, p. 299 *Pwy bynnac a vynno kwplav y y pyderav*. The definite article occurs at the end of the line and is repeated in error at the

beginning of the following line: this scribal error has been corrected in this edition. For the suggestion that the *Hystoria* may have been used as a sermon or reading on the feast of the virgins, see the Introduction.

273   **ddevddec pater ar hugain** 'thirty-two prayers'. Nasalization of <p-> would be expected after *devddec*, but does not occur here. The expected nasalization of <b-> after *devddeng* is marked in §14 above, *devddeng mrenin ar hugain*, 'thirty-two kings'.

273-74   **rhyf y gweryddon** 'the virgins' praise', not the number of virgins: see GPC Online, s.v. *rhif*¹ d.

§19

279-80   **y maent hefyd yn y dinas bonheddic Colen ynghwanec a chant o gapeloedd** 'there are also in the noble city of Cologne more than a hundred chapels': Pen. 182, p. 300 *y maent hefyd yn y dinas bonheddic Colen y maent ynghwanec A chant o gapeloedd*. Repetition of the verb present 3 pl. *y maent* has been deleted in this edition. This error may have crept in as a result of translating a text in which the location preceded the verb; in the Welsh translation, since the verb preceded the location, it was not needed after the place name. This section acts almost as an appendix to the *Hystoria*, providing information on the number of contemporary religious houses in Cologne, and precedes the Latin hymn *O vernantes Christi rosae*, which is also attributed to Hermann Joseph and which one can easily imagine would have been performed in honour of the virgins on their feast day; see Petit, *Spirituality of the Premonstratensians*, pp. 118-36 (especially p. 128).

281-83   **ac aneirif o bardynav gwedy i ymrafael baboedd i rhoddi. Pwy bynnac a vai tan not o'r pardynav hyn, ef allai gaffael gras yn y byd hwn ac yn y byd a bery byth** 'and countless pardons having been given by various popes. Whoever be designated [at] these pardons, he would receive grace in this world and in the world which lasts forever'. A more literal translation of *Pwy bynnac a vai tan not o'r pardynau hyn* would be 'Whoever be under the sign of these pardons', i.e. chosen or designated. It is surprising that Huw Pennant is still using <t> for /d/ in this period: one might have expected *nod* rather than *not* here. Cf. also his use of *bynnac* rather than *bynnag*. Once again the particle *a* is missing before the verb *allai*; see Notes 38, p. 69 above.

GLOSSARY

The arrangement of words in this glossary is according to graphic shape and follows the same order as that used in Modern Welsh dictionaries, namely a, b, c (k/), ch (/χ/), d, dd (/ð/), e, f (/v/), ff (/f/), g, ng (ŋ), h, i, l, ll (/λ/), m, n, o, p, ph, r, rh, (/r̥/), s, t, th, u (/ɫ/), w (/u/), y (/ə/ or /I/). Since <k> and <v> do not occur in Modern Welsh, <k> is recorded under <c>, whereas <v>, which represents /v/, /ɫ/ and /u/, is listed in its usual position in the English alphabet, between <u> and <w>. The selection of a head word in cases of text-internal variation is always a difficulty and I have attempted to give ample cross-references in this case, as well as in other cases of orthographical and morphological variation which may present problems. Finite verbal forms are entered under the verbal noun. Mutated consonants are restored to their radical forms, except in a few instances in which the mutated form has become petrified, for example *dros*. Words beginning with a mutated c/k (for example *garu* and *chaffael*) have generally been restored to forms beginning with k rather than c, since k occurs more frequently than c at the beginning of words in this particular text. Initial mutations that are expected after prepositions etc. have been indicated, even if these are not realized in the text. The gender of nouns provided here follows GPC Online: in the case of words that can be both masculine and feminine, a specific gender is only noted if this is discernible from mutations in the text. Line numbers are given for each word that occurs in the edition. In the cases of words that have a high frequency of occurrence, only the first three examples are provided. The meaning given is that relevant to the context.

Abbreviations

adj.	adjective
adv.	adverb
aff.	affixed
art.	article
asp.	aspirates
comp.	comparative
conj.	conjunction
cons.	consuetudinal
def.	definite
dem.	demonstrative
equat.	equative
f.	feminine

fut.	future
impf.	imperfect
indep.	independent
inf.	infixed
interj.	interjection
interrog.	interrogative
len.	leniting
lit.	literally
m.	masculine
ModW	Modern Welsh
MW	Middle Welsh
nas.	nasalizing
neg.	negative
neut.	neuter
num.	numeral
ord.	ordinal
pers.	personal
pl.	plural
plupf.	pluperfect
poss.	possessive
prep.	preposition
pres.	present
pret.	preterite
pron.	pronoun
rel.	relative
sg.	singular
subj.	subjunctive
suff.	suffixed
superl.	superlative
vn.	verbal noun

A

a¹ (asp.), **ac, ag** (before vowels) conj. *and* 4, 7, 8; with def. article **a'r** 4, 65, 69; with inf. poss. pron. 3 sg. m. **a'i** (len.) 8, 36, 39, 3 sg. f. **a'i** (asp.) 12, 14, 37

a² (len.) preverbal particle 11, 12, 22; with inf. obj. pron. 3 sg. m. **a'i** 199, with inf. obj. pron. 3 pl. **a'i** 43, 44, 176

a³ (len.) rel. particle *who, which, that* 3, 7, 10; with inf. obj. pron. 3 sg.m. 264; with inf. obj. pron. 3 pl. 172, 173

a⁴ (len.) vocative particle 93

a⁵ (asp.) **ac** (before vowels) prep. *with* 32, 116, 234, *as, that* after equative 43, 224, 229

GLOSSARY

abad m. *abbot* 265, 267
achos m./f. *cause, reason* 27
adnabod vn. *to know, recognise, be acquainted with*; pres. impersonal **adnabyddir** 244; impf. 3 sg. **adwyniad** 256 (variant of **atwaenat**, *GMW*, §132)
adref adv. *home, homewards* 38
adwyniad see **adnabod**
addaw vn. *to promise* 24, 32
addwyn adj. *elegant, excellent, splendid, gentle, noble* 93; equat. **addwyned** 14; superl. **addwynaf** 40
angav m. *death* 58, 67
angel m. *angel* 31, 33, 74; pl. **engylion** 46, 48, 51
anghevawl adj. *mortal, deathly* 102
angreistio vn. *to rebuke, reprove, chide* 133
angristynogawl adj. *unchristian* 87
ail (len.) ord. num. *second* 152, 190, 200
am (len.) prep. *for, about* 29; **am ben** *upon* 86
amdler m. *large number or amount, multitude* 210
amerodreth f. *empire* 96
amerodyr m. *emperor* 178
amgen adj. *different*; **nid amgen no** *namely, no less than* 212 (*GMW* §46, N2)
amgylch m. *vicinity, surrounding area* 111
amgylchyn m. *(surrounding) area, vicinity* 128
amraevael see **ymrafael**
amser m. *time* 2, 99, 132
amyn prep. *apart from, save, no fewer than* 279
aneirif adj. *innumerable, countless* 82, 280, 281
anffurvo vn. *to deform, disfigure* 246
anffyddlon adj. *unfaithful* 28
anffyddlonder m. *unfaithfulness, infidelity, disloyalty, lack of religious faith* 133
annoc m. *exhortation, urging, encouragement* 51
anobeithiol adj. *hopeless, despairing* 253
anrhydedd m./f. *honour, esteem* 184, 210
anvodd m. *displeasure, unwillingness, discontent*; **o anvodd** *against the wishes of* 177
anvon vn. *to send* 21, 42; impf. impersonal **anvonid** 46
ar prep. *on* 76, 98, 110; with suff. pers. pron. 3 sg. m. **arno** 114
ar dem. particle, serves as antecedent to a relative clause 89
arall adj. *another, other* 141, 142, 152; pl. **eraill** 5, 49, 50
archdiacon m. *archdeacon* 182
ardderchawc adj. *excellent* 17, 92, 149
arglwydd m. *lord*; pl. **arglwyddi** 41, 49, 147

arglwyddes f. *lady* 66, 89
arloesi vn. *to prepare or clear the way* 266
arver m./f. *habit, manner, reputation*; pl. **arveroedd** 15
arver vn. *to have a habit of, be used or accustomed to* 252; **arvero** pres. subj. 3 sg. 248
arverol adj. *usual, accustomed to* 23
arvollwr m. *sponsor, patron, ally* 181
asgwrn m. *bone*; pl. **esgyrn, eskyrn** 109, 217, 226
at, att (len.) prep. *to* 41, 43; with suff. pers. pron. 3 pl. **attaddunt** 46
ateb vn. *to answer, respond, reply*; impf. 3 sg. **atebai** 257, 258
ateb, atteb m. *answer, reply* 38, 39
athro m. *tutor, teacher* 12

B

bach, bychan adj. *small* 221; pl. **bychain** 216; equat. **kyn bychaned** 218
bedrod m./f. *tomb, grave* 116
bedyddiaw vn. *to baptise*; pret. 3 sg. **bedyddiodd** 176, 198; pret. impersonal **bedyddiwyd** 11
bedd m. *grave* 118, 120
bendigedic adj. *blessed, sacred, holy* 56, 85, 130
bendigiaw vn. *to bless*; pret. 3 sg. **bendigawdd** 125, 176; imperative 2 sg. **bendicka** 123
bendith f./m. *blessing, benediction* 79
beth interr. *what* 267
bevnydd adv. *daily* 272
biteiliaw vn. *to victual, supply with provisions, feed, stock up with food* 69
bod vn. to be 28, 68, 224; pres. 1 sg. **wyf** 258, pres. 2 sg. **wyd, yr wyd** 95, pres. 3 pl. **maent** 73, 220, 221, pres. rel. 3 sg. **sydd** 35, 245; cons. pres./fut. 3 sg. **bydd** 119, 251, 267; impf. 3 sg. **yr oedd, oedd, yttoedd** 2, 4, 6, impf. 3 pl. **yr oeddynt, oeddynt** 83, 87, 145; cons. impf. 3 sg. **byddai** 238, 253, 254, cons. impf. 3 pl. **byddynt** 8, 81; impf. subj. 3 sg. **bai, pe bai** 45, 233, 247, impf. subj. 3 pl. **baent, pe baent** 72; pret. 3 sg. **bu** 107, 114; plupf. 3 sg. **buassai** 94, 131
blaidd, bleidd m. *wolf*; pl. **bleiddiav** 86
blwydd see **blwyddyn**
blwyddyn f. *year*; pl. **blynyddoedd** 227; (after num.) **blynedd** 34, 68; **blwydd** f. *a year (of age)* 197; **chwe blwydd ar hugain** *twenty-six years old* 197
blynedd see **blwyddyn**
bodlonhav vn. *to satisfy* 39
bol m. *belly, stomach*; pl. **boliav** 217, 219
bonedd m. *nobility, aristocracy*; pl. **boneddigion** 34, 128, 195
bonheddic adj. *noble, aristocratic* 84, 142, 144

GLOSSARY

bore m. *morning, daybreak* ; **y bore drannoeth** *the following morning* 117, 129
brawd m. *brother* 3, 4, 142
brenhinawl adj. *royal* 18, 139, 190
brenhiniaeth f. *kingdom* 26
brenhines f. *queen* 9, 20, 89
brenin, brennin m. *king* 3, 6, 8; pl. **brenhinedd, brenhinoedd** 5, 6, 40
brevawl adj. *fragile* 89
bryd m. *mind, disposition* 113, 250
brys m. *haste;* **ar vrys** *in haste, hurriedly* 132
buchedd f. *life* 90, 265
bucheddawl adj. *devout, virtuous* 148
bychain see **bach**
bychodedd m. *small quantities, small amounts* 211
byd m. *world* 90, 108, 243
bydawl adj. *earthly, worldly* 19
bygwth vn. *to threaten* 25
bynnag see **pwy**
byth adv. *(for) ever, always* 91, 270, 283
byw vn. *to live;* adj. *alive* 229
bywyd m. *life, lifetime* 10, 29, 58

C/K

kadarn adj. *powerful, strong, steadfast* 155, 167, 202
kadarnhav vn. *to confirm* 46; pret. 3 sg. **kadarnhaodd** 123
kadw vn. *to keep, preserve* 13, 64; impf. 3 sg. **kadwai** 10; pret. 3 sg. **kedwis** 98
kaethiwed m./f. *incarceration, imprisonment* 110
kaffael vn. *to have, obtain, acquire, secure* 9, 34, 68; pres. 2 sg. **keffi** 96, pres. impersonal **keffir** 59; impf. 3 sg. **kai** 261; impf. impersonal **keffid** 42
kaled adj. *hard* 245
kaledi m. *hardship* 31
kalon, kallon f. *heart* 9, 106, 134; pl. **kalonnav** 62
cant num. *one hundred* 217; **pum cant** *five hundred* 217
kanmoladwy adj. *praiseworthy* 21, 206
kanvod vn. *to discover;* pret. 3 sg. **kanvu** 91
kanv vn. *to sing, chant* 262; imperative 3 sg. **kaned** 272
kanys conj. *because* 27, 58, 94
kapel m. *chapel;* pl. **kapeloedd** 280
kar m. *kinsman, relative, cousin* 190
kardinal m. *cardinal* 177; pl. **kardinaliaid** 177
kares f. *kinswoman, relative, cousin* 145, 170, 204; pl. **karessav** 151, 251
kariad m. *love* 57, 60, 66

karu, karv vn. *to love* 61, 259; impf. 3 sg. **karai** 114
Katholic adj. *Catholic* 13, 45, 55
kefnitherw, kefnither f. *cousin* 144, 157
kefnvor m. *ocean* 70
kefynderw m. *cousin* 191
keisiaw vn. *to try, attempt, seek* 22, 39, 48
kelennig m. *gift, present*; pl. **kelenigion** 24
kennad m. *messenger*; pl. **kennadav, kenadav** 23, 32, 38
kerdded vn. *to walk, travel, emanate, spread* 79; impf. 3 sg. **kerddai** 15
kerdd *song, poem, music*; pl. **kerddav** 107
kerddgar adj. *loving literature, poetry*; **rhai kerddgar** *cultured people, lovers of literature* 275
certaen, sertaen pron. also adj. *certain, a certain amount of* 132, 139, 222
ki m. *dog*; pl. **kwn** 246
kladdu vn. *to bury* 112, 116, 117; pret. 2 sg. **kleddaist** 109, pret. impersonal **kladdwyd** 111
klefyd m. *illness, sickness* 253, 255, 264
klo *lock, bolt*; pl. **kloav** 123
klust f. *ear* pl. **klustiav** 62
klyfychu vn. *to become sick, fall ill* 264
klywed vn. *to hear* 17
knawd m. *flesh* 50, 108, 127
knowdol adj. *fleshy, carnal, earthly* 89, 106
knwpae m. *club, cudgel* 234
kof m. *memory, mind* 254
kolli vn. *to lose* 130
korff, korph m. *body, corpse* 116, 118, 228; pl. **kyrff** 73, 222, 225
coron f. *crown* 130
koroni vn. *to crown* 54, 104
korphorawl adj. *corporeal* 58
kredadun adj. *believing* 28
krefydd f. *faith, religion* 52, 65; *order* 137, 252, 278; **a oedd mewn krefydd** *who was in religious orders* 137
krevlondeb m. *cruelty, oppression, persecution* 127
kri m./f. *cry, clamour* 85
Kristiawn, Kristion m. *Christian*; pl. **Kristynogion** 83, 283
Kristynoges f. *(female) Christian* 28
kroesawy vn. *to welcome, embrace* 78
kroessawys adj. *welcoming* 44
cubed, kubed m. *cubit* 120
kwbwl m. *the whole*; adj. *completely, entirely* 21, 232

kwfaint m./f. *monastery, convent, religious house* 265
kwmpeini f. *company*, *crew* 87
kwmpeniaeth f. *company* 131
kwplav vn. *to complete, finish, perform, conform* 68, 272; impf. 3 sg. **cwplae** 29
cwplae see **kwplav**
kyd-wyryf f. *fellow virgin, virginal companion*, pl. **kyd-weryddon** 62
kydymaith m. *companion*, pl. **kydymdeithion, cydymddeithion, kymedeithion** 61, 78, 90
kydymddeithas f. *communion, companionship* 35
kyfadnabyddus adj. *known, familiar, acquainted* 257
kyfamser m. *meantime, time*; **yn y kyfamser hwnnw, yn y kyfamser hyn** *at that time* 4, 16, 76
kyfan adj. *whole, in one piece* 228
kyfenw m. *cognomen, anniversary* 135
kyflawn adj. *full* 150
kyfodi vn. *to raise, lift up, start* 63, 76, 97; pret. 3 sg. **kyfodes** 120, 262
kyfoeth m. *wealth, riches, power* 211
kyfrannoc adj. *partaking, participating in* 270
kyfrif vn. *to count* 217
kyfywch see **uchel**
kyffrous adj. *excited* 266
kyngor m. *advice* 37, 209
kyhafal adj. *similar, alike, same* 56, 70, 106
kymaint adj. equat. (based on a noun) *as great, as large, as many* 43 (*GMW*, §41)
kymell vn. *to incite, encourage, urge, compel*; impf. 3 pl. **kymellynt** 50
kymen adj. *accomplished, wise, fair, dexterous* 150, 169, 189
Kymraec, Cymraec f./m. *Welsh, the Welsh language* 175, 275
kymryd vn. *to take* 133; imperative 2 sg. **kymer** 95
cyn, kyn with equat. adj. *so* 14, 218, 223
kynhorthwy m. *aid, succour, support* 31
kynifer m. *so great a number, so many* 131
kynnal vn. *to hold, support* 235
kynnullaw vn. *to collect, gather*; pret. 2 sg. **kynnullaist** 108
kynt prep. *before, previous to, earlier* 67, 94; superl. **kyntaf** *first* 121, 136, 174; **val kynt** adv. *as before* 21
kyntaf ord. num. *first* 121, 136, 174; **gyntaf** adv. 12
kynvigen f. *jealousy* 47
kynvlleidua, kynulleidua f. *audience, assembly, gathering* 173, 245
kyrchu vn. *to seek, approach, make for* 69
kyssegredic adj. *blessed, sacred, holy, consecrated* 73, 122, 176
kyssur m. *comfort, solace, consolation* 95

kyttunaw vn. *to agree* 32
kywoeth m. *wealth* 18, 210

CH

chwaer f. *sister* 161, 166, 170; pl. **chwioredd** 151, 153, 156
chwarel m./f. *arrow*; pl. **chwarelav** 242
chwe, chwech num. *six*; **chwech ar hugain** *twenty-six* 197
chweched ord. num. *sixth* 160

D

da adj. *good, virtuous* 20, 51, 95; comp. **gwellwell** *better and better, progressively better* 51
daearol adj. *earthly* 112
dafad f. *sheep*; pl. **devaid** 86
dangos vn. *to show, demonstrate* 121, 218, 221; pres. 3 sg. **dengys** 31
dan, tan (len.) prep. *under* 85, 172, 282; **dan law** *under the care of, under the tutelage of* 12, 172
danvon vn. *to send*; pret. 3 sg. **danvones** 10
dav (len.) num. *two* 179, 180, 183
dawns f./m. *dance* 107
dayar f. *earth* 119
dec num. *ten* 33, 141, 146
dechrav vn. *to begin, start* 92
deddyf f. *law* 23
deffroi vn. *to wake*; impf. 3 sg. **deffroe** 61
derbyn vn. *to receive* 261; impf. 3 sg. **derbyniai** 44; pret. 3 sg. **derbyniodd** 175
devddeng (nas.), **devddeg** num. *twelve* 277; **devddeng mrenin ar hugain** *thirty-two kings* 212; **devddec pater ar hugain** *thirty-two prayers* 273
dewis vn. *to choose, select*; impf. 3 sg. **dywyssai** 172
diagon m. *deacon* 180
diflannv vn. *to disappear* 261
dilev vn. *to abolish, get rid, delete, remove* 90; pres. 3 sg. **dilea** 60
dilyn vn. *to follow*; impf. 3 pl. **dilynynt** 183
dim m. *anything* 61
dinas m. *city* 75, 81, 83
dinustyr m. *destruction, ruin* 25
dioddef vn. *to suffer* 55, 67; pret. 3 sg. **dioddefodd** 137
diolch m. *thanks, gratitude* 44, 259
diovalu vn. *to relieve (from care, solicitude)*; pres. 3 sg. **diovala** 36
disglair adj. *radiant, shining, bright* 255
diwair adj. *chaste* 192

dodi vn. *put, place* 101
doeth adj. *wise* 150, 169, 189; pl. **doethion** 148
dros (len.) *over, above* 55, 89, 133; **dros ben hynny** *furthermore* 53
drwy see **trwy**
dryllio vn. *to crush, shatter, destroy*; plupf. impersonal **drylliesid** 234
duc m. *duke* 142, 144, 153; pl. **dugieid, dugiaid** 41, 140, 195
dunystyr, dunvstyr vn. *to destroy* 84, 87
Duw m. *God* 9, 10, 13
dwfr m. *water, tears* 247
dwy (len.) num. f. *two* 155, 157, 159
dwyfron f. *chest, breast* 247
dwylaw see **llaw**
dwyn vn. *to carry away, steal, bring* 43, 255; pret. 3 sg. **duc** 264; **dwyn ynghyd** *to bring together, gather* 43
dwywawl, dwywol adj. *devout, pious, religious* 8, 162
dy (len.) poss. pron. 2 sg. *your* 36, 93, 94
dyall vn. *to understand* 276
dydd m. *day* 35, 52
dyfod, dyvod vn. *to come, arrive* 23, 132; pres. 1 pl. **down** 261, pres. subj. 1 pl. **delom** 270, 283; impf. 3 pl. **devynt** 48, impf. subj. 3 pl. **delynt** 45; pret. 3 sg. **doeth** 178, 185, pret. 3 pl. **daethont, doethant** 88, 119, 121
dyfodiad m. *coming, arrival* 78, 84, 124
dylyn vn. *to follow* 168
dylyu vn. *should, ought, to have a right to*; pres. 3 sg. **dyly** 57; pres. impersonal **dyleir** 121
dyn m. *man, person, human being* 57, 112, 248
dynessav vn. *to approach, draw near* 81
dyrnod m./f. *blow, a pounding, battering* 231
dysgv, dysgu vn. *to learn, teach, instruct* 35, 45, 46; impf. 3 sg. **dysgai** 12, 173; plupf. 3 sg. **dysgyssai** 23
dywededic, dywedic adj. (verbal) *aforementioned* 81, 222, 265
dywedud vn. *to say, speak, recount* 11, 257; pres. impersonal **dywedir** 139, 173, 188; pret. impersonal **dywetpwyd** 84, 263; imperative 2 sg. **dywaid** 259

E

e see **i**[1]
eb see **heb**
ef[1] indep. pron. 3 sg. m. 43, 77, 82
ef[2] aff. pron. 3 sg. m. 20, 23, 28
ef[3] expletive pron. 216 (*GMW*, §191)
eglwys f. *church* 117, 221; pl. **eglwyssi** 277, 279; **eglwyssi coleds** *church colleges*

277; **eglwysi plwyf** *parish churches* 279
egored adj. *open* 238
ehun, e hun pron. 3 sg. *himself, herself* 276
eisioes, eissioes adv. *already* 11; *however, yet, nevertheless* 68
eithyr prep. *but, except* 5, 18, 20
emelldigedic see **ymelldigedic**
enaid m. *soul* 58, 104, 261; pl. **eneidiav** 184
eneidiol adj. *soulful, of the soul, psychological* 90
enill, ynill vn. *to win, conquer* 83, 104; impf. 3 pl. **ynillai** 58, impf. 3 pl. **ynillynt** 54; pret. 2 sg. **ynillaist** 110
enw m. *name* 77, 135, 160; pl. **enwav** 139, 149, 188
er prep. *for the sake of* 65, 99, 121
erbyn prep. *by* 35, 119, 198; **yn erbyn** *against* 212
erchi vn. *to ask, request, beg* 33, 137, 266; impf. 3 sg. **archai** 32
ergrynu vn. *to tremble, quake*; pret. 3 pl. **ergrynant** 96
esgob m. *bishop* 185, 186, 187; pl. **esgyb** 188
esgrifenedic adj. (verbal) *written, recorded* 59
etifedd m. *heir, progeny* 9, 10
ev see **i**
evduned m./f. *vow, wish, pledged word* 65
ewyllys f./m. *will, desire* 29, 50, 63
ewyrth, ewythyr m. *uncle* 142, 187, 192; **ewyrth vrawd tad** *paternal uncle* 142; **ewyrth vrawd i mam** *maternal uncle* 187

Ff

ffenaf see **pen**
ffieiddiaw vn. *to despise, hate, abhor* 99
ffiolen f./m. *the bony structure covering the head, skull* 232
ffo vn. *to flee* 71
ffoeri vn. *to spit* 132
ffurfaidd adj. *shapely* 225
ffydd f. *faith* 13, 45, 47
ffyddlawn adj. *faithful* 31

G

gadaw vn. *to leave, abandon, relinquish*; imp. 3 pl. **gedewynt** 67, 75; pret. 3 sg. **gedewis** 177
gair m. *word* 267, 268; pl. **geiriav** 62
galw vn. *to call, to name*; pres. impersonal **gelwir** 198, 205, impf. impersonal **gelwit, gelwid** 3, 11, 126; pret. 3 sg. **gelwis** 199
gallu m. *ability, power, authority, property, wealth* 19, 97, 100

gallu vn. *to be able (to), can*; impf. 3 sg. **gallai** 35, 43, 89; pret. 3 sg. **gallodd** 262
gan prep. *with, by, from* 19, 107, 246; with suff. pers. pron. 3 sg. m. **gantav** 82, 3 sg. f. **genthi** 21, 1 pl. **genym** 259, 3 pl. **ganthunt** 49; preceding vn. to perform function of participle 9, 44, 98
gelyn m. *enemy*; pl. **gelynion** 82, 110, 132
gellwng vn. *to release, set free* 85
genav m. *mouth* 238
geni vn. *to be born*; plupf. impersonal **ganyssid** 99
ger bron prep. *before, in front of, in the presence of* 243
gida (asp.) **gidac** (before vowels) prep. *with, in the company of, alongside* 55, 131, 148
gilidd see **i gilidd**
glan adj. *pure, clean* 60, 269
gofal m. *fear, anxiety, concern, solicitude* 60
gofyn vn. *to ask, request* 24, 33; impf. 3 sg. **gofynnai** 256
gognwd m. *trust, faith, mind* 64, 98, 115 (see Notes 64, p. 73)
golwc m. *sight, vision, gaze* 64, 97; **mewn golwc** *in view, on display* 231
gorchymyn m. *commandment* 13
gordderch m./f. *lover, adulterer; lust, fornication, adultery* 50
gorffowys, gorffywys, gorphowys vn. *to rest, lie* 74, 226, 230
goruc see **gwneuthur**
goruchel adj. *almighty* 30, 44
gorvod m./f. *victory, success, triumph* 105
gorvod vn. *to triumph, prevail, be victorious*; pret. 2 sg. **gorvuost** 109
gosgedd f. *appearance, image, demeanour* 93
gradd f./m. *dignity, worth, merit*; pl. **graddav** 107
gras m./f. *grace* 51, 73, 282
gwaed m. *blood, ancestry* 7, 18, 140
gwallt m. *hair* 224, 225, 228
gwarae, gware m./f. *game, prank, trick*; pl. **gwareav** 70
gwarandaw vn. *to listen* 62
gwasgu vn. *to press* 226
gwedy, wedy prep. *after* 23, 39, 42
gwedd f. *manner* 60, 72, 86
gweddi f. *prayer, supplication, adoration* 136
gweddiaw, gweddio vn. *to pray* 9, 30, 88
gweithred f./m. *action, act, deed* 244; pl. **gweithredoedd** 100
gweld, gweled vn. *to see* 94, 107; pres. impersonal **gwelir** 120; impf. 3 sg. **gwelai** 245, impf. impersonal **gwelid** 71; pret. 3 sg. **gweles** 72, 127, 134; plupf. 3 sg. **gwelsai** 255
gweledigaeth f. *vision* 56, 268

gwellwell see **da**
gweryddawl adj. *virginal* 51
gwlad f. *country, land*; pl. **gwledydd** 214, 215, 216
gwledd f. *feast* 270
gwneuthur vn. *to do, make*; impf. 3 sg. **gwnai** 33, 42, 45, imp. 3 pl. **gwneynt** 66, 70, impf. sub. 3 sg. **gwnelai** 28, impf. impersonal **gwnaid** 42; pret. 3 sg. **goruc, gorug, gwnaeth** 36, 79, 85, pret. 3 pl. **gorugant, gwnaethont** 12, 22, 39, pret. impersonal **gwnaethbwyd** 138
gwr m. *man* 6, 163, 170; pl. **gwyr** 278
gwra vn. *to seek or take a husband, marry* 14
gwraic f. *woman, wife* 7, 202, 203
gwreika vn. *to seek or find a wife, marry* 17
gwrthod vn. *to refuse*; pret. 3 sg. **gwrthodes** 176
gwrthwyneb adj. *opposite, antithesis* 19; **yn gwrthwyneb** *opposed, contrary* 72
gwybod vn. *to know, be aware of* 68; pres. 3 sg. **gwybydd** 77; pret. 1 sg. **gwybu** 100
gwyl f. *feast (of a patron saint), holy-day, festival* 135, 138; **gwyl y gweryddon** *feast of the virgins* 138
gwyn adj. *blessed*; **gwyn dy vyd** *blessed are you* 108
gwyrthuawr adj. *precious, valuable* 104
gwyryf f. *virgin* pl. **gweryddon** 1, 54, 62
gyd see **y gyd**

H

hallt adj. *salty* 247
hanvot vn. *to descend from*; pres. 3 pl. **henynt** 223; impf. 3 sg. **hanoedd, hannoedd** 7, 77, 189, impf. 3 pl. **hanoeddynt** 78; pret. impersonal **hanwyd** 93
heb¹ prep. *without* 27, 217
heb², eb def. verb *said* 93, 95, 258 (*GMW*, §170)
hebyrgofi vn. *to forget*; pres. impersonal **hebyrgofir** 243
heddiw, heddyw adv. *today* 120, 218, 221
heddychu vn. *to make or restore peace*; pret. 3 sg. **heddychodd** 124
hefyd adv. *also* 43, 180, 181
help m./f. *help, assistance* 251; pres. 3 pl. **helpant** 268
helynt m./f. *trouble, worry, predicament* 71
hen adj. *ancient, old* 7, 47
hi¹ indep. pers. pron. 3 sg. f. 151, 153, 156
hi² aff. pers. pron. 3 sg. f. 11, 14, 15
hir adj. *long* 110
hithav¹ indep. conjunctive pers. pron. 3 sg. f. 25, 43, 55
hithav² aff. conjunctive pers. pron. 3 sg. f. 12, 20, 45

hollawl adj. *whole, complete* 64
hon dem. pron. sg. f. *this, she* 6, 11, 13
hwn dem. pron. sg. m. *this, he* 3, 7, 8
hwnnw dem. pron. sg. m. *that* 16, 17
hwyl f. *sail*; pl. **hwyliav** 70, 75
hwylwynt m. *favourable sailing wind* 69
hwynt[1] indep. pers. pron. 3 pl. *them* 109, 219 (also 71, 135 if the preceding *y* does not act as both particle and obj. pron.)
hwynt[2] aff. pers. pron. 3 pl. *them* 44, 45, 47
hwyntav conjunct. indep. pron. 3 pl. *them* 61
hyd prep. *until, as far as* 99, 129, 198; **hyd pan** conj. *until, so that* 87, 232
hyn dem. pron. neut. sg. *this* 4, 35, 36
hysbyssol adj. *well-known, familiar* 243
hysbyssu vn. *to inform, announce, declare, point out*; impf. 3 sg. **hysbyssai** 267, 3 pl. **hysbyssynt** 53
hystoria see **ystoria**

I

i[1] (len.) poss. pron. 3 sg. m. *his* 3, 7, 8
i[2] (asp.) poss. pron. 3 sg. f. *her* 12, 14, 43
i[3], **ev** (h-) poss. pron. 3 pl. *their* 42, 43, 62
i[4], **y** (len.) prep. *to* 17, 22, 26; with def. art. **i'r** 24, 36, 44; with inf. poss. pron. 2 sg. **i'th** 261, 3 sg. m. **y'w** 31, 61, 3 sg. f. **y'w** 24, 25, 168, 3 pl. **y'w** 46, 218, 221 (*GMW*, §56, N2); with suff. pers. pron. 1 sg. **ymi** 94, 3 sg. m. **iddo** 82, 84, 3 sg. f. **iddi** 32, 33, 256, 3 pl. **vddunt, vddynt** 56, 62, 69
i gilidd pron. *each other, the other* 52
iach adj. *healthy, in good health, free from illness* 262
iaith f. *language* 276
iarll m. *earl* 143, 155, 158; pl. **ieirll** 41, 140, 195
iawn adv. *very* 48
iechyd m./f. *health, salvation* 260
iefanc, iefanck adj. *young* 113, 126

Ll

Llading f./m. *Latin* 175, 275
lladd vn. *to kill* 86; pret. impersonal **llas** 216, 219, **lleasswyd** 95; plupf. impersonal **lladdyssid** 94
llaw f. *hand; authority, care, protection, tutelage* 12; pl. *hands* **dwylaw** 63, 200
llawen adj. *merry, joyful* 44, 79
llawenhav vn. *to rejoice, be joyful* 37
llawn adj. *full* 240

lle m. *place* 73, 88, 244
lledu vn. *to spread, broaden, expand*; **lledu hwyliav** *to set sail* 70
llinyn m. *bow-string* 101
llong f. *ship*; pl. **llongav, llongev** 69, 75, 129
llu m. *host, large number of people* 82
llw m. *oath, vow* 65
llyfasu vn. *to dare, risk*; pres. impersonal **llyfesir** 111
llyfr m. *book* 211
llygad m./f. *eye*; pl. **llygaid** 133, 240
llywenydd m. *joy, mirth, delight* 90, 108
llywodraeth f. *governance, authority, jurisdiction* 172
llywodraethv vn. *to govern*; imp. 3 sg. **llywodraethai** 173

M

mab m. *son, boy, youth, man* 16, 22, 24; pl. **meibion** 49
maen m. *stone, gem* 103
maes m. *field, battlefield* 103, 105, 212
maint m. *size, magnitude* 47
mal, val prep. *like, as* 21, 59, 104; **mal y, yr, val y, yr** conj. *when, while* 8, 26, 30; conj. *so that* 12, 15, 34; + neg. **val nad** *so that...not* 57
mam f. *mother* 3, 12, 24; pl. **mammav, mamav** 41, 140, 214
marchoc m. *knight* 4; pl. **marchogion** 41, 140, 214
marvolaeth f./m. *death* 133
mawr adj. *great, large, big, long (of hair)* 114, 221, 237; comp. **mwy** 18, 215; adv. **mwy no chynt** *more than ever before* 95, 254
medru vn. *to be able to*; impf. 3 sg. **medrai** 11; pret. 3 sg. **medrodd** 274
meddwl m. *mind, thought* 27, 63, 269
meddyliaw, meddylied vn. *to think* 9, 106, 130
melldigedic see **ymelldigedic**
merch f. *girl, daughter* 2, 11, 13; pl. **merched** 34, 40, 145
merthyr m. *martyr* 179; pl. **merthyri, merthyry** 109, 111, 122
merthyrv vn. *to martyr, kill cruelly* 55; pret. impersonal **merthyrwyd** 135, 174, 200
mewn prep. *in* 27, 111, 129
mil num. f. *one thousand* 148, 172; **vn vil ar ddec** *eleven thousand* 33, 141, 146
mingamv vn. *to mock, scoff, make a wry smile* 101
mis m. *month* 197
misyriad m. *a month old* 219
mor m. *sea, ocean* 69, 197; pl. **moroedd** 214
mor adv. *as* 17, 92, 244
morwyn f. *maid, virgin* 88, 93, 97; pl. **morynion** 33, 86, 89

morwyndawd m. *virginity, chastity, purity* 98
mwy see **mawr**
mwyn m. *benefit, advantage* 65, 99; **yr mwyn** prep. *for the sake of* 65, 99
mynach m. *monk* 266, 267, 269
mynaches f. *nun, female religious* 137
mynachlog f. *monastery, convent* 278; pl. **mynachlogoedd** 278
myned vn. *to go* 74, 116, 117; pres. subj. 3 sg. **el** 261; impf. 3 pl. **aent** 254; pret. 3 sg. **aeth** 197, pret. 3 pl. **aethont** 38, 73, 76
mynegi vn. *to express, explain, declare, narrate* 56; pres. 3 sg. **mynaic** 94
mynnu vn. to wish, desire, insist; pres. subj. 2 sg. **mynech** 259, pres. subj. 3 sg. **mynno** 272; pret. 3 sg. **mynnodd** 114
mynwgl m. *neck, throat* 233
mynych adj. *frequent* 46, 47

N

na, nad (before vowels) subordinating negation *that not* 57, 121, 136; relative 89
nachaf, nychaf interj. *lo, behold* 31
naill, y naill (len.) pron. *the one* 118, 151, 159
nawed ord. num. *ninth* 165, 205
neb pron. *anyone* 112; **y neb** (before relative clauses) *the one* 98, 256
nebun pron. *someone, somebody, anyone* 96
nef f. *heaven* 31, 53, 131; pl. **nefoedd** 45, 46, 55
nev (len.) conj. *or* 106
newydd adj. *new*; + vn. prep. *just, recently* 233
ni[1] indep. pron. 1 pl. 261
ni[2], **nid** (asp./len.) neg. part. 29, 94, 111; **nis** neg. + inf. pron. 3 sg. f. **os hithav nis rhoddid** *if she were not given* 25
no, noc (before vowels) (asp.) conj. used after comp. degree of adj. *than* 19, 95, 216 (*GMW*, §46); **nid amgen no** *not otherwise, namely* 212 (comp. in meaning *GMW* §46 N2)
nombyr m. *number* 220
not m. *mark, symbol, sign* 282

O

o[1] (len.) prep. *of, from, by, as a result of* 2, 6, 7; with def. art. **o'r** 11, 31, 39; with suff. pers. pron. 3 pl. **ohonvnt, onaddunt** 68, 151, 153; **o'r** (o + ar) **o'r pan** *from when* 11 (*GMW*, §84)
o[2] interj. *oh* 108, 123
o[3] see **os**
oddyno adv. *from there* 75, 76
oedran m. *age* 13, 17, 197

ofynhav, ofni vn. *to fear* 61; impf. 3 pl. **ofynheynt** 57
ofn m. *fear, terror* 89
ofnus adj. *afraid* 28
offrwm vn. *to sacrifice, offer* 184
oherwydd prep. *because, since* 17, 23, 47
ol m. *track, trail*; prep. **yn ol** *after, following, in accordance with* 38, 50, 105; prep. **ar ol** *after* 146
oll adj. *all* 209, 220, 270
os, o conj. *if* 25, 27, 29 (*GMW*, §272b)

P

pab m. *pope* 76, 79, 80; pl. **paboedd** 281
pader m./f. *prayer, rosary* 260; pl. **pederev, pyderev** 260, 263, 272
pan (len.) temporal conj. *when, as* 11, 72, 77; **pan yw** *that it is* 53 (*GMW*, §87); **hyd pan** see **hyd**
paratoi vn. *to prepare* 69
pardwn m. *pardon, feast*; pl. **pardynav** 282
parhav vn. *to last*; pres. 3 sg. **pery** 91, 270, 282
parod adj. *ready, prepared* 63, 69
parth a prep. *towards* 64, 80, 97
pawb pron. (sg. pl.) *everyone, all, everybody* 68, 184, 244
pe, bai conj. *if* 72, 94, 232; see also **bod**
pechadur m. *sinner* 121
pechod m. *sin*; pl. **pechodav** 48, 50
pedair num. f. *four* 164
pedwaredd ord. num. f. *fourth* 143
pen m. *head* 86, 231, 232; pl. **pennav** 224, 225, 241; **pennav saethav** arrow-heads 242; adj. *chief*; superl. **pennaf, ffennaf** *foremost* 140, 145
peregil m. *danger, risk* 29
pererindod m./f. *pilgrimage* 74
perffaith adj. *perfect* 57, 60
peri vn. *to cause, bring about* 39, 115
pla f. *plague* 85
plentyn m. *child*; pl. **plant** 125, 216
plwyf m. *parish* 279
pob pron. *each, every, all, every type of* 31, 172
pobyl f. *people, inhabitants* 31
porth m. *gate, gateway, portico*; pl. **pyrth** 124
pregethu vn. *to preach* 56
pres m. *brass* 257
pressennol adj. *present, current* 30

priawd, priod adj. *married, wedded, betrothed* 22, 24, 96; **gwr priod** *married man, betrothed, fiancé* 170, 188, 193
priodas f. *marriage, matrimony, wedlock* 33
priodi vn. *to marry, wed* 35, 49
prophwydaw vn. *to prophesy, foretell*; impf. 3 pl. **prophwydynt** 53
pum, pvm, pvmp num. *five* 145
pwy interr. pron. *who* 106, 244; pron. **pwy bynnag** *whosoever* 272, 281
pygan, pagan m. *pagan* 16, 19, 28; pl. **pyganieid** 85, 92, 127
pymed ord. num. *fifth* 144

Rh

rhag prep. *before, because of, from, against* 52; with suff. pers. pron. 3 sg. m. **rhacddaw** 97
rhagorawl adj. *excellent, splendid, outstanding* 52
rhai pron. *some* 40, 215, 217; **y rhai hyn** *these, these ones* 35, 42, 223
rhaid m. *necessity, obligation*; adj. superl. **rheitia** *most necessary* 251
rhain pron. *these* 34, 147, 151
rhandir f./m. *part of a country, area, region*; pl. **rhandiredd** 124
rhieni m./f. pl. *parents* 93
rhinwedd f. *virtue, moral excellence, characteristic*; pl. **rhinweddav** 20, 150
rhinweddawl adj. *virtuous, worthy, impeccable* 20
rhoddi vn. *to give, place* 12, 27, 64; impf. 3 sg. **rhoe** 43, impf. impersonal **rhoddid** 25; plupf. 3 pl. **rhoessynt** 65
rhwng prep. *between* 57, 200, 221
rhwygo vn. *to rip, tear, hack* 127
rhwymo vn. *to bind, tie, secure*; **rhywmo'r gwallt ynghyd** *to mat the hair together* 225
rhybydd m. *warning, advice, instruction* 60
rhybuddiaw vn. *to warn*; impf. 3 sg. **rhybuddiai** 74
rhydd-deb m. *freedom, liberation* 110
rhyf m. *praise, honour* 274
rhyfeddu vn. *to wonder, marvel, be astonished, astounded* 267
rhyngu bodd vn. *to please, give pleasure*; pres. 3 sg. **rhyng bodd** 36
rhyw pron. used adjectivally *kind of* 112, 231, 245 (*GMW*, §99)

S

saeth f./m. *arrow* 101, 102, 236; pl. **saethav** 242
saethu vn. *to shoot* 101
sampyl f./m. *example, sample, instance* 112, 121, 251
sanctaidd, santaidd adj. *holy* 6, 8, 26
sant m. *saint* 4; pl. **saint** 87, 107, 116

santes f. *saint* 262, 268; pl. **santesav, santessav** 87, 126, 128
sawl, y sawl (len.) pron. *such, those* 125, 268
sef *that is, namely* 16, 36, 76; substantival *it is this, thus* 59, 97, 128, adverbial 10, 255, 257, adjectival 70, 74 (*GMW*, §55f)
sefyll vn. *to stand* 125, 268
son m. *rumour, word, talk* 15
sorri vn. *to offend, anger*; impf. 3 sg. **sorrai** 29
sydd see **bod**
syr m. *sir, title given to priests or clerics (as well as knights)* 275
syrthio vn. *to fall*; pret. 3 sg. **syrthiodd** 102, 253

T

tad m. *father* 10, 12, 26
tafawd m./f. *tongue* 106
tair num. f. *three* 34, 68, 168
talu vn. *to pay*; impf. 3 sg. **talai** 104
taraw vn. *to strike, hit* 103; impf. impersonal **trewid** 239
tebygu vn. *to suppose, assume, think*; pres. impersonal **tybygir** 218
tec adj. *pretty, fair* 22; equat. **tecked, kyn decked** 14, 223, 228; superl. **teckaf** 40
teilwng, teylwnc, teilwnc adj. *worthy, praiseworthy, deserving* 6, 8, 96
tervynu vn. *to end*; pres. 3 sg. **teruyna** 274; impf. 3 sg. **tervynai** 269
teyrnas f. *kingdom* 6; pl. **tyrnassoedd** 15, 40
ti[1] indep. pers. pron. 2 sg. 96, 110
ti[2] aff. pers. pron. 2 sg. 258
tiriaw vn. *to land, come ashore*; impf. 3 pl. **tirynt** 75
tithav aff. conjunctive pers. pron. 36
torri vn. *to cut, break, smash* 233; pret. 3 sg. **torres** 232
traethu vn. *to speak, express, relate* 106; pres. impersonal **treithir** 195
tragywyddawl, tragywydd, tragwyddol adj. *eternal, everlasting* 58, 130, 264
trannoeth, tranoeth adv. also adj. *the following day, the next day* 117; **y bore drannoeth** *the following morning* 117
tref f. *town* 83, 198
trewid see **taraw**
tri num. *three* 181, 212, 218
trigianwr m. *inhabitant, resident*; pl. **trigianwyr** 83
trigo vn. *to live, dwell*; pres. 3 pl. **trigant** 125
troed m./f. *foot*; pl. **traed** 76
troi vn. *to change, alter, turn, convert*; pret. 3 sg. **troes** 199, 209
trugaredd m./f. *mercy, compassion* 134
trwm adj. *heavy, severe* 27, 253
trwssiedic adj. *well-dressed, adorned* 42

trwy prep. *through, throughout, by means of, via* 15, 24, 35
trydedd ord. num. f. *third* 155
trydydd ord. num. *third* 3, 182, 191
tu m. *side*; **tu draw** *the other side* 214
tuedd m. *region, district* 7
twyllaw vn. *to trick, deceive* 48
tyngu vn. *to vow* 66
tyner adj. *tender* 128
tynnv vn. *to pull, take; translate* 275
tyrnassu vn. *to reign, govern* 57
tywyllwc m. *darkness* 48
tywyssog, twyssoc, tywyssawc m. *prince* 157, 162, 183; pl. **tywyssogion** 41, 171 (here *leaders*), 213
tywyssoges f. *princess* 62, 140, 143

Th

'th inf. pron. 2 sg. 110, 261

U

uchel adj. *high*; comp. **kyfywch** 120
ugain, vgain num. *twenty* 197, 212, 279
urddas m. *honour, dignity, reputation* 15

V

val see **mal**
vchelwaed (**vchel** adj. + **gwaed** m.) *noble blood* 196
velly adv. *so, thus, therefore* 138, 274
verch see **merch**
vfyddhav vn. *to obey, submit to* 37
vn (len.) num. *one* 129, 148, 149; **vn ar ddec** num. *eleven* 147, 171; **vn vil ar ddec** num. *eleven thousand* 33, 141, 146; **vn vil ar bymtheg** num. *sixteen thousand* 220
vniawnvryd m. *in unison, with one accord* 9
vnoliaeth f. *solidarity, unanimity* 22, 63, 66
vnved ar ddec ord. num *eleventh* 169
vrddedig adj. *ordained, noble* 157, 162, 190
vrddol adj. *noble, dubbed* 4; pl. **vrddolion** 41, 140, 215
vry adv. *above, (mentioned) above, earlier* 84
vwchben prep. *above, on top of* 120, 265
vy (nas.) poss. pron. 1 sg. *my* 95
vyny, i vyny adv. *up* 262

W

'w inf. pron. 3 sg. 24, 25, 31
weithiav, weithiev adv. *sometimes, occasionally, at times* 48, 49, 70
weithion adv. *now, henceforth* 139, 195
wrth prep. *by, at* 226; *in a context denoting obedience, consent* 37; with suff. pers. pron. 3 sg. m. **wrtho** 251; **wrth hynny** *therefore, on account of this* 220
wylo, wylaw vn. *to weep*; impf. 3 sg. **wylai** 246
wyneb m. *face, surface* 118, 119; **yn wyneb** *facing, opposing* 71
wythved, wythued ord. num. *eighth* 164, 204

Y

y¹, i, yr def. art. *the* 1, 2, 4
y², yd, yr affirm. preverbal part. 2, 5, 6
y³, yr rel. part. 45, 88, 99
y⁴ subordinating part. 8, 12, 15
y⁵ see yn⁴
y gyd a (asp.), ac (before vowels) prep. *together with* 82
yma adv. *here* 139
ymchwel vn. *to return, go back*; impf. impersonal **ymchwelud** 80
ymddangos vn. *to appear* 137
ymddiddan vn. *to converse, talk* 32, 92
ymddygiad m. *behaviour* 14, 21
ymelldigedic, emelldigedic, melldigedic adj. *accursed, cursed, damned* 82, 91, 100
ymgeleddu vn. *to treasure, cherish, lay out*; pret. 3 sg. **ymgeleddaist** 109
ymguddiaw vn. *to hide, conceal oneself* 129
ymladd vn. *to fight* 72
ymlaen prep. *before, ahead of, in preference to, above* 61
ymlid vn. *to chase, pursue* 71
ymplith prep. *among, amidst* 5
ymrafael, ymravael, amraevael adj. *various, different, many* 5, 50, 213
ymroi vn. *to dedicate oneself; give in to*; pret. 3 sg. **ymroes** 178
ymysc prep. *among, amidst* 103, 117, 121
yn¹, ym, y' (before m-) (nas.) prep. *at, in, into* 2, 4, 5; with suff. pers. pron. 2 sg. **ynod** 125, 3 pl. **ynddunt** 242
yn² (len.) with adjectives forming adverbs 42, 43, 44
yn³ part. preceding vn. 9, 26, 30
yn⁴ predicative part. 3, 4, 6
yna adv. *then* 37, 107, 248
ynghwaneg adj. *additional, more, a greater quantity* 220, 225, 280
ynghwanegu vn. *to increase, enlarge, add (to)* 107

ynghyd adv. *together* 42, 43
ynghylch prep. *around* 233
ynill see **enill**
yno adv. *there* 75, 87, 174
yntev[1] indep. conjunctive pers. pron. 3 sg. m 29 (see also *GMW*, §55, p. 51 N
    yntev can also be used adverbially to mean *therefore*)
yntev[2] aff. conjunctive pers. pron. 3 sg. m. 8
ynys f. *island*
ysbi m. *(information gained by) spying*; **kaffael ysbi** *to be informed* 84
ysbrydawl adj. *spiritual* 63
ysgrowlingo vn. *to stick, glue, join, mat together* 235
ysgymvn adj. *wicked, heinous, abhorrent, villainous* 81
yspas m. *gap, interval, respite* 34
ystaciwn f./m. *stational churches of Rome* 79
ystoria, hystoria f. *story, history, chronicle* 1, 274

INDEX OF PERSONAL NAMES

Aldwlff *Adulphus, king* 205
Ambrosius *patron* 181
Amic *Avitus, king* 205
Arthimia *one of the 11,000 virgins whose relics in Cologne are noted* 228

Balbina *one of the wives who accompanied Ursula* 203
Barthimia *one of the 11,000 virgins whose relics in Cologne are noted* 227
Benedicta *one of the 11,000 virgins and one of the leaders who led 1,000 virgins* 161
Benigna *one of the 11,000 virgins whose relics in Cologne are noted and one of the leaders who led 1,000 virgins* 152, 229
Blandina *one of the wives who accompanied Ursula* 202
Brytanieid pl. *Britons,* **yr hen Vrytanieid** *the ancient Britons* 7, 77, 141

Calixtus *deacon* 180
Canutus *king* 203
Carpophora *one of the 11,000 virgins and one of the leaders who led 1,000 virgins* 159
Katrin *one of the 11,000 virgins whose relics in Cologne are noted* 236
Celindys *one of the 11,000 virgins and one of the leaders who led 1,000 virgins* 166
Kilianus *deacon* 181
Kiric, Ciriacus *Curig, Cyriacus, pope* 77, 174, 175
Clemencia *one of the 11,000 virgins whose relics in Cologne are noted and one of the leaders who led 1,000 virgins* 155, 234
Clodonius *king* 202
Columba *one of the princesses who accompanied Ursula* 206
Colu[m]banus *Columbanus, bishop, Ursula's cousin* 190
Colwmba *one of the 11,000 virgins and one of the leaders who led 1,000 virgins (possibly the same character as Columba above)* 160
Cordula¹ *one of the principal virgins* 126, 137, 143
Cordula² *Colwmba's sister; one of the princesses who accompanied Ursula* 161
Cornula *one of the 11,000 virgins* 163
Krist, Crist, Iessu *Christ, Jesus* 66, 82, 98
Cristina *one of the 11,000 virgins whose relics in Cologne are noted* 233
Cristianus *patron* 182
Crophorus *king* 201

Dronisia *Dionysia, one of the wives who accompanied Ursula* 205

Index of Personal Names

Eleutherius *bishop* 191
Elevtheria *one of the principal virgins* 143
Etherius (formerly known as **Oloffernes**) *son of the king of England and Ursula's fiancé* 196, 199
Ewffrofnia *Euphrosyna, one of the 11,000 virgins* 154
Ewgeina *one of the 11,000 virgins* 168
Ewgenius *prince* 183
Ewlalia *one of the 11,000 virgins* 158
Ewstachia *one of the 11,000 virgins* 154
Ewtropiam *Europia, one of the 11,000 virgins* 159

Fflorencia *one of the principal virgins* 145
Fflorentius *Roman archdeacon* 183
Ffolarius *bishop of Luws/Loon* 193

Genimiana *one of the 11,000 virgins* 152

Illwstris *one of the 11,000 virgins* 164
Iacobus, Iago *Jacobus, James, bishop of Antioch and one of the martyrs whose relics in Cologne are noted* 186, 240
Iota *one of the 11,000 virgins and one of the leaders who led 1,000 virgins* 149
Iuductam *one of the 11,000 virgins* 156
Iulia *one of the 11,000 virgins* 168
Iusticia *one of the 11,000 virgins* 152
Iustinus *patron* 181

Lotarius *bishop, Etherius' uncle* 192
Lucia[1] *Sibilia's sister, one of the 11,000 virgins* 168
Lucia[2] *vorwyn one of the 11,000 virgins and one of the leaders who led 1,000 virgins* 169
Luctus *king* 201

Mair, Mair Vorwyn *Mary, Virgin Mary* 66, 250
Margaret *one of the wives who accompanied Ursula, a relative of Ursula* 204
Mawricius *Maurisius, bishop of Levitan (Levicana)* 193
Mihangel *Michael the Archangel* 250
Mobilia *one of the 11,000 virgins* 154

Nicostrastus *prince* 183
Nothus *Ursula's father* 141
Odilia *one of the 11,000 virgins and one of the leaders who led 1,000 virgins* 164

Olifer *Oliver, king* 200
Oloffernes see **Etherius**

Paladoram *Palladora, one of the 11,000 virgins* 160
Pantulus *bishop of Basel and one of the martyrs whose relics in Cologne are noted* 185, 231
Petrus *cardinal* 180
Placida *one of the 11,000 virgins* 170
Poncius *cardinal* 179
Prudencia *one of the 11,000 virgins* 164
Pupinus *king* 203
Pynnosa *Pinnosa, one of the principal virgins* 142

Reffridus *Refridus, king* 208

Sapiencia *one of the 11,000 virgins* 164
Sattan *Satan* 47
Serena *one of the 11,000 virgins* 158
Sibilia[1] *Benigna's sister, one of the 11,000 virgins* 154
Sibilia[2] *sister of Iulia, Lucia and Ewgenia; one of the 11,000 virgins and one of the leaders who led 1,000 virgins* 167
Sibli *one of the wives who accompanied Ursula* 208
Silian[1] *Clemencia's sister, one of the 11,000 virgins* 156
Silian[2] *Odilia's sister, one of the 11,000 virgins* 165
Sophia *one of the 11,000 virgins whose relics in Cologne are noted* 237
Sulpicius *bishop of Raben* 194
Syrianus *king* 207

Virgilia *one of the 11,000 virgins* 167

Wiliam *William, bishop* 189
Wrsia *Ursitia, one of the 11,000 virgins* 165
Wrsla, Wrsula, Vrsla *Ursula* 11, 18, 19

INDEX OF PLACE NAMES

Antiocha, Antioetsia *Antioch* 186, 240

Basil *Basel* 75, 185, 231
Braban *Brabant* 216

Caer Sallawc *Caernarfon*. In ModW Caer Sallog has come to mean *Salisbury* 2, see Notes 2, p. 62 above
Cesilia *Sicily?* 223
Kolen, Cwlen, Kwlen, Colen *Cologne* 54, 73, 80

Fflandrys *Flanders* 215
Ffrisia *Frisia* 216

Iewerddon *Ireland* 215

Levitan 193
Luws *Loon* from French Looz, roughly equivalent with the modern Belgian province of Limburg 194, see Notes 193–94, p. 90 above

Lloegyr, Lloegr *England* 16, 196

Magwnsia *Mainz* 198
Maritene *Maritene or Maritime regions?* 230
Melden *Melden* 187

Normandi *Normandy* 215

Prydyn *Britain*

Raben *Ravenna* 194

Rhufain *Rome* 74, 77, 96

Ynys y Kedyrn *the Island of the Mighty (i.e. Britain)* 5
Yr Almaen *Germany* 1, 54, 73

BIBLIOGRAPHY

Manuscripts

Aberystwyth, National Library of Wales, MS 3108B
Aberystwyth, National Library of Wales, MS 1641B I
Aberystwyth, National Library of Wales, MS 17110E
Aberystwyth, National Library of Wales, MS 17520A
Aberystwyth, National Library of Wales, MS Cwrtmawr 44
Aberystwyth, National Library of Wales, MS Llanstephan 28
Aberystwyth, National Library of Wales, MS Llanstephan 34
Aberystwyth, National Library of Wales, MS Llanstephan 117
Aberystwyth, National Library of Wales, MS Peniarth 5
Aberystwyth, National Library of Wales, MS Peniarth 27ii
Aberystwyth, National Library of Wales, MS Peniarth 54
Aberystwyth, National Library of Wales, MS Peniarth 182
Aberystwyth, National Library of Wales, MS Peniarth 215
Bangor University MS 1267
Cardiff, Central Library, MS 3.11
Cardiff, Central Library, MS 2,629
Clitheroe, Stonyhurst College, MS 'Tragedies, Gallicanus, etc.'
Liège, Bibliothèque de l'Université, MS 366
London, British Library, MS Cotton Tiberius E. i
London, British Library, MS Cotton Vespasian A. xiv
London, British Library, MS Harley 2059
London, British Library, MS Harleian 4181
Milano, Bibl. Pinacoteca Ambr. MS 12
Oxford, Jesus College, MS 119

Printed Primary and Secondary Sources and Websites

ARNOLD, JOHN CHARLES, *The Footprints of Michael the Archangel: The Formation and Diffusion of a Saintly Cult, c. 300–c. 800* (Basingstoke: Palgrave Macmillan, 2013)

ATHANASIUS OF ALEXANDRIA, 'Life of St. Antony of Egypt', trans. by David Brakke, in *Medieval Hagiography: An Anthology*, ed. by Thomas Head (New York and London: Routledge, 2001), pp. 1–30

BARING-GOULD, SABINE, and JOHN FISHER, *Lives of the British Saints*, 4 vols (London: Cymmrodorion, 1907–1913)

BARTLETT, ROBERT, *Why Can the Dead Do Such Great Things? Saints and Worshipper from the Martyrs to the Reformation* (Princeton and Oxford: Princeton University Press, 2013)

BARTRUM, PETER C. (ed.), *Early Welsh Genealogical Tracts* (Cardiff: University of Wales Press, 1966)
—— 'Y Pedwar Brenin ar Hugain a Farnwyd yn Gadarnaf', *Études Celtiques*, 12 (1968-1971), 157-94
—— 'Some Studies in Early Welsh History', *Transactions of the Honourable Society of Cymmrodorion* (1949), 279-302
—— *A Welsh Classical Dictionary: People in History and Legend up to about A.D. 1000* (Aberystwyth: National Library of Wales, 1993)
—— (ed.), *Welsh Genealogies AD 1400-1500*, 18 vols (Aberystwyth: National Library of Wales, 1983)
BEDE, *The Life of St Cuthbert*, trans. by J. Stevenson (London and New York: Burns & Oates, 1887)
BELL, JENNIFER, 'Here, There or Nowhere: The School of St Illtud', unpublished paper delivered at the XVIth International Congress of Celtic Studies, University of Bangor, 23 July 2019
BONIFACE VIII, *Sermones et bulla de canonisatione sancti Ludovici, Recueil des historiens des Gaules et de la France* 23 (Paris: Imprimerie Nationale, 1894), pp. 148-60
BORSLEY, ROBERT D., ET AL. (eds), *The Syntax of Welsh* (Cambridge: Cambridge University Press, 2007)
BOWEN, GERAINT, 'Y Drych Cristianogawl: Astudiaeth', *The Journal of Welsh Ecclesiastical History*, 5, supplementary volume (1988), 1-66
—— (ed.), *Y Drych Kristnogawl* (Cardiff: University of Wales Press, 1996)
BOYER, RÉGIS, 'An Attempt to Define the Typology of Medieval Hagiography', in *Hagiography and Medieval Literature: A Symposium*, ed. by Hans Bekker-Nielsen et al. (Odense: Odense University Press, 1981), pp. 27-36
BRAY, DOROTHY A., *A List of Motifs in the Lives of the Early Irish Saints* (Helsinki: Suomalainen Tiedeakatemia, 1992)
BREEZE, ANDREW, 'The Virgin's Rosary and St Michael's Scales', *Studia Celtica*, 24 (1989-1990), 91-98
BRIE, FRIEDRICH W. D. (ed.), *The Brut, or The Chronicles of England*, EETS o.s. 131 and 136 (1906, 1908; repr. as one volume, Woodbridge: Boydell & Brewer, 2000)
BROMWICH, RACHEL (ed.), *Trioedd Ynys Prydein*, 3rd edn (Cardiff: University of Wales Press, 2006)
BROMWICH, RACHEL, and D. SIMON EVANS (eds), *Culhwch ac Olwen* (Caerdydd: Gwasg Prifysgol Cymru, 1988)
BROWN, PETER, *The Cult of the Saints: Its Rise and Function in Latin Christianity* (Chicago: University of Chicago Press, 1981)
BRYAN, ELIZABETH J., 'Ursula in the British History Tradition', in *The Cult of St Ursula and the 11,000 Virgins*, ed. by Cartwright, pp. 117-42
BRYANT-QUINN, PAUL (ed.), *Gwaith Ieuan Brydydd Hir* (Aberystwyth: Canolfan Uwchefrydiau Cymreig a Cheltaidd Prifysgol Cymru, 2000)
CAESARIUS OF HEISTERBACH, *Dialogue on Miracles*, trans. by H. von E. Scott and C. C. Swinton Bland, 2 vols (New York: Harcourt, Brace and Company, 1929)
CALLANDER, DAVID (ed. and trans.), *Vita Sancte Wenefrede*, Seintiau yng Nghymru / Saints in Wales / Vitae Sanctorum Cambriae website <http://www.seintiaucymru.ac.uk/> / <http://www.welshsaints.ac.uk/> (forthcoming)

CARTWRIGHT, JANE, 'Buchedd Gwenfrewy: The Life of St Winefride in NLW MSS Peniarth 27ii and Llanstephan 34', unpublished paper delivered at XVI Celtic Congress, University of Bangor, 25 July 2019

—— (ed. and trans.), *Buchedd Gwenfrewy*, Seintiau yng Nghymru / Saints in Wales / Vitae Sanctorum Cambriae website <http://www.seintiaucymru.ac.uk/> / <http://www.welshsaints.ac.uk/> (forthcoming)

—— (ed. and trans.), *Buchedd Ieuan Gwas Padrig*, Seintiau yng Nghymru / Saints in Wales / Vitae Sanctorum Cambriae website <http://www.seintiaucymru.ac.uk/> / <http://www.welshsaints.ac.uk/> (forthcoming)

—— (ed.), *Celtic Hagiography and Saints' Cults* (Cardiff: University of Wales Press, 2003).

—— (ed.), *The Cult of St Ursula and the 11,000 Virgins* (Cardiff: University of Wales Press, 2016)

—— *Feminine Sanctity and Spirituality in Medieval Wales* (Cardiff: University of Wales Press, 2008)

—— (ed. and trans.), *Mary Magdalene and her Sister Martha: An Edition and Translation of the Medieval Welsh Lives* (Washington, DC: Catholic University of America Press, 2013)

—— 'The Middle Welsh Life of St Ursula and the 11,000 Virgins', in *The Cult of St Ursula and the 11,000 Virgins*, ed. by Cartwright, pp. 163–86

—— 'Santesau Ceredigion', *Ceredigion*, 14 (2001), 1–36

CHARLES, B. G., 'The Second Book of George Owen's Description of Penbrokeshire', *National Library of Wales Journal*, 5, part iv (1948), 265–85

CHOTZEN, T. M., '"La Querrelle des femmes" au pays de Galles', *Revue Celtique*, 48 (1931), 42–93

CLARK, ANNE L., *Elizabeth of Schönau: A Twelfth-Century Visionary* (Philadelphia: University of Pennsylvania Press, 1992)

CLEMEN, PAUL (ed.), *Die Kunstdenkmäler der Stadt Köln. Im Auftrage des Provinzialverbandes der Rheinprovinz und der Stadt Köln* (Düsseldorf: L. Schwann, 1934)

COGITOSUS, 'Cogitosus: Life of Saint Brigit', trans. by J.-M. Picard, *The Journal of the Royal Society of Antiquaries of Ireland*, 117 (1987), 11–27

COLGRAVE, BERTRAM (ed. and trans.), *Two Lives of Saint Cuthbert: A Life by an Anonymous Monk of Lindisfarne and Bede's Prose Texts, Translations and Notes* (Cambridge: Cambridge University Press, 1940)

CROMBACH, HERMANN, *S. Ursula vindicate. Vita et martyrium S. Ursulae et sociarum undecim millium virginium* (Cologne: Hermann Mylii Birckmann, 1647)

DAVIES, JAMES CONWAY, *Episcopal Acts and Cognate Documents Relating to Welsh Dioceses 1066–1272*, 2 vols (Cardiff: Historical Society of the Church in Wales, 1946)

DAVIES, JOHN REUBEN, *The Book of Llandaf and the Norman Church in Wales* (Woodbridge: Boydell Press, 2003)

—— 'Cathedrals and the Cult of Saints in Eleventh- and Twelfth-Century Wales', in *Cathedrals, Communities and Conflict in the Anglo-Norman World*, ed. by Paul Dalton et al. (Woodbridge: Boydell Press, 2011), pp. 99–116

—— 'The Saints of South Wales and the Welsh Church', in *Local Saints and Local*

Churches in the Early Medieval West, ed. by Alan Thacker and Richard Sharpe (Oxford: Oxford University Press, 2002), pp. 361–95

DAVIES, SIONED, *Pedeir Keinc y Mabinogi* (Caernarfon: Gwasg Pantycelyn, 1989)

DAY, JENNY (ed.), *Buchedd Marthin*, Seintiau yng Nghymru / Saints in Wales / Vitae Sanctorum Cambriae website <http://www.seintiaucymru.ac.uk/> / <http://www.welshsaints.ac.uk/> (forthcoming)

DE BUCK, VICTOR, ET AL. (eds), *Acta sanctorum octobris tomus IX* (Antwerp, Brussels, Tongerloo, Paris: Brussels Greuse, 1858)

DELEHAYE, HIPPOLYTE, *Cinq leçons sur la méthode hagiographique* (Bruxelles: Société des Bollandistes, 1934)

—— *Les légendes hagiographiques*, 4th edn (Bruxelles: Société des Bollandistes, 1955)

—— *The Legends of the Saints*, trans. by Donald Attwater (Dublin: Four Courts Press, 1998)

DELPINO, MARY I. R., 'A Study of "Ystorya Collen" and the British Peregrini' (unpublished PhD thesis, University of Pennsylvania, 1980)

DE VORAGINE, JACOBUS, *The Golden Legend*, ed. and trans. by W. Granger Ryan, 2 vols (Princeton: Princeton University Press, 1993)

—— *Legenda aurea*, ed. by Giovanni Paolo Maggioni, 2nd edn, 2 vols (Florence: Sismel edizioni del Galluzzo, 1998)

Dictionary of Welsh Bibliography <https://biography.wales/> (accessed 7 July 2019)

DOBLE, G. H., *Lives of the Welsh Saints*, ed. by D. Simon Evans (Cardiff: University of Wales Press, 1971)

DUCHESNE, L. (ed.), *Liber Pontificalis*, c. 39 Bibliothèque des Écoles françaises d'Athènes et de Rome, 2nd edn, 3 vols (Paris: E. de Boccard, 1955–1957)

DUFFY, EAMON, *The Stripping of the Altars: Traditional Religion in England 1400–1580* (New Haven and London: Yale University Press, 1992)

DUMVILLE, D. N., 'Sub-Roman Britain: History and Legend', *History*, 62 (1977), 173–92

DUNN-LARDEAU, BRENDA (ed.), *La légende dorée: édition critique, dans la revision de 1476 par Jean Batailler, d'après la traduction de Jean de Vignay (1333-1348) de la Legenda aurea (c. 1261-1266)* (Paris: H. Champion, 1997)

EDWARDS, ALAW MAI (ed. and trans.), *Buchedd Collen*, Seintiau yng Nghymru / Saints in Wales / Vitae Sanctorum Cambriae website <http://www.seintiaucymru.ac.uk/> / <http://www.welshsaints.ac.uk/> (forthcoming)

EDWARDS, NANCY (with contributions by Heather Jackson, Helen McKee and Patrick Sims-Williams), *A Corpus of Early Medieval Inscribed Stone Sculpture in Wales Vol II: South-West Wales* (Cardiff: University of Wales Press, 2007)

EDWARDS, OWAIN TUDOR, *Matins, Lauds and Vespers for St David's Day: The Medieval Office of the Welsh Patron Saint in National Library of Wales MS 20541E* (Cambridge: Brewer, 1990)

—— 'The Office of St David in Paris, Bibliothèque Nationale, MS Lat. 17294', in *St David of Wales*, ed by Evans and Wooding, pp. 233–52

ELIZABETH OF SCHÖNAU, *The Complete Works*, trans. by Anne L. Clark, Preface by Barbara Newman (New York: Paulist Press, 2000)

ENNEN, LEONARD, and GOTTFRIED ECKERTZ, *Quellen zur Geschichte der Stadt Köln*, 6 vols (Cologne: M. DuMont-Schauberg, 1860–1879)

Evans, D. Simon, *A Grammar of Middle Welsh* (Dublin: Dublin Institute for Advanced Studies, 1964)

Evans, Emrys, 'Cystrawennau "sef" mewn Cymraeg Canol', *BBCS*, 18 (1958–1960), 38–54

—— 'Cystrawen y Rhagenw Personol yn Rhyddiaith Gymraeg y Cyfnod Canol' (unpublished MA thesis, University of Wales, Swansea, 1958)

Evans, George Eyre, *Cardiganshire* (Aberystwyth: The Welsh Gazette, 1903)

Evans, J. Gwenogvryn, *Report on Manuscripts in the Welsh Language*, 2 vols in 7 parts (London: Royal Commission on Historical Monuments, 1898–1910)

—— *White Book Mabinogion: Welsh Tales & Romances Reproduced from the Peniarth Manuscripts* (Pwllheli: privately printed, 1907)

Evans, J. G., and J. Rhŷs (eds), *The Text of the Book of Llan Dâv* (Oxford: John Bellows for J. G. Evans, 1893)

Evans, J. Wyn, 'Bishops of St Davids from Bernard to Bec', in *Pembrokeshire County History II*, ed. by R. F. Walker (Haverfordwest: Pembrokeshire Historical Society, 2002), pp. 270–303

—— 'The Early Church in Denbighshire', *Transactions of the Denbighshire Historical Society*, 35 (1986), 61–81

Evans, J. Wyn, and Jonathan M. Wooding (eds), *St David of Wales: Cult, Church and Nation* (Woodbridge: Boydell Press, 2007)

Felix, *Felix's Life of St Guthlac*, ed. and trans. by Bertram Colgrave (Cambridge: Cambridge University Press, 1956)

Field, Sean L., and Walter Simons, 'A Prophecy Fulfilled? An Annotated Translation of the Sources on the Death of the Crown Prince Louis of France (1276) and the Interrogations of Elizabeth of Spalbeek (1276–78)', *The Medieval Low Countries*, 5 (2018), 35–92

Flynn, William, 'Hildegard (1098–1179) and the Virgin Martyrs of Cologne', in *The Cult of St Ursula and the 11,000 Virgins*, ed. by Cartwright, pp. 93–118

Geoffrey of Monmouth, *The History of the Kings of Britain: An Edition and Translation of De gestis Britonum [Historia regum Britanniae]*, ed. by Michael D. Reeve, trans. by Neil Wright (Woodbridge: Boydell Press, 2007)

Godwin, Francis, *De praesulibus Angliae commentaries: ominium Episcoporum necnon ei cardinalium eivsdem gentis, nomina … per Franciscvm Godwinvm episcopum Landauensem* (London: William Stansby and Eliot's Court Press, 1616)

Goetinck, Glenys (ed.), *Historia Peredur Vab Efrawc* (Caerdydd: Gwasg Prifysgol Cymru, 1976)

—— 'Pedair Cainc y Mabinogi: Yr Awdur a'i Bwrpas', *Llên Cymru*, 15 (1987–1988), 249–69

Görlach, Manfred, *The Textual Tradition of the South English Legendary* (Leeds: University of Leeds, 1974)

GPC Online, *Geiriadur Prifysgol Cymru / A Dictionary of the Welsh Language*, Canolfan Uwchefrydiau Cymreig a Cheltaidd Prifysgol Cymru <http://www.geiriadur.ac.uk> (accessed 30 October 2019)

Griffith, John Edward (ed.), *Pedigrees of Anglesey and Carnarvonshire Families with their Collateral Branches in Denbighshire, Meirionethshire and Other Parts* (Horncastle: W. K. Morton, 1914)

GUY, BENJAMIN DAVID, 'Constantine, Helena, Maximus: On the Appropriation of Roman History in Medieval Wales, *c.* 800–1250', *Journal of Medieval History*, 44 (2018), 381–405
—— 'The Life of St Dyfrig and the Lost Charters of Moccas (Mochros), Herefordshire', *Cambrian Medieval Celtic Studies*, 75 (2018), 1–34
—— 'A Lost Medieval Manuscript from North Wales: Hengwrt 33, the Hanesyn Hên', *Studia Celtica*, 50 (2016), 69–105
—— 'Medieval Welsh Genealogy: Texts, Context and Transmission', 2 vols, (unpublished DPhil thesis, University of Cambridge, 2016)
—— 'The Vespasian Life of St Teilo and the Evolution of the *Vitae Sanctorum Wallensium*', unpublished paper delivered at the *Vitae Sanctorum Cambriae* Conference, University of Cambridge, 26 September 2019
HAMER, RICHARD (with the assistance of Vida Russell) (ed.), *Gilte Legend, Volume 1*, EETS (Oxford: Oxford University Press, 2006)
—— (ed.), *Gilte Legend, Volume 2*, EETS (Oxford: Oxford University Press, 2007)
—— (ed.), *Gilte Legend, Volume 3*, EETS (Oxford: Oxford University Press, 2012)
HARBUS, ANTONINA, *Helena of Britain in Medieval Legend* (Cambridge: D. S. Brewer, 2002)
HARRIS, SILAS M., 'Was St. David Ever Canonized?', *Wales* (June 1944), 30–32
HATFIELD, EDMUND, *Lyf of Saynt Vrsula* (London: Wynkyn de Worde, 1509?), Early English Books Online
HEAD, THOMAS (ed.), 'Hagiography', The ORB: On-Line Reference Book for Medieval Studies <http://www.the-orb.net/encyclop/religion/hagiography> (accessed 23 April 2018)
—— *Medieval Hagiography: An Anthology* (New York and London: Routledge, 2001)
HEFFERNAN, THOMAS J., 'Philology and Authorship in the *Passio Sanctarum Perpetuae et Felicitatis*', *Traditio*, 50 (1995), 315–25
HENKEN, ELISSA R., *Traditions of the Welsh Saints* (Cambridge: Brewer, 1987)
—— *The Welsh Saints: A Study of Patterned Lives* (Woodbridge: D. S. Brewer, 1991)
HERBERMANN, CHARLES, ET AL. (eds), *The Catholic Encyclopedia*, 15 vols (New York: Encyclopedia Press, 1913)
HOEFENER, KRISTIN, 'From St Pinnosa to St Ursula: The Development of the Cult of Cologne's Virgins in Medieval Liturgical Offices', in *The Cult of St Ursula and the 11,000 Virgins*, ed. by Cartwright, pp. 61–91
HOLT, GEOFFREY (ed.), *The Letter Book of Louis Sabran, S. J. (Rector of St. Omers College) October 1713 to October 1715* (St Albans: The Catholic Record Society, 1971)
HORSTMANN, CARL (ed.), *The Early South-English Legendary*, EETS o.s. 87 (London, 1887; reprinted Millwood New York, 1975)
—— *Nova Legenda Anglie*, 2 vols (Oxford: Clarendon Press, 1901)
HUGHES, IAN (ed.), *Bendigeiduran Uab Llyr* (Aberystwyth: CAA, Prifysgol Aberystwyth, 2017)
HUGHES, KATHLEEN, 'British Museum MS. Cotton Vespasian A. XIV ('Vitae Sanctorum Wallensium'): Its Purpose and Provenance', in *Studies in the Early British Church*, ed. by Nora Chadwick et al. (Cambridge: Cambridge University Press, 1958), pp. 183–200

HULL, VIDA J., 'Spiritual Pilgrimage in the Paintings of Hans Memling', in *Art and Architecture of Late Medieval Pilgrimage in Northern Europe and the British Isles*, ed. by Sarah Blick and Rita Tekippe, 2 vols (Leiden: Brill, 2005), I, pp. 29–50

HURLOCK, KATHRYN, *Medieval Welsh Pilgrimage, c. 1100–1500* (Basingstoke: Palgrave Macmillan, 2018)

HUWS, DANIEL, *A Repertory of Welsh Manuscripts and Scribes c. 800–c. 1800*, 3 vols (Aberystwyth: National Library of Wales, forthcoming)

—— 'St David in the Liturgy: A Review of the Sources', in *St David of Wales*, ed. by Evans and Wooding, pp. 220–32

ISAACSON, R. F. (ed. and trans.), *The Episcopal Registers of the Diocese of St. David's 1397–1518*, 3 vols (London: The Honourable Society of Cymmrodorion, 1917–1920)

JAMES, HEATHER, 'The Geography of the Cult of St David: A Study of Dedication Patterns in the Medieval Diocese', in *St David of Wales*, ed. by Evans and Wooding, pp. 41–83

JANKULAK, KAREN, *Geoffrey of Monmouth: Writers of Wales* (Cardiff: University of Wales Press, 2010)

JOHNSON, RICHARD F., *Saint Michael the Archangel in Medieval English Literature* (Woodbridge: Boydell Press, 2005)

JONES, D. J. (Gwenallt), 'Buchedd Mair Fadlen a'r *Legenda Aurea*', *BBCS*, 4 (1929), 325–29

—— 'Cerddi'r Saint a'r Bucheddau Cyfatebol', unpublished MA dissertation, University of Wales, Aberystwyth, 1929

JONES, NERYS ANN, and ANN PARRY OWEN (eds), *Gwaith Cynddelw Brydydd Mawr*, I (Caerdydd: Gwasg Prifysgol Cymru, 1991)

—— *Gwaith Cynddelw Brydydd Mawr*, II (Caerdydd: Gwasg Prifysgol Cymru, 1995)

JONES, NERYS ANN, and MORFYDD E. OWEN, 'Twelfth-Century Welsh Hagiography: The Gogynfeirdd Poems to Saints', in *Celtic Hagiography and Saints' Cults*, ed. by Cartwright, pp. 45–76

JONES, T. (ed.), *Brut y Tywysogyon (Red Book of Hergest Version)* (Cardiff: University of Wales Press, 1952)

—— *Ystoryaeu Seint Greal* (Caerdydd: Gwasg Prifysgol Cymru, 1992)

JONES, T. GWYNN (ed.), *Gwaith Tudur Aled*, 2 vols (Caerdydd: Gwasg Prifysgol Cymru, 1926)

KENNEY, J. F., *The Sources for the Early History of Ireland* (New York: Columbia University Press, 1929)

KERLING, J., 'A Case of "Slipping": Direct and Indirect Speech in Old English Prose', *Neophilologus*, 66 (1982), 286–90

KIPLING, GORDON (ed.), *The Receyt of the Ladie Kateryne*, EETS o.s. 296 (Oxford: Oxford University Press, 1990)

KITZLER, PETR, *From 'Passio Perpetuae' to 'Acta Perpetuae': Recontextualizing a Martyr Story in the Literature of the Early Church* (Berlin: De Gruyter, 2015)

KLINKENBERG, J. (ed.), 'Studien zur Geschichte der Kölner Märterinnen', *Bonner Jahrbücher*, 89 (1890), 118–24

KRACHT, HANS-JOACHIM, and JAKOB TORSY, *Reliquiarium Coloniense* (Siegburg: Verlag Franz Schmitt, 2003)

KRAJEWSKI, ELIZABETH M. G., *Archetypal Narratives: Pattern and Parable in the Lives of Three Saints* (Turnhout: Brepols, 2018)

LAKE, A. CYNFAEL (ed.), *Gwaith Siôn ap Hywel ap Llywelyn Fychan* (Aberystwyth: Canolfan Uwchefrydiau Cymreig a Cheltaidd Prifysgol Cymru, 1999)

LAȜAMON, *Laȝamon: Brut*, ed. by G. L. Brook and R. F. Leslie, EETS o.s. 250, 277 (London: Kegan Paul, Trench, Trübner & Co, 1963)

LECLERCQ, H., 'Station Days', *CE*, XIV, pp. 268–69

LEVISON, WILHELM, 'Das Werden der Ursula-Legende', *Bonner Jahrbücher*, 132 (1927), 1–164

LEWIS, BARRY (ed. and trans.), *Medieval Welsh Poems to Saints and Shrines* (Dublin: School of Celtic Studies, Dublin Institute for Advanced Studies, 2015)

LEWIS, HENRY (ed.), *Brut Dingestow* (Caerdydd: Gwasg Prifysgol Cymru, 1942)

LEWIS, HENRY ET AL. (eds), *Cywyddau Iolo Goch ac Eraill* (Caerdydd: Gwasg Prifysgol Cymru, 1937)

LHUYD, EDWARD, *Archaeologia Cambrensis: Parochialia*, 3 parts (London: Cambrian Archaeological Society, 1909–1911)

LLANBEBLIG BOOK OF HOURS, NLW MS 17520A, National Library of Wales <https://www.llyfrgell.cymru/?id=258&L=1> (accessed 25 January 2018)

LOOKER, R., 'Huw Pennant ('Syr') (*fl.* during the second half of the 15th century), cleric, poet, and antiquary', *The Dictionary of Welsh Biography* (1959) <http://biography.wales/> (accessed 23 April 2019)

LUFT, DIANA, 'Treating the Stone in Sixteenth-Century Wales (According to the Vicar of Gwenddwr)', *The Recipes Project* <https://recipes.hypotheses.org/tag/diana-luft> (accessed 1 October 2019)

MARVIN, JULIA (ed. and trans.), *The Oldest Anglo-Norman Prose Brut Chronicle: An Edition and Translation*, Medieval Chronicles, 4 (Woodbridge: Boydell Press, 2006)

MARX, WILLIAM, 'Saint Ursula and the Eleven Thousand Virgins: The Middle English *Legenda aurea* Tradition', in *The Cult of St Ursula and the 11,000 Virgins*, ed. by Cartwright, pp. 143–63

MAZZONIS, QUERICIOLO, 'The Impact of Renaissance Gender-Related Notions of the Female Experience of the Sacred: The Case of Angela Merici's Ursulines', in *Gender, Catholicism and Spirituality: Women and the Roman Catholic Church in Britain and Europe, 1200–1900*, ed. by Laurence Lux-Sterrit and Carmen Mangion (Basingstoke: Palgrave Macmillan, 2011), pp. 51–67

—— *Spirituality, Gender, and the Self in Renaissance Italy: Angela Merici and the Company of St. Ursula (1474–1540)* (Washington, DC: Catholic University of America Press, 2007)

MEHAN, JEANNE, 'The Enduring Meme of the Saintly Daughters of Brychan Brycheiniog' (unpublished PhD thesis, University of Wales Trinity Saint David, forthcoming)

MERDRIGNAC, BERNARD, 'The Process and Significance of Rewriting in Breton Hagiography', in *Celtic Hagiography and Saints' Cults*, ed. by Cartwright, pp. 177–97

MERLO, J. J., 'Johann Crane und seine Stiftungen in der Ursulakirche zu Köln', *Zeitschrift für christliche Kunst*, 2 (1889), 105–10

MILITZER, KLAUS, 'The Church of St Ursula in Cologne: Inscriptions and Excavations', in *The Cult of St Ursula and the 11,000 Virgins*, ed. by Cartwright, pp. 29–39

MONASTIC WALES <http://www.monasticwales.org> (accessed 5 June 2018)

MONTGOMERY, SCOTT B., *St. Ursula and the Eleven Thousand Virgins of Cologne: Relics, Reliquaries and the Visual Culture of Group Sanctity in Late Medieval Europe* (Bern: Peter Lang, 2009)

—— 'What's in a Name? Navigating Nomenclature in the Cult of St Ursula and the Eleven Thousand Virgins', in *The Cult of St Ursula and the 11,000 Virgins*, ed. by Cartwright, pp. 10–28

MORGAN, T. J., *Y Treigladau a'u Cystrawen* (Caerdydd: Gwasg Prifysgol Cymru, 1952)

MORRIS-JONES, JOHN, *A Welsh Grammar* (Oxford: Clarendon Press, 1913)

MORRIS-JONES, JOHN, and JOHN RHŶS (eds), *The Elucidarium and Other Tracts in Welsh From Llyvyr Agkyr Llandewivrevi A.D. 1346* (Jesus College MS. 119) (Oxford: Clarendon Press, 1894)

MUIRCHÚ, *Muirchú Moccu Mactheni's 'Vita Sancti Patriccii' Life of Saint Patrick*, ed. by David Howlett (Dublin: Four Courts Press, 2006)

MUSURILLO, HERBERT (ed. and trans.), *The Acts of the Christian Martyrs* (Oxford: Clarendon Press, 1972)

NICHOLSON, H., 'St Ursula and the Military Religious Orders', in *The Cult of St Ursula and the 11,000 Virgins*, ed. by Cartwright, pp. 41–59

NITZE, WILLIAM A., and T. ATKINSON JENKINS (eds), *Le Haut Livre du Graal: Perlesvaus* (Chicago: University of Chicago Press, 1932)

NOBLE, THOMAS F. X., and THOMAS HEAD, *Soldiers of Christ: Saints and Saints' Lives from Late Antiquity and the Early Middle Ages* (London: Sheed & Ward, 1995)

Nova Legenda Anglie (London: Wynkyn de Worde, 1516), Early English Books Online

NUECHTERLEIN, JEANNE, 'Hans Memling's St. Ursula Shrine: The Subject as Object of Pilgrimage', in *Art and Architecture of Late Medieval Pilgrimage in Northern Europe and the British Isles*, ed. by Sarah Blick and Rita Tekippe, 2 vols (Leiden: Brill, 2005), I, pp. 51–75

O'LOUGHLIN, THOMAS, 'Rhygyfarch's *Vita Dauidis*: An Apparatus Biblicus', *Studia Celtica*, 32 (1998), 179–88

PARRY, JOHN JAY (ed.), *Brut y Brenhinedd Cotton Cleopatra Version* (Cambridge, Mass.: The Medieval Academy of America, 1937)

PARRY OWEN, ANN (ed. and trans.), 'Canu i Cadfan', Seintiau yng Nghymru / Saints in Wales / Vitae Sanctorum Cambriae website <http://www.seintiaucymru.ac.uk/> / <http://www.welshsaints.ac.uk/> (forthcoming)

—— (ed. and trans.), 'Canu i Ddewi', Seintiau yng Nghymru / Saints in Wales / Vitae Sanctorum Cambriae website <http://www.seintiaucymru.ac.uk/> / <http://www.welshsaints.ac.uk/> (forthcoming)

—— (ed. and trans.), 'Canu i Tysilio', Seintiau yng Nghymru / Saints in Wales / Vitae Sanctorum Cambriae website <http://www.seintiaucymru.ac.uk/ / <http://www.welshsaints.ac.uk/> (forthcoming)

PARRY-WILLIAMS, T. H., *Rhyddiaith Gymraeg Y Gyfrol Gyntaf Detholiad o Lawysgrifau 1488–1609* (Caerdydd: Gwasg Prifysgol Cymru, 1954)

PETIT, FRANÇOIS, *Spirituality of the Premonstratensians: The Twelfth and Thirteenth Centuries*, trans. by Victor Szczurek, ed. by Carol Neel (Collegeville, Minnesota: Liturgical Press, 2011)

PHILIPPART, GUY (ed.), *Hagiographies: International History of the Latin and Vernacular Hagiographical Literature in the West from its Origins to 1550* (Turnhout: Brepols, 1994–2010)

PHILLIMORE, EGERTON, 'Notes by the Editor', in J. W. Willis-Bund, 'The True Objects of Welsh Archaeology', *Y Cymmrodor*, 11 (1890–1), 103–32 (pp. 125–32)

POPPE, ERICH, 'Slipping in Some Medieval Welsh Texts: A Preliminary Survey', in *Le slipping dans les langues médiévales*, ed. by Jürg Rainer Schwyter, Erich Poppe and Sandrine Onillon (Lausanne: Université de Lausanne, Faculté des Lettres, 2005), pp. 119–51

POPPE, ERICH, and REGINE RECK (eds), *Selections from Ystorya Bown o Hamtwn* (Cardiff: University of Wales Press, 2009)

PROSPER OF AQUITAINE, *Chronica Minora*, ed. by Th. Mommsen, Monvmenta Germaniae Historica, 11 vols (Berlin: Weidmannos, 1892)

PRYCE, A. I., *The Diocese of Bangor in the Sixteenth Century* (Bangor: Jarvis & Foster, 1923)

PRYCE, HUW, 'A New Edition of the *Historia divae Monacellae*', *Montgomeryshire Collections*, 82 (1994), 23–40

REAMES, SHERRY L., *The Legenda Aurea: A Reexamination of its Paradoxical History* (Madison: The University of Wisconsin Press, 1985)

RICHARDS, MELVILLE (ed.), 'Buchedd Fargred', *BBCS*, 11 (1939), 324–34

RICHES, SAMANTHA, 'Male Martyrs, Female Models? St Ursula and St Acacius as Leaders and Victims', in *The Cult of St Ursula and the 11,000 Virgins*, ed. by Cartwright, pp. 245–61

—— 'Relics of Gender Identity: Interpreting a Reliquary of a Follower of St Ursula', in *Matter of Faith: An Interdisciplinary Study of Relics and Relic Veneration in the Medieval Period*, ed. by James Robinson, Lloyd de Beer and Anna Harnden (London: British Research Publication No. 195, 2014), pp. 143–50

RICHMAN, G., 'Artful Slipping in Old English', *Neophilogus*, 70 (1986), 279–91

ROBERTS, BRYNLEY F. (ed.), *Breudwyt Maxen Wledic* (Dublin: School of Celtic Studies, Dublin Institute for Advanced Studies, 2005)

—— (ed.), *Brut y Brenhinedd* (Dublin: Dublin Institute for Advanced Studies, 1971)

ROBERTS, THOMAS, and IFOR WILLIAMS (eds), *The Poetical Works of Dafydd Nanmor* (Cardiff: University of Wales Press, 1923)

RUSSELL, PAUL, 'The After-Life of St Melangell/Monacella', unpublished paper delivered at the *Vitae Sanctorum Cambriae* Conference, University of Cambridge, 26 September 2019

SÁGHY, M., '*Scinditur in partes populus*: Pope Damasus and the Martyrs of Rome', *Early Medieval Europe*, 9 (2000), 273–87

SALIH, SARAH, 'Introduction: Saints, Cults and *Lives* in Late Medieval England', in *A Companion to Middle English Hagiography*, ed. by Sarah Salih (Cambridge: D. S. Brewer, 2006), pp. 1–23

SANOK, CATHERINE, *New Legends of England: Forms of Community in Late Medieval Saints' Lives* (Philadelphia: University of Pennsylvania Press, 2018)

SAXER, VICTOR, 'Damase et le calendrier des fêtes de martyrs de l'église romaine', in *Saecularia Damasiana: atti del convegno internazionale per il XVI centenario della morte di papa Damaso*, Studi di antichità Cristiana 39 (Città del Vaticano: Pontificio istituto di archeologia cristiana, 1986), pp. 61–88

SCHMITZ, WINFRIED, 'Die spätantiken und frühmittelalterlichen Grabinschriften in Köln (4.-7. Jahrhundert n. Chr.)', *Kölner Jahrbuch*, 28 (1995), 643-776
SEINTIAU YNG NGHYMRU / SAINTS IN WALES / VITAE SANCTORUM CAMBRIAE WEBSITE <http://www.seintiaucymru.ac.uk/> / <http://www.welshsaints.ac.uk/> (forthcoming)
SHARPE, RICHARD, and JOHN REUBEN DAVIES (ed. and trans.), 'Rhygyfarch's *Life* of St David', in *St David of Wales*, ed. by Evans and Wooding, pp. 107-55
SHEINGORN, PAMELA, and MARCELLE THIÉBAUX (trans.), *The Passion of Saint Ursula and The Sermon on the Birthday of Saint Ursula*, 2nd edn (Toronto: Pergrina Publishing, 1996)
SIMS-WILLIAMS, PATRICK (ed.), *The Book of Llandaf as a Historical Source* (Oxford: Boydell Press, 2019)
—— (ed.), *Buchedd Beuno* (Dublin: School of Celtic Studies, Dublin Inst. for Advanced Studies, 2018)
SINDERHAUF, MONICA, *Die Abtei Deutz und ihre innere Erneuerung: Klostergeschichte im Spiegel des verschollenen Codex Thioderici* (Vierow: SH-Verlag, 1996)
STANCLIFFE, CLARE, *St Martin and his Hagiographer: History and Miracle in Sulpicius Severus* (Oxford: Clarendon Press, 1983)
STEIN, ALBERT GEREON, *The Church of Saint Ursula and her Companions in Cologne: Its Memorials, Monuments and Curiosities* (Cologne: H. Theissing, 1896)
STEPHANUS, *The Life of Bishop Wilfrid*, ed. and trans. by Bertram Colgrave (Cambridge: Cambridge University Press, 1927)
STURZER, NED, 'How Middle Welsh Expresses the Unexpected', *Cambrian Medieval Celtic Studies*, 41 (2001), 37-53
SULPICIUS SEVERUS, *Sulpicius Severus' 'Vita Martini'*, ed. by Phillip Burton (Oxford: Oxford University Press, 2017)
TERVARENT, GUY DE, *La légende de Sainte Ursule dans la littérature et l'art du moyen-âge*, 2 vols (Paris: Les Éditions G. van Oest, 1931)
THACKER, ALAN, '*Loca Sanctorum*: The Significance of Place in the Study of the Saints', in *Local Saints and Local Churches in the Early Medieval West*, ed. by A. Thacker and R. Sharpe (Oxford: Oxford University Press, 2002), pp. 1-43
THOMAS, OWEN (ed.), *Gwaith Dafydd Epynt* (Aberystwyth: Canolfan Uwchefrydiau Cymreig a Cheltaidd Prifysgol Cymru, 2002)
THOMAS, PETER WYNN, '(GWNAETH): Newidyn Arddulliol yn y Cyfnod Canol', in *Cyfoeth y Testun: Ysgrifau ar Lenyddiaeth Gymraeg yr Oesedd Canol*, ed. by Iestyn Daniel et al. (Caerdydd: Gwasg Prifysgol Cymru, 2003), pp. 252-80
—— 'Middle Welsh Dialects: Problems and Perspectives', *BBCS*, 40 (1993), 17-50
THOMPSON, D., 'Cistercians and Schools in Later Medieval Wales', *Cambridge Medieval Celtic Studies*, 3 (1982), 76-80
THURSTON, H. H., 'Names, Christian', *CE*, x, pp. 673-75.
TOCH, MICHAEL, 'The Medieval German City under Siege', in *The Medieval City under Siege*, ed. by Ivy A. Corfis and Michael Wolfe (Woodbridge: Boydell Press, 1999), pp. 35-48
TOUT, MRS T. F. (Mary), 'The Legend of St Ursula and the Eleven Thousand Virgins', in *Historical Essays by Members of the Owens College, Manchester*:

Published on Commemoration of its Jubilee (1851–1901), ed. by T. F. Tout and J. Tait (London: Longmans, Green, and Co., 1902), pp. 17–56

TÜSKÉS, ANNA, 'The Cult of St Ursula in Hungary: Legends, Altars and Reliquaries', in *The Cult of St Ursula and the 11,000 Virgins*, ed. by Cartwright, pp. 187–204

URSINUS, *Passio Leudegarii*, ed. by B. Krusch and W. Levison (Hanover and Leipzig: Impensis Bibliopolii Hahniani, 1910)

USUARDUS, *Acta sanctorum iunni VII, Martyrologii Usuardini*, ed. by Jean-Baptiste Sollerius (Antwerp: J. P. Robin, 1717)

VANHERLE, OLGA, '*Ystoria o Wyrthie Mihangel*: Trawsysgrifiad a Golygiad (Peniarth 182) gyda Nodiadau, Geirfa a Chyfieithiad, Cyd-destunoli'r Testun a Golwg ar Dystiolaeth Farddonol a Llenyddol, Materol a Chelfyddydol Cwlt Mihangel yng Nghymru'r Oesoedd Canol', (unpublished PhD thesis, University of Wales Trinity Saint David, forthcoming)

WADE-EVANS, A. W. (ed. and trans.), *Vitae Sanctorum Britanniae et Genealogiae* (Cardiff: University of Wales Press, 1944)

WATKINS, T. ARWYN, 'The *sef* [...] Realization of the Welsh Identifactory Copula Sentence', in *Dán do Oide: Essays in Memory of Conn R. Ó Cléirigh*, ed. by A. Ahlqvist and V. Capková (Dublin: Institiúid Teangeolaíochta Éireann, 1997), pp. 579–93

WILLIAMS, GLANMOR, *The Welsh Church from Conquest to Reformation* (Cardiff: University of Wales Press, 1976)

WILLIAMS, GRUFFYDD ALED, 'The Bardic Road to Bosworth', *Transactions of the Honourable Society of Cymmrodorion* (1986), 7–31

WILLIAMS, IFOR (ed.), *Pedeir Keinc y Mabinogi* (Caerdydd: Gwasg Prifysgol Cymru, 1930)

WILLIAMS, R., 'Historiae Monacellae', *Archaeologia Cambrensis*, 3 (1848), 139–42

WILLIAMS, ROBERT (ed. and trans.), *Y Seint Greal: The Holy Greal* (Gwynedd, 1897; repr. Pwllheli: Jones, 1987)

WILLIAMS, STEPHEN J. (ed.), *Ystorya de Carolo Magno* (Caerdydd: Gwasg Prifysgol Cymru, 1968)

WILLIAMS, TALIESIN (ed.), *Iolo Manuscripts: A Selection of Ancient Welsh Manuscripts* (Llandovery: William Rees, 1848)

WILLIS, DAVID W. E., *Syntactic Change in Welsh* (Oxford: Oxford University Press, 1998)

WINWARD, FIONA, 'The Lives of St. Wenefred (BHL 8847–8851)', *Analecta Bollandiana*, 117 (1999), 89–132

WOGAN-BROWNE, JOCELYN, 'Saints' Lives and the Female Reader', *Forum for Modern Language Studies*, 4 (1991), 314–32

WOODING, JONATHAN M., 'The Figure of David', in *St David of Wales*, ed. by Evans and Wooding, pp. 1–19

www.ingramcontent.com/pod-product-compliance
Lightning Source LLC
Chambersburg PA
CBHW071511150426
43191CB00009B/1485